Essays Mostly on Periodical Publishing in America

Essays Mostly on Periodical Publishing in America

A collection in honor of
CLARENCE GOHDES

Edited by
JAMES WOODRESS
with the assistance of
TOWNSEND LUDINGTON
and JOSEPH ARPAD

DUKE UNIVERSITY PRESS
Durham, N. C.
1973

L.C.C. card no. 72–96683
I.S.B.N. 0–8223–0281–0

Printed in the United States of
America by Heritage Printers, Inc.

Foreword

The twelve essays collected in this volume have been written to honor Clarence Gohdes, whose retirement from Duke University in 1971 brought to a close forty-five active years as teacher, scholar, and editor. His career began at a time when American literature was scarcely considered a respectable subject for scholarly attention, and it ended well after the Americanists had won their battles and consolidated their position. Clarence Gohdes was a leader in the growth of American literature as a field of study, and his writings contributed significantly to this discipline. There is no serious student of American literature anywhere who does not know his name. As author or editor of thirteen literary and bibliographical studies, he has played an important part in disseminating a broader knowledge of American literature and in interpreting it to successive generations of students. His studies of *The Periodicals of American Transcendentalism* (1931) and *American Literature in England* (1944) are significant books that have not been superseded. His editorial labors on behalf of Sidney Lanier and Walt Whitman have helped make those authors more readily available for serious study. His contribution to *The Literature of the American People* (1951) for which he wrote "The Late Nineteenth Century," his *Bibliographical Guide to the Study of the Literature of the U.S.A.*, and other compilations have provided useful tools for the study of American literature. But perhaps most important were his more than three decades as managing editor and then editor of *American Literature*, a journal which from its beginning has been the chief organ for the publication of American literary scholarship.

All three of the editors of this volume were students of Clarence Gohdes at Duke University, and their debt to him goes beyond the impact of his scholarship. We can testify that he was more than a scholar: he was a man strongly committed to teaching. His courses were models of clarity and cogency and rested on a solid command of his field of specialization. The high standard of excellence that he set for himself in his teaching he also demanded of his undergraduates in their papers and examinations and his graduate students in their theses and dissertations. Certainly he has cast his shadow in higher education through his shaping influence both on the students who sat in his classes and on those who pursued advanced degrees under his direction.

One of Clarence Gohdes's continuing interests has been periodical publishing, and it seemed appropriate in the planning of this volume to invite essays on this subject. Nine of the twelve contributions gathered here deal with periodical publishing in one way or another, and together they make a significant study of this important topic. They cover more than a century of magazine history and examine the subject from several viewpoints—from the angle of editors and contributors, from the standpoint of social mores and public taste, from the perspectives of art and economics. Because periodicals always have played a more important role in the cultural life of America than in other nations, a study of magazine publishing in the United States has unusual relevance for the study of our civilization.

These essays begin with Randolph Randall's close scrutiny of Joseph Dennie's opinions expressed in the contents and in the editorial apparatus of his *Port Folio* (1801–1827), the first important American critical journal; and they end with C. Hugh Holman's study of Thomas Wolfe's short novels and their appearance in *Scribner's Magazine* a generation ago. In between are seven interesting, significant, and sometimes ground-breaking studies of writers from Thoreau to Dreiser. Charles Anderson's "Thoreau and the *Dial*: The Apprentice Years" provides important new documentation and insight into Thoreau's development as a writer through his periodical contributions. Here is new light on an author already extensively studied. Kimball King's essay deals generally with the impact the vogue for local color fiction had on the development of post-Civil War writers and provides an introduction to the essays by Rayburn Moore and Harriet Holman, which illuminate with some rather sharp detail the relations between northern editors and the southern writers Paul Hamilton Hayne and Thomas Nelson Page in the late nineteenth and early twentieth centuries. Edwin S. Cady and his daughter, Elizabeth Saler, have written a fascinating article—with some surprises—about *St. Nicholas* magazine. James Woodress focuses on the most successful of all the editor-promoters during the age of the monthly magazine in a profile of S. S. McClure. Donald Pizer has significant observations to make about Dreiser's early stories, originally published in magazines, and their relationship to his later novels.

The other three essays, with which we have begun this collection, were written by old friends of Clarence Gohdes on several other subjects that long have interested him: Walt Whitman, America's literary foreign relations, and the presentation of previously unpublished literary manuscripts. The opening piece is Floyd Stovall's essay on Whitman, the ripe distillation of a lifetime of scholarship and a long and fruitful devotion to Whitman's life and works. Because its subject is also the topic of one of Clarence Gohdes's own books, we have put it first. The second essay is Lewis Leary's captivating article on the expatriate diary kept in Florence in the 1850's by Elizabeth Stedman Kinney, mother of the poet Edmund Clarence Stedman. Finally, Part I ends with Herbert Brown's essay introducing the first publication of a manuscript by Charles Brockden Brown, "The Story of Julius."

JAMES WOODRESS
TOWNSEND LUDINGTON
JOSEPH ARPAD

Contents

Notes on Contributors

Charles R. Anderson was born in Macon, Georgia, in 1902. He holds a B.A. and an M.A. degree from the University of Georgia, a Ph.D. from Columbia University. He taught briefly at the University of Georgia, for ten years at Duke University, and from 1941 until retirement in 1969 at Johns Hopkins, where he was Chairman of the English Department from 1950 to 1956 and Caroline Donovan Professor of American Literature since 1956. He has been visiting professor at Columbia, the University of Southern California, and Hawaii; abroad at Heidelberg, the Universities of Rome, Torino, Kyoto, and Doshisha; and State Department lecturer in European and Far Eastern countries. He has held several fellowships, including Guggenheim, Huntington, and Fulbright, and has served on the editorial boards of several journals. His books include *Melville in the South Seas* (1939), *Emily Dickinson's Poetry: Stairway to Surprise* (1960), *The Magic Circle of Walden* (1968). He edited with others *The Centennial Edition of the Works of Sidney Lanier* (1945); he was general editor of a two-volume anthology, *American Literary Masters* (1965).

Herbert Brown was Edward Little Professor of Rhetoric and Oratory at Bowdoin College until he retired in 1972. He remains Managing Editor of the *New England Quarterly*. He is the author of *The Sentimental Novel in America: 1789–1860* (1940) and *Sills of Bowdoin* (1964); he has also edited Hawthorne's *The Snow Image*, Holmes's *The Autocrat of the Breakfast Table*, W. H. Brown's *The Power of Sympathy*, H. W. Foster's *The Coquette*, and coedited *The Heritage of American Literature*. He has been visiting professor at Duke, Columbia, Harvard, the University of Minnesota, and the Bread Loaf School of English at Middlebury. A member of the American Academy of Arts and Sciences, he was Chairman of the American Literature Group of the Modern Language Association in 1955 and an American Specialist at major universities in India in 1968–1969.

Edwin H. Cady was born in Old Tappan, New Jersey, in 1917. He has an A.B. degree from Ohio Wesleyan University, an M.A. from the University of Cincinnati, and a Ph.D. from the University of Wisconsin. He has taught at Syracuse University and is presently Rudy Professor of English at Indiana University. He has served as member of the editorial board of *American Literature* (1960–1963), as general editor of *A Selected Edition of William Dean Howells* (1964–1968), and is on the executive committee of the Center for Editions of American Authors. His books include *The Gen-*

tleman in America (1949), *The Road to Realism: The Early Years, 1837–1885, of William Dean Howells* (1956), *The Realist at War: The Mature Years, 1885–1920, of William Dean Howells* (1958), *Stephen Crane* (1962), *John Woolman: The Mind of the Quaker Saint* (1965), and *The Light of Common Day: Realism in American Fiction* (1971).

C. HUGH HOLMAN was born in South Carolina in 1914 and was educated at Presbyterian College (B.S., 1936; B.A., 1938) and the University of North Carolina at Chapel Hill (Ph.D., 1949). He has taught at Presbyterian College, where he was Academic Dean, and, since 1949, at the University of North Carolina, where he is now Kenan Professor of English, and where he has been Chairman of the English Department, Dean of the Graduate School, and Provost. He has been bibliographer for the American Literature Section of the Modern Language Association, and chairman of that section. He is the author of *Thomas Wolfe* (1960), *The American Novel Through Henry James: A Bibliography* (1966), *Three Modes of Modern Southern Fiction* (1966), *A Handbook to Literature* (3rd edition, 1972), and *Novelists of the American South* (1972). He has edited *The Short Novels of Thomas Wolfe* (1961), *The Thomas Wolfe Reader* (1962), and (with Sue F. Ross) *The Letters of Thomas Wolfe to His Mother* (1968). He has held a Guggenheim fellowship, is advisory editor for American literature for the *Encyclopedia Americana*, and is co-editor of the *Southern Literary Journal*.

HARRIET R. HOLMAN was born in Anderson, South Carolina, in 1912 and earned her A.B. degree from Winthrop College, her A.M. from the University of Michigan, and her Ph.D. from Duke University. She has taught in public schools and at Winthrop College, been a reference librarian at Duke University, served as Chairman and Professor of English at Erskine College, and is now Professor of English at Clemson University. In addition to articles on Poe and other nineteenth-century figures, she has written *John Fox and Tom Page: As They Were* (1970). She has also edited several volumes, including Page's *North African Journal, 1912* (1970) and *Mediterranean Winter, 1906* (1971).

KIMBALL KING was born in Princeton, New Jersey, in 1934. He was graduated from Lawrenceville School, attended Yale University, and received his B.A. degree from Johns Hopkins University. He received his M.A. degree from Wesleyan University and his Ph.D. from the University of Wisconsin. He has edited Thomas Nelson Page's *In Ole Virginia* (1969) and has recently completed a biography of Augustus B. Longstreet. His articles, reviews, and bibliographies have appeared in *American Literature*, *Mississippi Quarterly*, *Modern Drama*, *Genre*, and other periodicals. Since 1969, he has been bibliographer for the American Literature Section of the Modern Language Association, and he is regional chairman for the South Atlantic states of the *American Literary Manuscripts* revisions project.

Lewis Leary was born in Blauvelt, New York, in 1906. He took his bachelor's degree from the University of Vermont and his A.M. and Ph.D. degrees from Columbia University. After teaching at the American University in Beirut and the University of Miami, he was a member of the faculty of Duke University for eight years and of Columbia University for seventeen (seven as chairman of his department) until he took up his present position at the University of North Carolina in 1969. Among the books he has written are *That Rascal Freneau* (1941) and *The Literary Career of Nathaniel Tucker* (1951); among those he has edited are *Mark Twain's Letters to Mary* (1961), *Articles on American Literature, 1900–1950* (1954), and *Articles on American Literature, 1950–1967* (1970). He has served on the editorial board of *American Literature*, has contributed frequently to periodicals, and is the author of several of the University of Minnesota Pamphlets on American Writers.

Rayburn S. Moore was born in Helena, Arkansas, in 1920. He holds the A.B. and M.A. degrees from Vanderbilt University and the Ph.D. degree from Duke University. He taught at Hendrix College from 1954 to 1959 and subsequently at the University of Georgia, where he is Professor of English. From 1964 to 1969, he was director of graduate studies in English. He was secretary of the American Literature Section of the South Atlantic Modern Language Association in 1967 and chairman in 1968. He is the author of *Constance Fenimore Woolson* (1963) and *Paul Hamilton Hayne* (1972); the editor of *For the Major and Selected Short Stories of Constance Fenimore Woolson* (1967); a contributor to the annual MLA bibliography on Literature and Society (since 1961) and to *A Bibliographical Guide to the Study of Southern Literature* (1969); and the author of articles and reviews in *American Literature*, *American Quarterly*, and other journals. He is editing *Guy Rivers* for the Centennial Edition of the Writings of William Gilmore Simms.

Donald Pizer, who was born in New York City in 1929, received his B.A., M.A., and Ph.D. degrees from the University of California, Los Angeles. After service in the army, he joined the faculty of Newcomb College, Tulane University, in 1957, where he is now Professor of English. He was a Guggenheim Fellow (1962), a Rosenbach Fellow (1971), and a Fellow of the American Council of Learned Societies (1971–1972). During 1967–1968, he was a Fulbright Lecturer at the University of Hamburg. Among his books are *Hamlin Garland's Early Work and Career* (1960), *Realism and Naturalism in Nineteenth-Century American Literature* (1966), *The Novels of Frank Norris* (1966), and editions of works by Hamlin Garland, Frank Norris, Theodore Dreiser, and Stephen Crane. He is currently preparing a critical study of the novels of Theodore Dreiser.

Randolph C. Randall was born at Arcadia, Indiana, in 1900. He was educated at Indiana University (A.B., 1922) and at Columbia University

(A.M., 1926 and Ph.D., 1955). After teaching briefly in Puerto Rico, he was a member of the faculty at Centenary College of Louisiana from 1926 to 1931. From 1931 to 1965 he was Professor of English and chairman of his department at Fenn College, where he took part in the formation and development of the College of Arts and Sciences. When Fenn became Cleveland State University in 1965, he continued in his position until retirement in 1970. He is the author of several articles in periodicals and of *James Hall: Spokesman of the New West* (1964).

ELIZABETH C. SALER, the daughter of Edwin H. Cady, was born in Syracuse, New York, in 1947. She received her B.A. degree from Ohio Wesleyan University in 1969 and her M.A. degree from Duke University in 1970. The jointly authored essay which appears in this volume grew out of a paper she presented in one of Professor Gohdes's last graduate seminars at Duke; she has also published in *The Stephen Crane Newsletter*. She presently resides with her husband in Olney, Illinois, where she plans to begin a teaching career.

FLOYD STOVALL was born in Texas on July 7, 1896, and educated in the public schools and at the University of Texas, where he received his B.A., M.A., and Ph.D. degrees. He taught for several years at the University of Texas and then at North Texas State College. Later he went to the University of North Carolina in 1949 and to the University of Virginia as Edgar Allan Poe Professor of English in 1955. He retired in 1967. Although his first book was on Shelley, his publications have been chiefly in American literature, including the following: *American Idealism* (1943); an edition of Poe's poems, with variant readings and textual notes (1965); an edition of Whitman's major prose works (1962–1963); and a critical work, *Edgar Poe the Poet* (1969). Professor Stovall also was the original editor of *Eight American Authors* (1956) and has served on the editorial board of *American Literature*.

JAMES WOODRESS was born in Webster Groves, Missouri, in 1916, and educated at Amherst College (A.B., 1938), New York University (A.M., 1943), and Duke University (Ph.D., 1950). After a period in journalism with the United Press and in the army in World War II, he taught at Grinnell College, Butler University, and San Fernando Valley State College before joining the English faculty at the University of California at Davis, where he is now Chairman. His books include *Howells and Italy* (1952), *Booth Tarkington: Gentleman from Indiana* (1955), *A Yankee's Odyssey: The Life of Joel Barlow* (1958), and *Willa Cather: Her Life and Art* (1970). He was editor of *American Literary Scholarship* (1965–1969), *Eight American Authors* (1971), compiler of *Dissertations in American Literature* (1957, 1962, 1968), and has held fellowships from the Guggenheim and Ford foundations and Fulbright appointments in France and Italy.

I. A Trio of Essays on Whitman, an Expatriate Diary, and Charles Brockden Brown

Floyd Stovall

Whitman and the Poet in Leaves of Grass

Every poet reveals something of himself in his poems, no matter how transformed by the creative imagination. Whitman was no exception. Yet it is a mistake to interpret his poems, as some critics have done, as authentic biographical documents. The "I" who speaks in them, the "Poet," is not Walter Whitman of Brooklyn, sometime schoolmaster, printer, and journalist, who invented a new kind of verse and called himself "Walt," but a mythical person composed of the qualities that in 1855 Whitman supposed to be appropriate to the ideal poet of democracy in the New World. This Poet announces himself in the chief poem of the 1855 edition, later "Song of Myself," as "Walt Whitman, an American, one of the roughs, a kosmos, / Turbulent, fleshy, sensual, eating and drinking and breeding"; as going about "hankering, gross, mystical, nude"; as the poet of wickedness as well as of goodness; as the poet of the body and of the soul. He boasts: "Divine am I inside and out, and I make holy whatever I touch or am touched from, / The scent of these arm-pits is aroma finer than prayer." He says he was in Texas during the revolution of 1836, and he identifies himself with the crucified and resurrected Christ. He represents himself as the new Adam, a natural god-like man, a transcendental Davy Crockett, with the characteristics of Dionysus and Satan as well as the sympathy and benevolence of Jesus. In so far as he is physically described he resembles Walter Whitman, and he has Whitman's independence and faith in democracy. But the real Whitman, though something of an egotist, wearing his hat as he pleased, was not the supreme egotist we meet in the poems, and he was not one of the "roughs." He might have been called "fleshy," but he was neither gross nor sensual.

This mythical Poet was conceived in the mind of his creator like any other fictional hero, and he emerged full grown though not yet spiritually mature in the poems of 1855. He was sensitive to beauty, especially the beauty of nature, but the spiritual qualities which he manifested in the new poems of the 1860 edition and later were in 1855 only potential, still unrealized.

I do not pretend to know why or how this remarkable creation came about. Whitman's family on both his father's and his mother's side were ordinary people of intelligence and sound character but in no exceptional way different from most other Americans of their time. One must suppose that by some combination of genetic circumstances Walter Whitman was endowed with a lively imagination and an unusual capacity for intellectual and spiritual development. Environment also played its part. He grew up during the period, 1820 to 1840, when the forces of individualism, democracy, and nationalism were rampant in America. Although political independence had been achieved earlier, it was only then that the United States began to establish a cultural identity independent of England and Europe.

As a political journalist he was reasonably successful; yet journalism, like schoolteaching, was only a livelihood, not a chosen vocation. His tastes and his ambitions, even as a boy, were literary. As an apprentice printer and helper in newspaper offices he was close to the literary scene. When only thirteen or fourteen he contributed "a piece or two" to George P. Morris's fashionable paper *The Mirror*.[1] Already he was a confirmed reader. Among the books that most delighted him and influenced him permanently were Walter Scott's novels and his collection, *Minstrelsy of the Scottish Border*. He must have begun to read Scott's novels and other writings when only ten or twelve years old, and he continued to read them even into old age.[2] These books helped to arouse his interest in history and especially in the feudal life of the Middle Ages. This interest, which led inevitably to Shakespeare's historical plays, and eventually to Homer, Ossian, the *Nibelungenlied*, and primitive poetry in general, was not shared by the Poet of *Leaves of Grass*, although it had much to do with the writing of the book. The Poet had no love for the past. He

1. See *Specimen Days, Prose Works 1892*, ed. Floyd Stovall (New York, 1963), I, 287.

2. Ibid., I, 13. See also "A Backward Glance O'er Travel'd Roads," ibid., II, 722–723. He told Horace Traubel in 1888, "If you could reduce the Leaves to their elements you would see Scott unmistakably active at the roots." (*With Walt Whitman in Camden*, I, 96–97.)

understood that it was the foundation on which the present rested, but his main concern was the future, and he hoped to be the prophet preparing the way to its greatness. Whitman early developed an intense love of the heroism reflected in primitive poetry and the pageantry of the feudal world as described in Scott's novels and in Shakespeare's historical plays. This love he never outgrew although his role as the poet of democracy required that he should condemn its undemocratic character. He conceived of *Leaves of Grass* as a kind of primitive American poem that should function for American culture as Homer's poems functioned for Greek culture or as the *Nibelungenlied* for medieval Germany. He thought of Shakespeare as the poet of English feudalism, and he conceived of himself as the poet of American democracy. His verse owed little or nothing to Shakespeare's, but he thought his role in the New World was parallel with that of Shakespeare in the Old.

Precisely when Whitman first read Shakespeare I do not know, but I suspect it was not until he began to attend the theaters across the river in New York. He says in *Specimen Days*, "As a boy or young man I had seen, (reading them carefully the day beforehand,) quite all Shakspere's acting dramas, play'd wonderfully well."[3] The first theater he attended was the Park, where the actors were mostly English and their style in the formal tradition of the London stage. It can be established that he went there as early as the spring of 1833, before his fourteenth birthday.[4] In *Specimen Days* he says that Fanny Kemble thrilled his "boyish heart" and that he saw her "nearly every night that she played." She played only at the Park. She appeared there many times with her father, Charles Kemble, in plays of Shakespeare, but he liked her best in other plays then popular but now nearly forgotten. The Kembles made their last appearance on the New York stage June 20, 1834.[5]

One might reasonably expect that in the 1830's his favorite actor would have been the American, Edwin Forrest, whose imposing presence and stentorian voice made him a favorite with the many, especially the young and the unsophisticated, who crowded the Bowery Theater. That was apparently not the case, although the young Whitman did see him frequently and remembered him in such

3. Ibid., I, 21.
4. For details see my essay "Walt Whitman and the Dramatic Stage in New York," *Studies in Philology*, L (July, 1953), 515–539.
5. George C. D. Odell, *Annals of the New York Stage*, III, 604f.

strong parts as the Gladiator and Metamora. He also liked the English actor, William Charles Macready, whose traditional style was the exact opposite of Forrest's. But the actor who aroused his greatest enthusiasm and influenced him most was Junius Brutus Booth, also an Englishman, but resident in the United States during Whitman's time, and father of the better known American actor, Edwin Booth. He praised Booth's acting in the roles of King Lear, Iago, and Shylock, and indeed in every part he played, but he liked him best as King Richard III. This was also Booth's favorite role and the one in which he appeared most frequently. Whitman saw many performances of *Richard III* during the 1830's with Booth as the King, but the one he remembered best and considered the highlight of his experience as a theater-goer occurred on June 8, 1835, at the Bowery Theater. On this memorable evening Booth's acting so impressed him that later, in *Specimen Days*, he compared its effect on him to that of his first sight of Niagara Falls.[6]

By 1846 the theater in New York no longer satisfied Whitman. As editor of the Brooklyn *Eagle*, where he sometimes reviewed theatrical performances, he demanded reform in the management and style of acting then prevalent, which he said were dominated by outmoded English precedents. He called vigorously for a native American drama. Yet, surprisingly, he did not cite as a model to be followed the distinguished American actor Forrest but rather Macready, the English formalist and great rival of Forrest. Whitman liked Macready's "mental style," as he called it, because, though it was quiet and restrained, it "touched the heart, the soul, the feelings, the inner blood and nerves" of his audience.[7] He acknowledged that Forrest had "high talent in his profession," but he feared that because he had become identified with an American style of acting "the crowd of vapid imitators may spread quite all the faults of that style, with none of its excellences." To men of taste, he declared, the "loud mouthed ranting style" designed to "tickle the ears of the groundlings" is ridiculous. What he wished in American acting was both power and art, and he felt that J. B. Booth's manner, when at his best, was perfectly balanced, having great power with no sacrifice of art.[8]

6. *Prose Works 1892*, I, 236.

7. From the *Eagle* of August 20, 1846; reprinted in *The Gathering of the Forces*, ed. Cleveland Rodgers and John Black (New York, 1920), II, 321–325.

8. From the *Eagle* of December 26, 1846; reprinted in *The Gathering of the Forces*, II, 330–334.

I do not know why Whitman did not name him as the perfect model for an American style. Among actresses of the middle 1840's Charlotte Cushman, an American, was his favorite because, like Booth, she had both power and art. In old age he remembered the Bowery Theater with fondness, but on the scene in 1847 he found its bad taste and vulgarity "beyond all toleration." The same was true of all other theaters in New York except the Park, where the audiences were "always intelligent" and there was a "dash of superiority thrown over the performances."[9] If we may judge by his taste in native American drama in 1847, we can hardly believe that his conception of the ideal American poet as "one of the roughs" dates from that year.

One reason for the decline of dramatic performances during the late 1840's was the fact that cultivated theater-goers deserted them for opera, which was made more attractive about that time by the successful introduction of the Italian opera. Whitman occasionally attended the Italian opera performances during these years, but he still preferred a simpler kind of music. "Songs whose words you can hear and understand," he declared, "are preferable to a mass of unintelligible stuff, (for who makes out even the libretto of English opera, as now given on the stage?) which for all the sense you get out of it might as well be Arabic."[10] He preferred the music of feeling—"heart music as distinguished from art music"—as exemplified in the singing of such family groups as the New England Cheneys and Hutchinsons.[11] Jenny Lind, who took New York by storm in 1850, astonished him by her "vocal dexterity" but never touched his heart.[12] He was not really a lover of opera until he heard the Italian tenor Alessandro Bettini in June, 1851. During the next two years his enthusiasm grew until it reached its climax when he heard Marietta Alboni in the early months of 1853. He was most deeply moved by her singing in the title role of *Norma.* This she sang only twice in New York, on

9. From the *Eagle* of February 8, 1847; reprinted in *The Gathering of the Forces,* II, 310–14.

10. From the *Eagle* of December 6, 1846; reprinted in *The Gathering of the Forces,* II, 348.

11. See Whitman's article "Art-Singing and Heart-Singing," published in Poe's *Broadway Journal* on November 29, 1845. Parts of this early article were reprinted in the *Eagle* articles of December 6, 1846, and September 8, 1847 (*The Gathering of the Forces,* II, 345–346).

12. See "Letters from Paumanok," No. 3, published in the New York *Evening Post,* August 14, 1851; reprinted in *Uncollected Poetry and Prose,* ed. Emory Holloway (Garden City, N.Y., 1921), I, 255–259.

January 27 and 28, 1853. The best musical critics of the time were equally impressed. Richard Grant White, of the *Courier and Enquirer*, said that "in her style her singing is as purely and absolutely beautiful as it is possible for anything earthly to be."[13] Much as he loved her singing and praised it in later years, Whitman wrote nothing in the 1855 poems that certainly reflects her influence. He was probably remembering Bettini, however, when he wrote in "Song of Myself," "A tenor large and fresh as creation fills me / The orbic flex of his mouth is pouring and filling me full."[14]

Beyond question, Whitman was deeply affected by music. He even found more than usual pleasure in what seemed to him the harmonies of nature. It would have been strange if he had not loved the magnificent sound effects of grand opera, the orchestra as well as the singers. Yet it is an exaggeration to assert, as one critic has done, that grand opera "made a poet of him."[15] It undoubtedly contributed much to the cultivation of his sensibility, as did also the dramatic stage, and in that way it increased his potential for poetic expression. But the early poems owed far more to ordinary experiences, the sights and sounds of the street and the countryside in Long Island. They also owed more to his reading than he was willing to admit. Before 1855 he had read most of the great English poets, particularly Wordsworth, Shelley, and Tennyson, as well as the Bible, Carlyle, and Emerson. He reviewed several of Carlyle's books in the *Eagle* in 1846–1847 and probably studied them carefully during the next six or eight years. J. T. Trowbridge stated, on the authority of Whitman's conversations with him in 1860, that he began to write out *Leaves of Grass* in the summer of 1854, immediately after having read Emerson's *Nature* and some of the shorter essays.[16] This is not the place to enter

13. White quoted this from his newspaper review in "Opera in New York," the *Century Magazine*, XXIV (May, 1882), 38–39.

14. Lines 601–602. In the "Letter from Paumanok" cited above he was referring to Bettini when he wrote of "the vast, pure Tenor,— identity of the Creative Power itself." At the end of his paragraph on "A Contralto Voice" in the manuscript of *Specimen Days* (1882) I found the following passage, deleted before publication: "(This kind of voice has always to me the sense of young maternity—the last art-sense of all. Alboni was its fruition and apex. I wonder if that lady will ever know that her singing, her method, gave the foundation, the start, thirty years ago, to all my poetic literary effort since?)." See *Prose Works 1892*, I, 235n. See also ibid., II, 772. It would appear that, remembering his enthusiasm for Alboni, Whitman was tempted to give her more credit than, after reflection, he decided was due.

15. Robert D. Faner, *Walt Whitman & Opera* (Philadelphia, 1951), p. 22.

16. J. T. Trowbridge, *My Own Story* (Boston, 1903), p. 367.

fully into the question of Whitman's indebtedness to Emerson, but it is true that the Poet of *Leaves of Grass* as he appears in the 1855 edition bears a striking resemblance to the American poet that Emerson called for and characterized in his essay "The Poet" first published in 1844. There Emerson called the poet the Sayer, as distinguished from the Knower and the Doer, although each of these is endowed with some degree of the powers of the other two. The Sayer both knows and tells. He announces what no man has foretold. He is also the joiner; he re-attaches things to nature and to the whole, and he is not only free himself but he makes others free. In so far as the poet is a knower, all things are fit for his use. "The vocabulary of an omniscient man," said Emerson, "would embrace words and images excluded from polite conversation." The universe is the externalization of the soul. "All the facts of the animal economy, sex, nutriment, gestation, birth, growth, are symbols of the passage of the world into the soul of man, to suffer there a change and reappear a new and higher fact." Looking ahead, Emerson said that "America is a poem in our eyes; its ample geography dazzles the imagination and will not wait long for metres. Some day this poem will find its voice, and a new and American poet will say, "It is in me, and shall out." The Poet of *Leaves of Grass* is a bit less refined than Emerson's mythical poet, but he is essentially the same.

In one of his early notebooks Whitman made two comments under the heading "American Opera" which show that he did not wholly accept for America the formal music of Italian grand opera. In the first one he said: "When a song is sung the accompaniment is to be by only one instrument or two instruments, the rest silent. The vocal performer to make far more of his song, or solo part, by the by-play, attitudes, expression, movements, &c. than is at all made by the Italian opera singers.—The American opera is to be far more simple, and give far more scope to the *persons* enacting the characters." In the second one he said: "American Opera.—put three banjos (or more?) in the orchestra—and let them accompany, (at times exclusively,) the songs of the baritone or tenor.—Let a considerable part of the performance be instrumental—by the orchestra only.—Let a few words go a great ways—the plot not complicated but simple—Always one leading idea—as Friendship, Courage, Gratitude, Love—always a distinct meaning.—The story and libretto as now are generally of no account.—In the American Opera the story and libretto must be the *body* of the performance."[17] A reference to sick and wounded British soldiers in hospitals at Sebastopol proves that a part of the notebook at least was written after the battle of Balaklava, which occurred in October, 1854. It contains versions of lines of verse used in "Song of Myself," "I Sing the Body Electric," and "Song of the Answerer." It also contains fragments suggestive of the Preface to the 1855 edition, which must have been written only a few months after the notebook. The "appropriate native grand-opera" which he called for in the Preface would have been such as he prescribed in the passages quoted above, both simple and original.

It is not possible to determine just when Whitman conceived his ideal of the native American poet, but it was probably not before, or not long before, he began to write down ideas and verse patterns looking toward *Leaves of Grass.* In the notebook which Holloway calls "the earliest and most important" (item 80 of the Harned Collection in the Library of Congress), Whitman begins by describing the "noble expanded American Character," also in terms suggestive of the Preface. Holloway dates this notebook as early as 1847–1849, but I suspect it belongs rather to the years 1853–1854. It seems improbable that verse of this degree of finish should have been composed as early as 1847–1849, or that after eight years of experimenting he should have composed no more than the twelve poems of the first edition. He was trained as a journalist, and therefore would not have been likely to hoard his compositions. In later years he usually published, if possible, soon after its composition whatever he thought worthy of publication. I have already referred to the statement of J. T. Trowbridge that Whitman told him he began to write *Leaves of Grass* in the summer of 1854. Dr. R. M. Bucke's categorical statement in his biography, which Whitman approved before publication, confirms Trowbridge's memory: "In 1854 he commenced definitely writing out the poems that were printed in the first edition."[18] If we can credit the statement Whitman set down in his manuscript of *Specimen Days* and then cancelled before publication, that the singing

17. This notebook is item No. 84 of the Harned Collection as listed in the 1955 catalog of the Whitman Collections in the Library of Congress. I quote from a microfilm made for me by the Library in 1934, but both these comments on American opera were printed by C. J. Furness in *Walt Whitman's Workshop* (Cambridge, Mass., 1928), pp. 201–202, n. 37, although arranged in reverse order.

18. *Walt Whitman* (Philadelphia, 1883), p. 24.

of Alboni gave "the foundation, the start" for all his poetry, that start could not have been before 1853.[19]

Near the end of the notebook that Holloway called No. 1 (item 80 in the Harned Collection) Whitman wrote: "(Criticism on *Myself*)," putting the words in parentheses because they were out of context. Some commentators have thought "Myself" was underlined because it referred to the poem later titled "Song of Myself." This is unlikely. It may be a reference to the first line of that poem, "I celebrate myself." There is a possibility, however, that it is a reminder to himself to write such an anonymous criticism of his poems and their Poet-Hero as he actually wrote and published in 1855. Just preceding this entry is the line, "Literature is full of perfumes," which was expanded into the 1855 line, "Houses and rooms are full of perfumes . . . the shelves are crowded with perfumes." Several lines in the notebook at this point have been pasted over. If we knew what is covered up we might possibly learn what he meant by "*Myself*."

The first edition was advertised for sale in the New York *Tribune* on July 6, 1855. In the Preface Whitman called for American poets with the largeness of nature who shall be spokesmen for democracy and who shall address the people in a language transcendent and now. The United States themselves, he announced, "are essentially the greatest poem." The poet of America, he added, "incarnates its geography and natural life and rivers and lakes." Although a great poem is for the future as much as for the present, "the direct trial of him who would be the greatest poet is today." The Preface concludes with the sentence, "The proof of a poet is that his country absorbs him as affectionately as he has absorbed it." He made no claims for himself in this Preface, but in the poems themselves the Poet who speaks in the first person proffers himself as the first of a new kind of poets, obviously such as he had called for in the Preface. Whitman had, in his own way, absorbed his country affectionately. The country, however, was unresponsive and needed some reminding that its poet had arrived. Reviews of the book were few and mostly unfavor-

19. *Prose Works 1892*, I, 235n. In an article published in the New York *Tribune* on May 10, 1879, speaking of the acting of Fanny Kemble, he wrote: "(Strange—but certainly true—that her playing, and the elder Booth's, with Alboni's and Bettini's singing, gave the first part of the influences that afterwards resulted in my 'Leaves of Grass.')." This sentence was lined out on the clipping of the article when Whitman prepared it for use in *Specimen Days*. (See *Prose Works 1892*, I, 20n.)

able. Some of the reviewers charged that the poems were not only crude but indecent, and that the poet was a rowdy or a villain.[20] Whitman must have anticipated such unresponsiveness, and in order to educate the public taste he very promptly wrote three reviews of his own book and published them anonymously in friendly periodicals.

The first of these to appear in print was published in the September issue of the *United States Review*.[21] It is not printed among the literary notices but like an essay, with the title "Walt Whitman and His Poems." This article must have been written before Whitman had seen any reviews of his book, unless he saw a review in the *Tribune* on July 23, possibly by C. A. Dana.[22] The review begins by announcing, "An American bard at last!" It goes on to characterize this bard in words borrowed from the poems as "self-reliant, with haughty eyes, assuming to himself all the attributes of his country. . . . One of the roughs, large, proud, affectionate, eating, drinking, and breeding." It says little of the poet's style except that it is "transcendent and new."

The second review, which appeared in the Brooklyn *Times* on September 29, is somewhat less excessive in its praise and more personal, describing the poet's appearance and habits, as if the reviewer appealed particularly to the people of Brooklyn who might know him.[23] He is described as "a person singularly beloved and looked

20. Emerson had no doubt raised great expectations and confirmed Whitman's opinion of his poems by praising them in his famous letter of July 21, 1855; and another New Englander, Charles Eliot Norton, reviewed the book in *Putnam's Magazine* for September, describing the poems rather accurately as "a mixture of Yankee transcendentalism and New York rowdyism." But outside of New England, transcendentalism was not much more popular than New York rowdyism.

21. This was, in effect, the same magazine as the *Democratic Review*, which Whitman had contributed to frequently during the 1840's. The first issue with the new title appeared in January, 1853. In 1856 the new magazine was reunited with the old. The editor in 1855 was D. W. Holly. (See Frank Luther Mott, *A History of American Magazines*, Cambridge, Mass., 1928, I, 678n.) I presume Holly was a friend of Whitman's.

22. The September number of the *United States Review* must have gone to press in late August or very early September, for it contains an announcement that Mrs. Gibbs, formerly Miss Graddon, "is now in New York, and about to give a series of entertainments," etc. Her forthcoming appearances were also announced in the *Herald* on September 19, just preceding her first appearance. (See Odell, VI, 498.)

23. The *Times* was owned by George C. Bennett, like Whitman an advocate of Free-Soil principles. Charles Gayler, the editor, was Whitman's immediate predecessor. (See *I Sit and Look Out*, ed. Emory Holloway and Vernolian Schwarz, New York, 1932, p. 10.) They were later not very friendly, but at this time they probably had no ill feelings. On December 17, 1856, before Whitman became editor, the *Times* printed a rather discriminating review of the 1856 edition of *Leaves of Grass*. The style is unlike Whitman's and I doubt that he wrote it, but who did write it, whether

toward, especially by young men and the illiterate," who "does not associate with literary people," and who takes "with easy nonchalance" the chances of his book's reception, "preferring always to speak for himself rather than have others speak for him."

The third review embraced a commentary on Tennyson's poems, especially *Maud*, in comparison with *Leaves of Grass*, and was titled "An English and an American Poet." It was published in the *American Phrenological Journal* for October, 1855, and was reprinted in the 1856 edition.[24] The tone of this review is somewhat subdued, as if Whitman had become less confident than he had been in the earlier reviews. This suggests that it was written after he had read some reviews of his book not written by himself. He begins with the sentence, "It is always reserved for second-rate poems immediately to gratify." The implication is clear that *Maud* is a second-rate poem. Since *Leaves of Grass* is first-rate, it is less popular at first, but it will last longer. It must wait for "the voice of the few rare and controlling critics, and the voice of more than one generation of men" to be justified.

One of the more significant passages in this review is a quotation of nineteen lines from the English poet Alexander Smith containing a prophecy of the coming of a "mighty poet" who shall be the spokesman of this age to all coming times, whose love shall "sphere the world" as the air, and who will reflect humanity as the lake reflects the heaven. How carefully Whitman read Smith's poems I cannot say, but in a manuscript note dated 1854, obviously made while reading them, he wrote: "There is one electric passage in this poetry, where the announcement is made of a great forthcoming Poet, and the illustration given of a king who, about dying, plunges his sword into his favorite attendant, to send him on before."[25] The insertion of this long quotation, together with the adjective "electric" in his note,

---

Gayler or Bennett or some one else, I cannot say. Gayler, like Whitman, was one of the patrons of Pfaff's restaurant and continued to be long after most of the bohemians had dispersed.

24. Fowler and Wells, who published this journal, were the agents through whom Whitman sold the 1855 and 1856 editions of his poems. *Maud* was published near the end of July, 1855.

25. The passage is from the second scene of *A Life-Drama*, which Whitman probably read in *Poems*, by Alexander Smith (Boston, 1853, reprinted in 1854). The note is in *Complete Writings*, IX, 156. Whitman adds in the same note a comment on Smith, who he thinks "is imbued with the nature of a Tennyson," and who "seems to be neither better nor worse than the high average." This appraisal was perhaps higher than Smith merited.

can mean nothing less than that Whitman hoped to be recognized eventually as the forthcoming poet. The doubtful note on which the review concludes, however, indicates that for the present he is not overconfident: "His is to prove either the most lamentable of failures or the most glorious of triumphs in the known history of literature. And after all we have written we confess our brain-felt and heart-felt inability to decide which we think it is likely to be."[26]

Whitman may have been encouraged to review and defend his own work by the examples of Wordsworth and other English poets. In his "Essay, Supplementary to the Preface," originally published in the 1815 edition of his poems, Wordsworth stated his belief, based on his own experience and on his knowledge of older poets, especially Milton, "that every Author, as far as he is great and at the same time *original*, has had the task of creating the taste by which he is to be enjoyed."[27] In Whitman's notebook cited above as item 84 of the Harned Collection I find the following sentence: "Always any great and original person, teacher, inventor, artist or poet, must himself make the taste by which only he will be appreciated, or even received."[28] This is closely parallel to Wordsworth's statement. Wordsworth meant, of course, that the excellence of the author's work created the taste; yet his influential prefaces and essays defending the *Lyrical Ballads* and his later poems might have encouraged Whitman to write as he did in his own Preface and to believe he could promote the success of *Leaves of Grass* by publishing favorable reviews of it anonymously. Although he was not a great admirer of Wordsworth's poetry, he must have had some acquaintance with it.[29] One of Whit-

26. These reviews have been reprinted in various places, most conveniently perhaps in the volume of essays, *In Re Walt Whitman*, edited by Whitman's literary executors (Philadelphia, 1893), pp. 13–21, 23–26, and 27–32. In Bucke's *Walt Whitman*, p. 26, Whitman is quoted as saying that "when the book aroused such a tempest of anger and condemnation everywhere" he went off to the east end of Long Island and "spent the late summer and all the fall," and then came back to New York confirmed in his resolution to go on in his own way to complete his poetic work. Since Moncure Conway visited him in Brooklyn about September 10–12, the poet's sojourn on the east end of Long Island must have begun after that date. Charles A. Dana printed Emerson's letter to Whitman in the *Tribune* on October 10, but whether Whitman gave him the letter at that time or earlier I cannot say. (See Conway's *Autobiography*, Boston, 1904, I, 196 and 215–216.)

27. This essay might have been most conveniently read by Whitman in Henry Reed's American edition in one large volume of *The Poetical Works of Wordsworth* (Philadelphia, 1851; first published in 1837 and frequently reprinted).

28. This is one of the passages reprinted in *Walt Whitman's Workshop* pp. 66–67.

29. There are several magazine clippings about Wordsworth and his poetry in the Trent Collection. On another clipping (listed by Bucke but not in the Trent Col-

man's Wordsworth clippings from the *American Whig Review* for May, 1851, consists only of that part, the last three pages, which was devoted to a brief account of Wordsworth's life and literary work. The remaining and larger part of the review, not clipped, is a discussion of *The Prelude* containing considerable quotation from the poem. Apparently Whitman was more interested in Wordsworth's life than in his poem, although he may well have read the poem in Reed's edition. Beside the paragraph telling of Wordsworth's legacy from a friend and his appointment as Distributor of Stamps and later Poet Laureate, Whitman noted: "So it seems Wordsworth made 'a good thing,' from the start, out of his poetry, legacies! a fat office! pensions from the crown!" In such accounts, not always accurate, Whitman may have found the basis for an unfavorable opinion of Wordsworth.

Pasted to the clipping of the article on Wordsworth's *Prelude* is another (possibly Bucke's No. 342, which he thinks is from a newspaper and titles "Leigh Hunt") at the head of which Whitman has written in ink: "Leigh Hunt criticising his own poems—Also the same sort of self-criticism by other poets." The clipping is really a paragraph from the first column of page 53 of a review of Leigh Hunt's *Autobiography* in the January issue, 1851, of the *American Whig Review* (pp. 34–53). The paragraph reads as follows: "We will not go with Mr. Hunt into the critical analysis of his own poetical productions, though many of his remarks thereon are as racy as the poems themselves. This method of commenting upon one's own productions is not altogether unauthorized. Mr. Hunt gives for it the example of the old Italian poets with Dante at their head. He regrets that Shakespeare had not been his own commentator, and Spenser given elucidations respecting his Platonic mysticisms on the nature of man. He would have enjoyed 'a divine gossip with him about his woods, and his solitudes, and his nymphs, his oceans, and his heaven.'" At the bottom of this clipping Whitman has written in pencil: "Spenser criticised himself." He also underlined the second and third sentences of the paragraph, beginning "This method," etc.[30]

lection), a poem entitled "To My Sister," but better known by its first line, "It is the first mild day of March," Whitman made the following annotation: "Wordsworth, it seems, is the originator of this kind of poem—followed here by Bryant and others" (*Complete Writings*, IX, 125).

30. Bucke printed this clipping, with Whitman's comments, in *Notes and Fragments*

It was not the 1855 edition only that Whitman sought to promote by his own anonymous writing. Throughout his life he continued to write anonymously about himself and his poems, or else he persuaded friends, under their own names, to publish manuscripts written by himself or based on notes that he provided. In the late 1850's he made friends among the literary bohemians of New York. One of these, Henry Clapp, editor of the *Saturday Press*, did much to promote *Leaves of Grass*, including the publication of Whitman's "A Child's Reminiscence" (later "Out of the Cradle Endlessly Rocking") on December 24, 1859, and the anonymous essay "All About a Mocking-Bird" two weeks later. Whitman scholars believe that Whitman either wrote this essay himself or collaborated with Clapp in writing it. In it the poetry of *Leaves of Grass* is said to be hard to understand because, like the Italian opera, it appeals to the soul rather than to the intellect.[31]

It is well known that Whitman wrote a considerable portion of John Burroughs's *Notes on Walt Whitman as Poet and Person*, published in 1867. When near the end of that year W. M. Rossetti agreed to select and edit for publication a collection of poems from *Leaves of Grass*, Whitman wrote to his friend W. D. O'Connor enclosing a critique of the poems with the request that he copy it and send it to Rossetti in the hope that he would use it as his own introductory essay. In this letter he insisted that he was not "rough," nor "eccentric," nor a "vagabond," but a man of "serenity & decorum, never defiant even to the conventions."[32] Rossetti, needless to say, wrote his own preface. While Whitman was visiting in New York in September, 1868, he sent his friend John Swinton of the New York *Times* a list of suggestions for an article on Whitman in that paper, and the

(see *Complete Writings*, IX, p. 119), but he or the printer changed Whitman's correct spelling of Spenser to "Spencer," possibly misreading Whitman's "s" for a "c", which is quite possible. Bucke lists another clipping from this review of the *Autobiography* (No. 27), at the head of which Whitman wrote: "Great Cockney Poets." It is clipped from page 47 of the review and reads as follows: "The Cockney school of poetry is the most illustrious in England; for to say nothing of Pope and Gray, who were both veritable cockneys, 'from within the sound of Bow Bell,' Milton was too; and Chaucer and Spenser were both natives of the city. Of the four greatest English poets, Shakspeare only was not a Londoner." I have not found this clipping in the Trent Collection.

31. The poem and the essay are reprinted, with some other Whitman materials, by Thomas O. Mabbott and Rollo Silver in a thin quarto with the title *A Child's Reminiscence* (Seattle, 1930).

32. *The Correspondence of Walt Whitman*, ed. E. H. Miller, (New York, 1961), II, 347–349. Whitman's draft of the letter is printed in *With Walt Whitman in Camden*, I, 383.

suggestions were faithfully followed by Swinton.[33] He did not wish one friend he had used to know how he had used another. On October 4, he wrote O'Connor, "Did you see John Swinton's warm paragraph about my illustrious self in *N.Y. Times*, 1st instant?"[34] On October 20 he wrote Charles W. Eldridge at Washington from Providence, where he was visiting: "If the next *Sunday Morning Chronicle* contains a 'personal' about me, would you do me the favor to get half a dozen copies, & keep for me?"[35] It is quite certain that Whitman either wrote out this item or provided the data for it. Whitman seems to have contributed numerous articles, or notes, about himself and his poems to the *Chronicle* and another Washington paper, the *Star*, during the period from 1868 to 1872. Emory Holloway, who examined many of these, says that Whitman "would criticize himself . . . inserting little harmless phrases of doubt or criticism as a smoke-screen to conceal his authorship."[36] This habit of criticizing his own poems favorably and anonymously continued long after he should have felt no need of it. He probably supplied information to O'Connor that was used in *The Good Gray Poet*, but given O'Connor's zeal for Whitman and his skill in composition, it is unlikely that Whitman would have needed to provide further assistance. But he not only supplied information for Dr. Bucke in the preparation of his biography, but revised the entire manuscript and was probably responsible, directly or indirectly, for some of the critical portions of the book, not so much to add to Bucke's extravagant praise, however, as to modify it and eliminate some of his mysticism. Unlike O'Connor, Bucke was not a skillful writer, and Whitman's revisions were mostly efforts to improve the style. The extent of Whitman's revision of Bucke's second version in manuscript is clearly indicated in his letter to Bucke, February 7, 1882.[37] The Springfield *Republican*, on July 23, 1875, printed an article entitled "Walt Whitman. His Life, His Poetry, Himself," which was widely circulated and quoted from.

33. *Correspondence*, II, 49–50.

34. Ibid., p. 54.

35. Ibid., p. 64.

36. "Whitman as His Own Press-Agent," *American Mercury*, XVIII (Dec., 1929), 482–488.

37. *Correspondence* (New York, 1964), III, 266–267. See also Harold Jaffe, "Bucke's *Walt Whitman*: A Collaboration," in the *Walt Whitman Review*, XV (Sept., 1969), 190–194. Jaffe says that Whitman "occasionally inserted exaggerated statements about himself." His article was written in the light of information derived from manuscripts now in the Trent Collection at Duke University and elsewhere, and also from data found in Whitman's *Commonplace Book* in the Feinberg Collection.

It was signed "J. M. S.," the initials of James Matlock Scovel, but it seems highly probable that it was written, in whole or in part, by Whitman.[38] On February 8, 1876, he wrote to Whitelaw Reid, the friendly editor of the New York *Tribune* at that time, about a review he had submitted, before its publication, of the 1876 edition of his works in two volumes, carefully marking the letter "private." The review was published in the *Tribune* anonymously on February 19, with the title "Walt Whitman's Poems. Extracts from 'Two Rivulets.' " Unlike Whitman's early reviews of his work, however, this one has little that could be called criticism, consisting almost wholly of extracts.[39] On February 28, 1885, an article appeared in the *Critic* by "George Selwyn" with the title "Walt Whitman in Camden." It had originally been submitted under the name of Whitman's friend J. M. Scovel, but the editors proposed a *nom de plume* and Whitman agreed.[40] Whitman himself, of course, was the real author. Although at the beginning of this article he said he had "decided to steer clear of any criticism of 'Leaves of Grass,' " he found, toward the end, that he had "slightly to infringe" that decision; on the whole, however, the article is devoted to the facts of his life, his personality, and his condition at the time. There was now no need for him to publicize himself or his book, but he continued, from time to time, to send small personal items to friendly editors, which they usually published.[41]

When Whitman first began to review his poems he clearly perceived the difference between the man he really was and the image of himself he projected as the Poet of *Leaves of Grass*. After 1856 both Whitman and his Poet changed, and as they changed the difference between them diminished. Yet he could not reject the image he so vividly delineated in the two early editions. Publicly, therefore, under the persuasion of Dr. Bucke and others, he came to accept the ideas that there had been no change and that he and his Poet were

38. *Correspondence*, II, 337, n. 54.

39. *Correspondence*, III, 23, and note 18. For particulars see Edwin Haviland Miller, "Walt Whitman's Correspondence with Whitelaw Reid, Editor of the New York *Tribune*," *Studies in Bibliography*, VIII (1956), 243–244. Miller prints in the same article, pp. 244–245, a personal item submitted by the poet in which he is rather flatteringly described in sentimental conversation with children on the occasion of the death of his brother's small son, Walt's namesake, Walter Whitman. This was printed on July 19.

40. See Whitman's letter to one of the editors, Joseph B. Gilder, February 18, *Correspondence*, III, 387, and n. 14.

41. For examples, see *Correspondence*, IV, 33, 66.

and always had been identical. Privately, however, he knew better, and in an emergency he would admit the difference. Such an emergency presented itself in September, 1871, when he received an ardent letter from an English lady, Mrs. Anne Gilchrist, to whom he had sent a volume of his poems and his photograph. In this letter, dated September 3, Mrs. Gilchrist professed her love for Whitman, or rather for the image of him which she derived from the poems, and offered herself in marriage as his ideal mate. Two months later he replied briefly, saying his book was his best letter. She persisted, and in a letter dated March 20, 1872, he told her, rather desperately: "Dear friend, let me warn you about myself—& yourself also. You must not construct such an unauthorized & imaginary ideal Figure, & call it W. W. and so devotedly invest your loving nature in it. The actual W. W. is a very plain personage, & entirely unworthy such devotion."[42] Although Whitman was evidently hard pressed to find reasons for rejecting Mrs. Gilchrist's offer without offending her, what he said was simply true. Never having known or even seen the real man, she had fallen in love with the ideal Poet of *Leaves of Grass*, especially the Poet of the early editions, who Whitman was in honor bound to say was not the real Walt Whitman and never had been.

The first evidence of change in the Poet is to be found in the Calamus poems, which he says he began to compose in September, 1859.[43] By that time the Poet was no longer one of the roughs, nor sensual, nor vulgar. The change is virtually completed in "Out of the Cradle Endlessly Rocking," where the Poet of 1855–1856 does not appear at all; in a sense he had died and a new Poet was born. In fact the last poem in the 1860 edition, "So Long!", reads as if Whitman wished his readers to understand that the Poet who first appeared in "Song of Myself" had now completed his work; he had prepared the way for greater Poets, and would now appear no more. The poem seems to say that whereas before, Walt Whitman had created in the Poet a *persona* different from himself, a mask, he would now and henceforth speak in his own person.

> My songs cease—I abandon them,
> From behind the screen where I hid, I advance personally.

42. *Correspondence*, II, 134–138, 140, 170.
43. See line 15 of "In Paths Untrodden."

The poem ends with the line, "I am as one disembodied, triumphant, dead." Whitman did not, I am sure, believe that his work as a poet was done. The death is purely symbolic so far as he was concerned, but it was real for the Poet-*persona* that he created in 1855. Henceforth the Poet of *Leaves of Grass* will be different and more like the actual Walt Whitman, who, though he has matured spiritually, is essentially the same as in 1855. It is this new Poet's birth that is celebrated in "Out of the Cradle Endlessly Rocking."

If my reading of *Leaves of Grass* is correct, the book was not intended to be an autobiography of the actual Walt Whitman, at least not in 1855. Yet it has often been called an autobiography, and two lines from "So Long!"—"This is no book, / Who touches this, touches a man"—have been cited as evidence. The man here is not the actual Whitman, however, but the Poet in the *Leaves*, who is the speaker in the poem. In a review of the 1860 edition by "January Searle" (George S. Phillips) in the New York *Illustrated News*, he termed *Leaves of Grass* "as genuine a piece of autobiography as that of Augustine, or Gibbon, or the Confessions of Rousseau." The review was reprinted, doubtless with Whitman's approval, in the *Saturday Press*.[44] In 1888 Dr. Bucke wrote Whitman that, in his opinion, *Leaves of Grass* was "a gigantic massive autobiography, the first of its kind (though the trick had been tried before by Goethe, Rousseau and others.)" Commenting on Bucke's statement, Whitman told Traubel that after thinking much about it, he had come to recognize "a more marked centrality" in his book than he had ever observed before, "a centrality actual, while not designed." He seemed to agree that his book might be an autobiography "in the high, the uncommon sense" in which Bucke meant it, but he modestly questioned the opinion that it excels those of Rousseau and Goethe.[45] The centrality he observed is more, I am sure, than would normally be found in a volume of poems on many subjects by a single author. But I gather from Whitman's comments on Bucke's theory—and he discussed it several times with Traubel—that he considered the Poet of *Leaves of Grass* as a projection of a self-image, somewhat idealized, not a representation of his actual self. Yet he and his Poet, as I have said, were more nearly a single identity after 1860 than they had been before. That may be

44. The review appeared in the *Illustrated News* on May 26, 1860, and was reprinted in the *Saturday Press* on June 30, 1860. See *A Child's Reminiscence*, p. 35.

45. Horace Traubel, *With Walt Whitman in Camden*, III, 354–355.

the chief reason he said in "A Backward Glance O'er Travel'd Roads" that without the three or four years of his experience during the Civil War, *Leaves of Grass* "would not now be existing."[46] In the army hospitals of Washington and the poems resulting from his experiences there and on the battle fields Walt Whitman and the Poet, for the time at least, became one. The new Poet who was born with "Out of the Cradle Endlessly Rocking" reached maturity in "When Lilacs Last in the Dooryard Bloom'd," but lost much of his vitality with the deterioration of Whitman's health after his paralysis.

46. *Prose Works 1892*, II, 724.

Lewis Leary

"The Congenial Few": An Expatriate Diary, 1854-1855

The history of American expatriates is yet to be written, and when it is, much fiction may be interspersed with fact. Away from home and close to springs from which their heritage has sprung, transatlantic wanderers have been tempted toward writing letters which reveal their satisfaction or surprise at European manners. Their diaries provide a storehouse of enthusiasm and disapproval through which native prejudice is often artlessly strung. Joel Barlow and Washington Irving were not the first among them, nor are the young men who today have fled from war to Sweden or Spain to be the last. Pilgrims from the new world, in innocence or guilt, have swarmed eastward as to a homeland, in search for a way of life which they have failed to discover at home. They are Ezra Pound and Gertrude Stein and Julian Green, but they are also Lambert Strether, Jake Barnes, and Sam Dodsworth, for fiction has improved the fact.

Germany for learning, France for fun and frolic, England for manners, but Italy for initiation to knowledge of the finest treasures wrought by the hand of man—this has been a familiar American formula. And Italy has had the added attraction of being inexpensive, so that it has drawn men of literature and art, as well as those who enjoy moving excitedly amid the reflection of other people's enterprise. The stream of Americans which flowed through Florence, Venice, and Rome in the nineteenth century has been expertly charted by Van Wyck Brooks in the *Dream of Arcadia.* What is here submitted is a footnote to that book, but a footnote which is worth recording because of what it suggests of an American of less talent than some of her contemporaries but with no less feeling or less appreciative response to what she was certain it was greatly her privilege

This essay in somewhat different form appeared as "A Gossip from Florence: 1854–1855" in the Columbia University *Library Columns,* XII (1963), 7–16.

to experience. If fiction guarantees the circumstance, her real adventures guarantee in turn the verisimilitude of pursuits which beguile Hilda in *The Marble Faun*, the little miniaturist in *Roderick Hudson*, even Isabel Archer, and especially Fran Dodsworth. Fiction has indeed been fathered by attitudes not distinguishably different from those which she reveals. Its longevity preserves fiction as the better witness, more convincing though not in every sense less true than her unformulated testimony.

I

Her name is Elizabeth Clementine Dodge Stedman Kinney, and she is the mother of the American critic, anthologist, and minor poet, Edmund Clarence Stedman. She attracts us immediately because she is sprightly, vain, pretty, and opinionated, proud that in her forties people thought she was in her twenties, proud also that few who first met her would believe that she was the mother of grown sons. Bred in New England, she had something of the Puritan in her, but something of the bluestocking as well, and she was a poet who published two volumes to prove it. She had a lively eye for people and a quick tongue for describing them, but the journal which she kept and the letters[1] which she wrote during a year of her residence in Florence reveal as much of herself as of the personages who fill so many of their pages.

We meet her first in Florence early in October of 1854, settled with her second husband, the Hon. William Burent Kinney, and their small children at Casa del Bello on Via Serragli, the same house in which Nathaniel Hawthorne would live not ten years later. She has decided that for one year she will keep a diary. Difficult as that may be for one of her disposition and domestic responsibilities, she will do it. And she does. Having procured a fat, hardcovered notebook, large enough to furnish her with a year's supply of blank pages, she begins: "For the past five years I have been living in Europe, four years at the court of Turin, where my husband was sent as minister for his government, and one year in this beautiful, this sacred city of Florence." Several pages are filled with reminiscent accounts of balls, receptions, and state dinners which as the wife of a diplomatic representative it had been her duty to attend at Turin. As a girl from the

1. The papers from which I quote are all included in manuscript in the Edmund Clarence Stedman Collection in the Columbia University Library.

New England provinces, accustomed to plainer living and more sedate thought, she had been horrified but fascinated by things which she had heard and seen among the *haute monde.* And Florence seemed even worse: "The morals of society here are even more corrupt than in Turin, but I am not *obliged* to come into contact with them as I was there—I am no longer the *slave* of high life; but can keep aloof from it, and choose my friends from the congenial few who resort to Florence as we do, to drink at her fountains—not to be infected by her pools."

She was indeed proud of these congenial few. Most intimate among them was young Hiram Powers, the American sculptor who would dash over from his studio across the street almost daily for tea and talk. He had been sent to Italy by the ladies of Virginia, commissioned to do a statue of their favorite patriot, Henry Clay, and though he seemed to Mrs. Kinney irresponsibly un-American because he had not yet put chisel to stone in beginning it, Powers was a fascinating companion, a good talker, occasionally a poet, and intriguingly Swedenborgian. The Brownings were also in Florence; the Trollopes, mother and son; and two brothers of Alfred Tennyson, both of them also poets. If not among the most congenial of the few, certainly often in their company was "Lytton son of Bulwer—himself the 'Owen Meredith' whose poems have recently made such a noise of praise"; Isabella Blagden, fervent as a poet and admired by the Brownings; James Jackson Jarvis, remembered today as one of America's most perceptive critics of art, but remembered by Mrs. Kinney, as we shall see, as the most gullible of men and also as a man "very difficult to please" when she read him verses of her own; and Thomas Buchanan Read, "a self-educated, self-made, or rather poetry-made man," who had written in *The New Pastoral* "the first purely American poem of length," but who was "excessively unquiet about it—so nervous that he is half sick" with fear that it would not be well received, which it was not. Such lack of confidence seemed to Mrs. Kinney unworthy of a man of letters.

She preferred someone like Charles Lever, the vivacious and popular Irish novelist, so stout and red-faced, and such a bonvivant, that Mrs. Kinney was sure he would die of apoplexy. She worried about what would happen then to his family of five plump children, but comforted herself with recollection that Lever had shown affectionate foresight by carrying a large life insurance policy. "There never was a jollier soul than he," thought Mrs. Kinney. "How he finds time to keep his two novels going monthly is more than I can divine—with his dinners, his champagne suppers, his rides—he keeps a whole stud of English horses—his morning calls and visits, his card parties and the opera." He told her one evening at dinner that not many months before "he started to go to the United States . . . but was stopped by the insurance company—they would not let him risk the life worth thousands to them in one of our ocean steamers." Providence of a kind which every New Englander could understand had intervened when, in spite of these objections, he had booked passage on the *Arctic* which on just the passage he had planned to take was lost at sea. Mrs. Kinney reported primly that it was in response to his wife's wise presentment that he had given up his plan for a transatlantic crossing and returned instead to Florence, "sacrificing all the fuss his story-telling fame might have made for him in America." But Lever's wife had been right, thought Mrs. Kinney. Her advice had "saved his life."

Mrs. Trollope particularly fascinated her. She was over seventy and lived just a few houses away in "her own beautiful *villino*—built from the product of her novels, and furnished with all the elegance and luxury which wealth and the scholarly taste of her son," Thomas Adolphus Trollope, and his pretty, talented wife, "could afford." The elder Mrs. Trollope, like Charles Lever, seemed to Mrs. Kinney one "of those off-hand writers . . . having published since the year 1830 one hundred volumes!" She was to be admired for the works of art she collected, especially the "Etruscan vases of immense value," but not for her writings. "For what are they?" asked Mrs. Kinney. Her answer was succinctly and austerely New England, as if it had been learned from Thoreau: "they are *novels*—and they sell." She remembered also that Mrs. Trollope had not always treated Americans kindly. In her earliest writings "she served up us Americans with bitter sauce; but we forgive her, for as her Western speculations fell to naught, so did the froth of her ill-humour, foam out at us. Besides, she now affects Americans greatly—as she does *cards*, and other amusements. She finds tongues in green ones; sermons in grave ones; and good in every one—that is, good subjects for her pen portraits. The old lady lives freely; but has free means to live on, thanks to her wit, or her industry."

The Tennyson brothers fascinated her also. They were odd individuals certainly, especially Frederick who loved music so much "that he was for years in the habit of listening alone several times a week to a picked company of twenty-five musicians, who played classic music for him." Such extravagance seemed outright sinful to a New England lady, bred to prudence even in financial affairs. There is an undertone of shock but of admiration also in her observation that Frederick Tennyson had "paid five hundred dollars at one time for a collection of the most celebrated compositions, and fifty dollars to the performers on each occasion, he being their sole audience." When Mrs. Kinney took him to task, however, for not sharing his good fortune with others, he mended his ways by inviting her and a few other friends "to these musical feasts, though with the strictest injunction that none should speak."

But Frederick Tennyson had troubles also. Not long before, one day on the countryside, he had seen a pretty peasant girl, had been infatuated, and had married her. "But . . . he found the face robbed of its charm when taken out of its rustic frame—he had married only the costume. He tried to have his peasant wife taught to read and write, but she was impatient and threw the book at the bore-of-a teacher's head." Here certainly was a situation borrowed perhaps from fiction, but which fiction would often borrow in return. "Poor Tennyson," moralized Mrs. Kinney, "he found it easier to get into a fix than to get out of it again. Why will geniuses do foolish things?"

Foolish things and shocking things distressed her—things like the sight of a person said to have been one of Byron's former mistresses, "now the wife of an old Marquis . . . and herself in good preservation, so as to be handsome at sixty, with fair hair hanging still in lover-catching curls." For individuals of this kind Mrs. Kinney had nothing but haughty disapproval: "She is much caressed and lionized," she said. In fact, "we have all sorts of 'lions' here, and some 'lionesses,' of the great world who in the United States would go by the name of a much *smaller* animal beginning with a B----. . . . Virtue is the rarest of rare Italian sights."

II

It was to the Brownings who lived only a few squares away "in the immortal Casa Guidi" that Mrs. Kinney most completely gave her heart. Mrs. Browning seemed to her "the most fragile-looking of human beings," so ill and wracked with cough that she seldom went out at all in winter—though recently she had been much improved by taking cod liver oil and was, said Mrs. Kinney, "really getting fat on it." Though his wife could speak "scarcely above a whisper . . . Mr. Browning talks enough and *well* enough for both." In fact, Mrs. Kinney thought him "a better conversationalist . . . than poet." His repertoire of small talk seemed inexhaustible; he talked incessantly. She admired him as a "wonderful man" of "intellectual resources, profound learning, tenacious memory, and fund of anecdote. For everything that occurs in the course of conversation, he has a quotation to apply or an illustrative illustration to tell." And "yet to look at him, none would suppose that he was either poet or humorist."

She described him carefully as "small, with a head that seems overgrown for his body, and set right on his shoulders." His "profusion of coarse waving black hair, sprinkled with grey, hides entirely from its length what a neck he has." His eyes were grey and expressive, "his beard nearly grey, his features ordinary, yet his mouth sometimes indicates humor, which he possesses, sometimes satire, and he has enough of this too—too much for keeping friends." Impulsive in manner, "his movements perpetual and wirey as a cricket's," he seemed to her "a very amusing man."

His poetry however seemed unnecessarily "obscure, metaphysical, studied, full of affectations." And purposely so: "He studies, *labors* on all he writes—not to *polish*, but to *roughen* it! His *condensation*—as some call it—would be wonderful, if it were *condensation*; but it really is failing purposely to fill up; his is the *dot and line* plan of writing—trying to give more force of expression—as painters do sometimes in sketches—without coloring." She talked with him one day about a young poet whose verses "seemed mostly to have been modeled on Browning's *Sordello*—that story in a mist—that enigmatical poem which none save himself has ever pretended to understand!" When Browning attacked the young man's lines as "grotesque, obscure, and full of odd conceits," Mrs. Kinney wanted, she said, to "ask him if he felt proud to be the leader of such a school of poets." She did not dare the question, but hoped he would see for himself "the ill effects of his own quaint and unintelligent writings."

Mrs. Browning was beyond doubt his superior: "Indeed," said Mrs. Kinney, "I think her the first of living female poets." Even Alfred Tennyson "must hide his diminished head" beside her, particularly now when he had forsaken his calling "to go off in *spasmodics*" as in "Maud" or into "crazy puerilities" as in "The Princess."

And "she is as good, too, as she is great; never speaks ill of anyone, and is kind, gentle, conciliating with all." Her lines came to her in quick flashes, as Mrs. Kinney's did, and she never stooped to roughen the melodies which sprang from her heart. How different in this and in temper from her husband who was "impulsive, often abusive in speaking of others, and unsparing in his ridicule and contempt of many whom the world calls poets."

Once he let his anger fall on Mrs. Kinney. The circumstance was this: some undiscriminating American traveler had written an article for Nathaniel P. Willis's New York *Home Journal* which had described Mrs. Browning as "an old moth—a crooked, dried up old woman, with a horrible mouth." Mrs. Kinney had risen loyally to the defense of her friend in a letter written to the Newark *Daily News*, which was edited by some of Mr. Kinney's family and to which she often sent accounts of her experiences abroad. What "lack of second sight must those have," she had written, "who see in Mrs. Browning only the frail form, shattered by disease, on which the strong workings of a true woman's heart have left deep traces in advance of time." But this did not please Robert Browning. Frail form, indeed! He wrote at once to Mrs. Kinney, a strong letter, "expressive of displeasure." She had failed to call his wife "beautiful in *person*" and "for this he could not," said Mrs. Kinney, "forgive me." To him his wife had no defect: "I won't concede for a moment," he wrote, "on account of any counter balance of mental qualifications that my wife may have, that 'her form is shattered by disease.' . . . *I* see well enough yet—as Benedick says—without spectacles, and yet see nothing of the matter." Mrs. Browning, however, "made apology to me for his ill-humor," said Mrs. Kinney somewhat archly, "and thanked me herself with feeling."

But sometimes it was difficult for her to understand even Mrs. Browning. The conversation at tea one afternoon turned to George Sand, "whom Mr. Browning said he had the pleasure of seeing recently when she passed through Florence *en route* for Venice.

" 'And I kissed her beautiful hand,' added he, with the satisfaction of one who deemed himself thereby honored.

" 'Pray, who is her lover now?' enquired I.

" 'I can't say,' he replied, 'since she has a new one every day.'

" 'What!' I exclaimed, 'is she so bad as that? I supposed she had never loved but one—certainly but one at a time.'

" '*One*? good heavens! Their name is legion. Put three ciphers to your one and that will not include the sum total of her loves.'

" 'And *you* kiss the hand of such a person—Robert Browning does this?'

" 'Yes, and Elizabeth Barrett Browning does the same, in respect to one of the greatest geniuses God ever made!' This he said with an air of surprise that I should question the act.

" 'Well, well,' I rejoined, 'the greater the genius, the greater the shame of yielding that body, which should be sacred as a temple for the consecrated mind, to the "lust of the flesh": to me George Sand is the worst of women.'

" 'Don't say that!' exclaimed Mrs. Browning, as if my lips had spoken a blasphemy. 'She is not a *bad* woman, but on the contrary, a good and charitable one.'

" 'Then what your husband has just said of her is not true,' I said.

" 'If it be true,' she answered, 'it is only because she has fallen under the dominion of a sensual appetite, which she cannot control; but it is no more than gluttony, or intemperance: I pity her more than I blame her for it. Her *mind* is none the less *godlike*.'

"A sigh was all that could for the moment escape me," said Mrs. Kinney, who must have remembered things which Emerson had written about the necessity of greatness and goodness combined, "so swollen was my heart with indignation, that Mrs. Browning—the truest, the purest of women—could so speak. When I recovered myself, I said freely that I could make no such abstraction of mind, as to separate it from the *morals* of the individual possessing it; at least in this case where the whole heart and mind must be alike depraved and polluted with the body: that a licentious appetite was not to be compared with other sensual appetites affecting merely the taste; that no one could be in act lascivious without having also a lascivious mind. This led to a long and warm discussion. I insisted that if George Sand had been led astray by misplaced affection, having had, as it is said, a husband uncongenial, *love*, even though unlawful, would have somewhat excused, if it did sanctify an unhallowed intercourse.

" 'Love!' they both exclaimed at once. 'She never loved anyone but herself.'

" 'Horrible!' was my reply, to which I added that had she pursued this vile course for bread, again there might have been some palliation for her crime, or even were the appetite which caused them love of gain, it were less bestial.

"'No! No!' rejoined Mrs. Browning. 'There's Rachel, the *tragedienne,* I would not visit her, for she leads a dissolute life . . . for gain.'

"I persisted that the other was the most debasing lust, and that had George Sand the genius of the Archangel, to me she was but the more the *monster.*

"The result was," Mrs. Kinney concluded, "that our discussion left each party fully persuaded in its own mind; but as for me, I could not sleep on retiring for the night, so dreadful does it seem for one whom God has given power to be superhuman, to become brutal through the most polluting of sensual passions, and that this should be a woman too, seemed to me a shame to her whole sex."

Most meetings with the Brownings seemed to have been unmarred, however, with argument or loyal anger. Sometimes they were idyllic, as when the four of them, the Kinneys and the Brownings, sat one evening "in the enchanted gardens of Pratolino, the summer villa of Francesco of Tuscany, where he idled the rosy hours of love with his beautiful mistress (afterwards wife) Bianca Capello." It was just the proper romantic setting for the story of the Browning's courtship and marriage, as Robert Browning told it to them then: how he "had fallen in love with Miss Barrett's poems and wrote requesting an introduction," how she at first refused because "she had scarce ever seen the face of a man, and, like Miranda, knew by sight only her father, having been always confined to the sofa, a desperate invalid," but how "she resented the offer, which seemed to mock her helpless state. So he left under her frown; but sent back his poems and a letter; while she read and mused the fire burned! She believed him true and again received him." But their troubles, as everyone knows, were not over. "He asked her father's consent and was peremptorily refused," but he received her consent which was enough, "took her in his arms, put her into a carriage, carried her to the parson, and the poets' love-knot was tied. Till then he had not known she could stand on her feet." The marriage over, "he bore her as tenderly as one would an infant—to Italy, where *love* and milder airs revived at once her drooping frame." Don't whisper this to a soul, she cautioned as she relayed the tale to her son in America: it was told to us in confidence, "for the Brownings dread getting their private affairs in newspapers."

III

Not long afterwards Florence was to be set to an uproar by the invasions of privacy resulting from the arrival of Daniel Home, the young American spiritualist who as the "Wizard of the West" had been attracting attention in the drawing rooms of England, where he was sponsored by no less a personage, said Mrs. Kinney, than Bulwer Lytton himself. The Trollopes had all crossed over to London, just to watch him tilt tables and spell out messages from the dead. James Jarvis, who was then also in England, sent Mrs. Kinney word that her own guardian-spirit had appeared at a seance there, with a special warning, which he felt that in all friendship he must send on to her, of something which would happen to her soon in Florence. "Perhaps it is some misfortune and he spares my feelings," she wrote. "Thank God, I am not afraid of it." But Daniel Home and his mysterious powers fascinated her, as they did so many of her friends. His arrival early in autumn was a greater event in Florence "than an overflow of the Arno or a revolution. At the club, in the drawing-room, in the servant's hall—court and town—the first question, before even 'Good Morning,' is—'Mr. Home, have you seen him? What has he done?' "

Mrs. Kinney's friends were divided in opinion. Hiram Powers, "being of the Swedenborgian faith, is of course pre-disposed to believe in communications pretending to come from the spiritual world, and he expressed boldly his acceptance of all the late manifestations . . . as veritable and supernatural." Mrs. Powers, "strong-minded, but nervous," could not make up her mind, but she was all of a flutter about it. Mrs. Browning, said Mrs. Kinney, "is half Swedenborgian and believes in 'the spirits,' " but Robert Browning, "a Presbyterian . . . protests them a humbug.' For once Mrs. Kinney agreed with him. But she was troubled because when Browning had seen Home at work in London some months before, even he had not been able to detect the exact nature of the fraud.

When Browning had then asked to see the "spirit hands" which rang bells and moved tables, "the request," he had written Mrs. Kinney, "was complied with, though the lamp was first extinguished, and all the light permitted for the experiment came through the muslin curtains, and that the dim light of a cloudy evening, so that the table could not be seen distinctly, nor anything save some object held up before the eyes." In such a situation, "presently a hand clothed to the elbows in white drapery appeared from the edge, not centre, of the table, but no one was permitted to touch it or to examine it closely." The mysterious hand then lifted a wreath from the table, and then Home solemnly remarked that the spirit wished to place it on Mrs. Browning's head."[2] Mrs. Kinney sniffed. "A very disconcerting spirit, to be sure," she said, "crowning the only lady poet present," especially when for this purpose Mrs. Browning had to "change her place and take the chair next to Mr. Home! Comments," she concluded archly, "are unecessary."

Browning had further written her that "knees were touched, and musical instruments played on; but these things were done *under* the table. In short, it was all *underhanded* work enough." And when Mr. Home had gone into his customary trance during which witnesses like the gullible Jarvis heard from him "eloquence such as no mere mortal ever uttered," his spiritual ecstasy produced to Browning "nothing more than a stupid, long-winded canting exhortation" which even Mrs. Browning admitted resembled a "dissenting sermon." Like Jarvis, the Trollopes, however, had been taken in completely—though later they were to change their minds—and wrote from London that when the medium came to Florence he would convince even the obstinate Mrs. Kinney, "sceptic as I am," she said, "that he is honest and his doings not *his*, but the *spirits*."

Her conversion was gradual but spectacular: when Mrs. Kinney fell, she fell all the way and all at once, like the "wonderful one-hoss shay" of which Oliver Wendell Holmes would write only a year later. As the time for Home's arrival in Florence approached, she became more apprehensive. She had been obdurate in her opinion that he was only an accomplished juggler, expert at sleight of hand, clever in using dim lights, and artful in allowing participants in his seance to betray themselves. But the more she heard, the more she worried,

2. Robert Browning's attitude toward Home is perhaps best expressed in his "Mr. Sludge, the Medium," which however in a review in the *Spiritual Magazine* for July, 1864, was said to have been inspired by the poet's jealousy because at the seance described above the spirit had chosen to place the wreath on Mrs. Browning's head instead of his own. See D. D. Home, *Incidents in My Life* (New York, 1872), pp. 105–107. "If I ever cross the fellow's path again," Browning later wrote Mrs. Kinney, "I shall probably be silly enough to soil my shoe by kicking him"—see *New Letters of Robert Browning*, ed. W. C. DeVane and K. L. Knickerbocker (New Haven, 1950), p. 199. He later still recalled "the rascality of Home and how his incredible stupidity wrought his downfall" (but that is another story)—see *Letters of Robert Browning*, ed. T. J. Wise (New Haven, 1933), p. 115.

and the more she worried the more she became convinced that perhaps he was not trickster at all, but a sorcerer, a wizard indeed, in league with forces of evil and a minion of Satan sent to distress good people. His sorcery was like the witchcraft which her colonial American ancestors had known, but came now in new form, with modern improvements, for "Sorcery was abroad in the land, and the days of Satanic incantations not past."

"When news came that Mr. Home was on his way hither, I almost determined," she wrote, "not to see him . . . not to let him into my own house, lest the spirit of evil should find admittance with him." But when Mrs. Trollope arranged a seance at her home, Mrs. Kinney did consent to attend. Seven of them—probably the Kinneys, the Powerses, and the three Trollopes—sat that evening around a heavy center table "which suddenly became agitated," reported Mrs. Kinney, "with a tremulous motion unlike anything I can suppose, unless it be the trembling produced by an earthquake; knocks were heard, first round the walls behind us, and in a few minutes on the table." The spiritualist himself seemed to her "apparently a simple as well as pleasing young man" who kept his hands the whole time visible on the table. She looked beneath the table, as Robert Browning had suggested, to see what caused the agitation, but she could find nothing. And then there came a tapping which indicated that the spirits were present, spirits who had come, said Mr. Home, especially to talk with her. When they tapped out her pet name, Libbie ("though no one but my husband knew I was so called") and when her foot was touched under the table by a strangely knotted handkerchief which no visible hand had placed there, then she cried out, "This is deviltry! . . . I am afraid of it!" Whereupon the spirits answered, "If you are good, evil can not come near you. God protects his own."

"I returned home," she reported later, "in a state of agitation, and as is my wont when perplexed, went to the Bible, opened it, and by chance put my finger on this passage—'Approve things which are excellent.' " It seemed a reproof to her scepticism and her suspicions of sorcery. She therefore arranged a private seance in which intimate details of her past life were disclosed by the spirits of departed friends, and she added thirty ecstatic pages to her journal to detail what happened in this and subsequent adventurings into the world of spirits. She wrote Mrs. Browning a long letter about her experience, her newfound belief. "Certainly," said the poet who was then in Paris, "if

Mrs. Kinney is convinced, we may despair of no one," and she wrote her sister an account of the conversion which, because Mrs. Kinney's own account is so long and so intimate, can be turned to as summary.

"The most private circumstances," wrote Mrs. Browning, "were referred to in messages from departed friends of the Kinneys . . . The raps which spelled out some sentences to Mrs. Kinney were made on Mr. Kinney's knee—he sitting the farthest off from the medium of all in the room. Mr. Kinney adroitly and rapidly, while he felt the raps, dropped his hand to his knee, and there came into sudden contact with another hand—the spiritual. . . . Young Mrs. Trollope's skirt was blown out. . . . The spirits said they could influence Mrs. Kinney's health beneficially—and they desired her to provide herself with a bottle of distilled water—which young Powers ran for to the chemists while the seance went on. . . . When the water came, Mrs. Kinney tasted it. Of course it was pure water. Left on the table to the eyes of all, there plainly arose a *vapour from the water.* Then she tasted it again, and there was a peculiar aromatic flavour. These spirits called it '*Odic* water,' and desired her to keep it in a dark place and take a tea spoon of it every day—which she *does.*"[3]

IV

The Odic water, or perhaps simply her sprightly interest in other people, preserved Mrs. Kinney in health for many years. She lived to be almost ninety, finally as proud of her literary son as she had formerly been proud of knowing the Trollopes, the Tennysons, and the Brownings. If she seems only another American innocent abroad and more naive than some of her twentieth-century countrymen may be likely to consider themselves, she provides spectacles through which can be seen a little more clearly, not only details in the life of artists who lived in Florence a hundred years ago as her gossip reveals them to us, but also something of a spirit of good-heartedness and good-will which are perhaps not always practical or even attractive native characteristics but which are underlined here only a little less effectively than when fashioned to fiction by countrymen who could examine their world more objectively than she.

3. *Elizabeth Barrett Browning: Letters to Her Sister, 1846–1859,* ed. Leonard Huxley (London, 1929), p. 23.

Herbert Brown

Charles Brockden Brown's "The Story of Julius": Rousseau and Richardson "Improved"

I

The name of Charles Brockden Brown is usually tagged with such familiar labels as "our first professional man of letters" and "the father of American fiction." His sensational treatment of dementia in *Wieland* (1798) and *Ormond* (1799), his grisly description of the ravages of yellow fever in *Arthur Mervyn* (1799–1800), his melodramatic account of Indian life in *Edgar Huntly* (1799), and his bold use of native materials to evoke intense horror have also earned him the title of "American Gothic novelist."

Brown, however, wore his Gothicism with a difference, discarding as untrue to nature the supernatural clap-trap of the popular goose-pimple school of fiction. As a child of the Enlightenment, he sought in *Arthur Mervyn* "to excite and baffle the curiosity, without shocking belief"; while in *Wieland*, he insisted that none of its seemingly "miraculous" incidents violated "the known principles of human nature." The author's importance in our literary history is owing to his ability to transcend the conventions of the Gothic novel and, as Richard Chase has noted, "to inaugurate that peculiar vision of things often found in American fiction—a vision of things that might be described as a mysteriously portentous representation of abstract symbols and ideas on the one hand and, on the other, the involutions of the private psyche."[1]

Although Brown has thus come to be rightly regarded as a pioneer in exploring the weird realm whose strands darken the work of Poe, Hawthorne, James, and Faulkner, it was only in the middle of his

1. Richard Chase, *The American Novel and Its Tradition* (New York, 1957), p. 30.

feverishly brief career that he achieved, and then only fitfully, his power as a recorder of the human conscience under the stress of overwhelming emotions. His first attempts at fiction in the early 1790's, as well as his last two novels, *Clara Howard* and *Jane Talbot* in 1800, are squarely in the sentimental tradition exploited by Rousseau and Richardson. The influence of both these writers is amply illustrated in the following sketch, "The Story of Julius," a tale of "fictitious adventures," here printed for the first time from a seventeen-page letter written on May 20, 1792, to Brown's intimate friend, Joseph Bringhurst, Jr., in Wilmington, Delaware.[2]

The sketch of "The Story of Julius" and a plan for its completion as a full-bodied, epistolary novel are embedded in a document of considerable biographical and critical interest.[3] As the self-revelation of an American Man of Feeling, it confirms the impressions the novelist made upon his other close friends, William Wilkins, Elihu Smith, and William Dunlap, who often complained about Brown's tendency to confuse truth with fiction and "to intertwine the real with the imaginary." The letter to Bringhurst also throws light on the novelist's love affair with "Henrietta G———," a shadowy lady who seems to have existed only in the world of Brown's ardent fantasies.[4]

Indeed, if the author's account of the inception of the sketch is not another of the many fictitious adventures with which Brown often puzzled and exasperated his friends, it was Henrietta who prompted the writing of "The Story of Julius." After listening to his rhapsodic

2. Joseph Bringhurst, Jr. (1767–1834) was Brown's fellow student at the Friends Latin School in Philadelphia, 1781–1786. The letters to Bringhurst are deposited in the Hawthorne-Longfellow Library of Bowdoin College by Mr. and Mrs. Gordon Hargraves of Wilmington, Delaware, to whose generosity I am indebted for permission to print "The Story of Julius."

3. "Julius" occupies only thirteen pages of the letter of May 20, 1792. I hope to print the entire correspondence consisting of a score of letters to Bringhurst, as well as four unusually revealing letters of the novelist to Deborah Ferris (1773–1844), who became the wife of Joseph Bringhurst, Jr., in 1799.

4. Evidence of the authenticity of the "love letters" between Henrietta and Brown is far from conclusive. Although a biographer of the novelist, David L. Clark, believes that they depict "one of the most momentous experiences in the young philosopher's life," the actual letters are not known to exist. The original correspondence is assumed to have been copied from the letters they exchanged with each other. They are printed as "Journal Letters" in Clark's *Charles Brockden Brown: Pioneer Voice of America* (Durham, N.C., 1952), pp. 53–107. For a devastating attack on the authenticity of Henrietta, see Eleanor M. Tilton's cogent article, "The Sorrows of Charles Brockden Brown," *PMLA*, LXIX (Dec., 1954), 1304–1308. Henrietta's romantic conduct, exquisite sensibility, and elegant epistolary style are so reminiscent of the attributes of countless sentimental heroines that the "Journal Letters" are probably another of Brown's attempts to write a sentimental novel in "the epistolary method."

praise of Rousseau's *La Nouvelle Heloise*, the outraged lady promised to forgive her lover only on the condition that he compose an antidote to the poison in that "seductive and pernicious book" by writing a tale inculcating "different maxims." Henrietta even went so far as to recommend that he take Rousseau or Richardson as a model for his performance, "either in the narrative or the epistolary method."

Brown's earlier letters had made Bringhurst familiar with his friend's admiration for Rousseau and Richardson. "I have been conversing with Rousseau," Brown wrote on May 5, 1792. "I have since ten o'clock been plying with rapturous attention through his impassioned and illumined pages.... What a model of pathetic eloquence!" His adoration of Richardson was equally fervid. On December 21 of the same year, the novelist startled his friend by declaring that as a picture of moral perfection for the instruction of mankind, *Sir Charles Grandison* exceeded in its power the biblical story of the life of "the divine son of Mary." "If glory be the recompense of actions beneficial to mankind," he continued, "who shall venture to dispute the palm with Richardson ... who is there who can stand in competition with the writer of *Clarissa*: the sublimest and most eloquent of writers? Nor can I have the least doubt that it is of more advantage to mankind that those celebrated works have been written, than that Galileo invented the telescope or that Newton surveyed the heavens through it."

Since Brown informed Bringhurst that "The Story of Julius" would be cast in the form of letters, he seems in at least one respect to have acted upon Henrietta's hint to use Richardson as his model. Gratefully acknowledging his friend's interest in the story on May 20, 1792, the author announced, "I have formed a list of all the letters of which it is to consist, their dates, the parties to them, their length, and the topics of which they are to treat.... I will shew this list to you if you have any inclination to see it." Brown viewed the completed project as a double-decked narrative. "The Story of Julius naturally divides itself into two parts," he told Bringhurst. "The second part beginning at the sickness of my hero, at a Glamorganshire village, I have already written: but the first part, which would commence at Julius' return from the Continent, is not yet composed. Whenever I have leisure I will complete the plan. I have already delineated a sketch of this performance."

If Brown actually completed the second part, which he said he had delivered in installments for Henrietta's entertainment, no trace of the manuscript seems to have survived. His explanation of its "irrecoverable" loss by "subsequent accidents" appears to have been cut from the same flimsy fabric as the lady herself whose "bright eyes" were "suffused with tears at the perusal of it." "How many sighs," Brown exclaimed, "did it draw from the bottom of her heart!" Had the novelist possessed the veriest smidgen of a sense of humor, Bringhurst might have known how to interpret his friend's remark that "the composition would be equal in extent to twenty duodecimo volumes. It would be a most delightful avocation which would quiet and soothe all my cares." Brown's cares, however, were not destined to be soothed by the composition of so ambitious an undertaking. Although the novelist promised his friend, "I will not despair of procuring for you the original performance," neither the completed portion which had edified Henrietta, nor a page of the projected "twenty duodecimo volumes" ever reached him. Later, when Bringhurst reported that he had dreamed of Julius, the flattered author responded in a note on May 30, 1792: "I am extremely pleased with your vision, and you cannot easily conceive how gratified I am in finding that the poor, neglected and desponding Julius is sometimes present in the airy porticos of slumbering fancy." Both friends, and perhaps, even Henrietta herself, were content to leave the neglected Julius slumbering in that nebulous region.

II

THE STORY OF JULIUS

The Plans of a Sketch of Fictitious Adventures

CHARLES BROCKDEN BROWN

It was in the summer of the year 1788, during my connection with the excellent and amiable Henrietta G——[5], that I first read the *Eloise* of Rousseau. I could never procure any more than the first & second volumes, but these I read with infinite avidity and delight. Miss G. had this work in the original, but notwithstanding all my solicitations and intreaties, she refused to lend it to me. She declared

5. This date seems to indicate that Brown's "connection" with Henrietta began at least four years before the time cited by Clark who conjectured, "Brown had apparently made the acquaintance of the beautiful Henrietta in the spring of 1792 . . . ," Clark, *Charles Brockden Brown*, p. 54.

that it was the most pernicious and seductive book that she had ever read, and that she would neither read it a second time nor suffer it to go out of her possession. This refusal and those invectives only heightened my desire to peruse it, and with some difficulty I obtained the sight of the translation of the first and second parts of that celebrated and fascinating performance. On my next visit to her she quickly discovered, by certain allusions which I made during the course of our conversation, that I had plucked the forbidden fruit. She, half angrily and half jocosely, upbraided my contumacy and repeated her opinion that the work was dangerous. This gave rise to an animated dispute, in which I endeavoured to maintain an opposite opinion, but I acted the part of an advocate with so much indiscreet vehemence as absolutely to offend this scrupulous and delicate fair one, and the only condition on which she would be persuaded to forgive me, was that I should compose a similar performance, in which different maxims should be incultivated, of which love and friendship in all their purity and sublimity should form the basis, and in which the triumph of virtue over the most lawless and impetuous passions, of duty over inclination, should be as vividly and forcibly described as I was able. She left me at liberty to make either Rousseau or Richardson my model, and to write either in the narrative or epistolary method.[6] Nothing could be more arrogant and audacious than for one of my youth and inexperience[7] to attempt to tread in the footsteps of these illustrious writers, and nothing but the necessity of submitting to absolute commands could induce me to engage in so arduous an undertaking. I accordingly immured myself in my chamber, placed a table opposite a window which overlooks the meeting streams of Delaware and Schuylkill and from which the eye might traverse the former river as far as Red Bank and Billingsport, and, by writing almost incessantly from sun rise to midnight for thirty days, in the finest season of the year, I performed the task which was imposed upon me, and finished a Romance, in the epistolary form and after

6. Brown relied awkwardly on "the epistolary method" in his full-length novels. Even in his personal letters, he enjoyed presenting ideas in the form of notes from imaginary correspondents. "I wanted to write an essay," he confessed to Bringhurst in a homily on December 22, 1792, "and have done it, you see, in epistolary form . . . ." He also amused himself by occasionally addressing his friends as though he were writing from the "Cuilli Pays de Vaud" in Geneva, Switzerland. A letter mailed to Bringhurst from Philadelphia on May 15, 1792, is headed "The Cocoa Tree, Pall Mall, London."

7. If 1788 *is* the date of the "connection" with Henrietta, Brown was only seventeen years old when he wrote "Julius."

the manner of Rousseau though somewhat more voluminous than 'Julie.'[8]

In a work, written with such haste, and with such little premeditation, defects must necessarily abound. I conceived a general idea of the plan as I walked homeward, one evening after visiting Miss G——. I, at that time lived four miles and an half from the city, and never left her till ten o'clock. Next morning I adjusted my table, furnished it with writing instruments, and began my work which I finished in the time which I have mentioned. I sent to Miss G—— in the evening all that I had written during the course of that day, without revision or correction, and waited on her personally once or twice a week, to hear her comments and remarks. I mention these circumstances as apologies for the defectiveness of the plan, for with regard to execution, the rapidity with which it was written rather added to its excellence than detracted from it, and all slighter inaccuracies of grammar, orthography and punctuation were amended by my fair critic, whose sagacity was equal to her taste.

The hero of my tale I distinguished by the name of Julius Brownlow. I believe in every work of this kind, the character of the writer, such as it really is, or such as he imagines, or wished to be, may be found.[9] I confess that this time my ambition extended no farther than to act and speak like *Julius.*

On the amiable Julius therefore I conferred every excellence, mental and corporeal, yet mingled with certain failings which I discovered in myself and which exalted this personage to the level of probability. I made his stature tall and majestic, his limbs graceful and exquisitely proportioned, his countenance beautiful and blooming, and his eyes full of sweetness and intelligence. He was the heir of an ancient and opulent family, whose patrimonial possessions lay near Keswick in Cumberland, one of the wildest and most romantic spots in Great Britain. His father died in the infancy of Julius, and left the guardianship of him and his sister Julietta, who were brought forth at a birth, to their mother: a woman of beauty and talents, but strongly addicted

8. Jean Jacques Rousseau, *Julie; ou, La nouvelle Heloise.*

9. The author's identification of himself with his hero by naming him "Brownlow" is not the first such instance in Brown's writings. In the early 1790's, he signed a playful letter to William Wilkins as "C. B. Brownlow." Quoted by Clark, *Charles Brockden Brown*, pp. 38–39. Four of Brown's early essays, "The Rhapsodist," published in the *Columbian Magazine* (Philadelphia, Aug.-Nov., 1789), were signed successively, B, R, O, W. See Harry Warfel, *The Rhapsodist* (New York, 1943), pp. vi, 1–24.

to the levities of fashion, of violent ambition, and full of the prejudices of birth.[10] She was passionately fond of her children, and displayed in their education, a true maternal tenderness and prudence.

Julius and Julietta, who, as I said before, were twins, so exactly resembled each other in their infancy, that one could scarcely be distinguished from the other, but as they grew up, Julietta retained only those features of her brother which were consistent with the highest degree of female softness and beauty. This angelick pair passed their childhood and learned the rudiments of education in the company of each other. Julius displayed many early tokens of future eminence, and Julietta displayed a memory not less tenacious, and an understanding not less vigorous than her brother. A conformity of dispositions and pursuits, the constant habit of living, learning, and playing together, gradually produced between these two, the most tender and inviolable union of which two persons, of different sexes are capable, and which does not absolutely deserve the appellation of love.

This union, my friend, formed one pillar of my performance and, in the conduct and characters of Julius and Julietta, I endeavoured to trace the effects of friendship of the purest and most exalted kind. I have, my dearest Bringhurst, long and deeply philosophised on love and friendship, but all my philosophy was merely the result of my own feelings. I have experienced all the effects which those passions can produce on a susceptible mind. I have not been an inattentive or unintelligent observer of my own emotions, and therefore do not want a guide in tracing all the mazes of the human heart when under the dominion of those seraphic passions.[11]

10. Mercenary parents, whose "violent ambition" and "prejudices of birth" cause the misery of their children by forcing them to marry wealthy but repulsive suitors, became stock figures in American fiction after the publication of Richardson's *Clarissa Harlowe*. See Herbert Brown, *The Sentimental Novel in America: 1789–1860* (Durham, N.C., 1940), pp. 28–57. The theme of parental control of marriage also appears in Brown's fragmentary "Sketches of the History of the Carrils and Ormes," printed in William Dunlap, *The Life of Charles Brockden Brown: together with Selections from the Rarest of His Printed Works, from His Original Letters, and from His Manuscripts before Unpublished* (Philadelphia, 1815), I, 299. ". . . the woes of Clarissa," Brown wrote to Bringhurst on December 21, 1792, "like the sufferings of Jesus, terminate only in death, and their virtues find their reward only in another region."

11. Brown's own letters provided such "a guide." "I never yet doubted that love and friendship were, in reality, the same," the novelist wrote in describing his feelings for William Wilkins. "I felt my self attracted to him by an inconceivable and irresistible charm that, like the lightning of love, left me not at liberty to pause or deliberate . . . . I can scarcely refrain from embracing him. Tears of affection start into my eyes, when I look upon him . . . ." In the same letter to Bringhurst on May 20,

With regard to Julius and Julietta, every cause existed from which sacred and celestial friendship naturally flows. Their personal resemblance, the conformity of tempers and pursuits, and their similarity with respect to age, and their constant and domestic intercourse, and all circumstances favourable in the highest degree, to the birth and nurture of this passion: of which the tenderness and delicacy must be greatly heightened by the difference of sexes, and their kindred, while it kept love (which, in the opinion of some is the only kind of friendship which can subsist between persons *unrelated*, and not of the same sex) at a sufficient distance, must be supposed to contribute to the strength of their attachment.

The situation was somewhat new, for Rousseau and Richardson had only described that friendship which may subsist between two men or two women, and have given us no striking pictures of sisterly and fraternal love, and of that refined and exquisite relation which must arise when the causes, producing friendship, operate in uniting two brothers or two sisters or a brother and a sister. That such causes may operate with regard to those, as well as with respect to absolute irrelatives is not to be denied, and the union, which results from those causes operating in the domestic sphere, must be proportionably more perfect, as opportunities are here afforded of more frequent converse and entire confidence than in other situations.

I have heard that Richardson, in his original plan, intended to have made Miss Howe the sister of Clarissa, but that he afterward found it expedient to alter his plan.[12] The alteration was doubtless proper, but had it not been made, we should have seen the description of a new kind of friendship. But to return to Julius—

Having in the first place, selected all the external circumstances proper for my design, it was next my province to endow them with corresponding talents and dispositions, with souls attuned to love and sympathy, and with virtues which, though heroic and uncommon, I contrived to render not romantic or incredible.

Julius, at a proper age, was sent to Eton: and his Mother and Sister

1792, Brown hastened to assure his friend that the attachment he cherished for his correspondent "is not so violent: so tender: so impassioned, but it is more rational and not less permanent."

12. In the list of characters prefacing *Clarissa*, Richardson described Miss Anna Howe as "the most intimate friend, companion, and correspondent" of the heroine. He later remarked in a letter to Sarah Chapone in 1751 that he hoped to create in Miss Howe "a lively Woman of Virtue," capable of refuting "the Notion of Rakes and Foplings that Womens Minds are incapable of fervent and steady Friendships."

removed from Cumberland to Middlesex, to a seat, which belonged to Julius, in the neighbourhood of London. The graceful student made a rapid progress in knowledge, and at fifteen was qualified for his entrance into the University. During his stay at Eton, Julius maintained a constant correspondence with his Sister, and spent every interval of leisure at his mother's house. Both Sister and Brother had acquired an exquisite taste for poetry, were adepts in English literature, and were highly skilled in penmanship and composition. Instead of going to the University of Cambridge or Oxford, [Julius] passed two years at Gottingen, under the tuition of a man eminent for knowledge and virtue whom I have distinguished by the name of Mr. Sutphen. He was a native of Switzerland, but had received an English education and was both a scholar and a gentleman. While at Gottingen, my hero continued to correspond with his sister, in like manner as at Eton. His letters were extremely copious and minute, containing a relation of every thing which respected himself, with strong and dramatic pictures of the characters and manners of his friends, associates and fellow students, and written with elegance and vivacity. Having resided for two years at Gottingen, he left it with his preceptor, and, after residing for twelve months in France, Italy, and Switzerland, he returned into England, and retired with his Mother and Sister to Brownlow Hall in Cumberland. There he devoted himself to the society of his Sister, to contemplation, and to the study of the sublimest sciences.

At Gottingen he became acquainted with Lauder Allen, the son of a Scottish Advocate, superior in age, and equal to Julius in virtue and accomplishments. Their acquaintance soon ripens into Intimacy, and on Julius' return to Keswick and Lauder's to Edinburg, they commence a correspondence with each other. Julius gives his friend, an account of his present Situation, of his resolutions and opinions with regard to study and to the conduct of life. He relates his daily avocations, his ramblings and his musings, and draws minute pictures of the adjacent country and of the manners of the Inhabitants.

With this correspondence, I at first intended to begin my work. There is no country in Great Britain, or perhaps in Europe that abounds with more magnificent and beautiful scenery amid rural grandeur and elegance than this part of Cumberland and the Neighbouring districts in Westmoreland, and none, in which the manners are more worthy of Philosophical observation. I had read but few accounts and those slender and imperfect of either the country or of the Inhabitants. But I was then possessed of a map of the northern provinces wonderfully extensive, accurate, and picturesque, and my fancy had long brooded on the scanty materials with which my various and diffusive reading had furnished me, with the utmost ardour and intensiveness.[13] I longed to reduce the vague but brilliant images, which had amused my visionary hours, into some form and order. I had often imagined myself wandering, by moonlight, along the shining and pebbly margin of the Darwent, or hanging over the verdant and precipitous banks of the Eden, and could have described a scene that would have equalled [it], were it possible to equal reality, but I was then doubtful of my skill, and began to think that before they could, with any propriety, be described, they must be actually visited.

I was also much delighted with the prospect of describing the meditations of a youth of the deepest penetration and the most vigorous imagination (who had studied books and conversed with mankind) on the sublimest subjects that can engage the human faculties, on the uses, bounds and relations of the Sciences and on the nature and capacity of the soul. I easily foresaw that this would furnish opportunity for forming, explaining and digesting my own opinions, and that I could, at all events, perform this part of my work by making judicious extracts from "The Journal of a Visionary," which I had written the year before, but I was quickly sensible that this would lead me too far from my principal design, that it would render my work too voluminous, and my plan too complicated.[14]

I therefore still postponed the opening of my work. Julius by his indefatigable application to his pen and his book, in a short time al-

13. Brown's fancy, brooding on scenes he had never visited, took the form of a letter sent to Bringhurst from the author's lodgings on Vine Street, Philadelphia, but headed "London, May, 1792," where he pretended to have been living for at least a year. "The approaching summer," he wrote, "I intend to pass in Westmorland and Durham, as I passed the last in Staffordshire and Wales, and the winter will be consumed at Edinburg . . . . After which I propose to loiter away several years in Switzerland and Italy . . . ."

14. If Brown's letter to Bringhurst on May 30, 1792, may be trusted as an accurate index to the "Journal of a Visionary," the author was judicious in refusing to make his hero the mouthpiece of the Visionary's meditations. Concluding that "grammar, Rhetorick and poetry were the sciences to which I felt the strongest attachment," Brown resolved "to form some regular and analytical System, which should furnish the material of reflexion, and which should serve as my lode star, my guiding luminary through the grammatical, Rhetorical and Poetical Library: by which I should be able to enroll in its proper class and assign its proper station to every new idea with which study and reflexion should furnish me."

most irreparably injured his constitution: which was naturally delicate and feeble. He was under a necessity of relinquishing his studies, and, for the sake of restoring his health, made an excursion into Wales and Cornwall. His indisposition increases, and he becomes dangerously sick in an obscure Inn at the Village of Mangam near the Severn Sea, in Glamorganshire. There then my performance opened and began with a letter from Julius written at Mangam, when he supposed his death to be near at hand, and expected to be carried from his apartment only to his grave, and addressed to the lovely Julietta, his sister and his friend. He however happily escapes the death which he imagined to be inevitably impending. And, in his subsequent letters informs his sister, that Mr. Wentworth the Rector of the parish, learning of his situation, visited him and prevailed upon him to suffer himself to be removed to his house, where by the benevolent and hospitable care of Mr. Wentworth and his daughter—

Ah! my friend! That daughter! Sophia Wentworth! With what a pen of passion did I describe her beauties! How liberally did I shower perfection on her mind and person! The Image of my Henrietta rose before me. Then did, I indeed, assume the person of my hero. Then quickly did the studious, philosophical Julius undergo a transformation, and become a tender, passionate, romantic lover like myself!—[15]

Julius quickly recovered and continuing his correspondence with his sister, relates the origin and progress of his passion for Miss Wentworth. The invitation which her father offers and he accepts to pass the summer at his house: describes the country and its Inhabitants, the manner in which he employs his time, and his long and interesting conversations with Sophia, and a variety of remarkable incidents which I, at this time, do not exactly recollect. I make the conduct of Sophia a pattern of prudence and delicacy, and though she is equally enamoured with Julius it is with the utmost difficulty the confession is extorted from her. At length however he prevails upon her to declare her sentiments: He then formally proposes himself to Sophia's father, and solicits her hand in marriage. The father after the discovery of his daughter's inclination scruples not to comply with this proposal pro-

15. The transformation of "the studious, philosophical Julius" to that of "a tender, passionate romantic lover" is paralleled by the author's similar metamorphosis. Brown confessed on May 30, 1792, that "the deity of Love" wrought havoc on his meditations. ". . . as soon as I began to riot in those intoxicating draughts which this divinity presented to my lips," he wrote his friend, "all my airy fabricks vanished, all my reveries were forgotten, and 'the journal of a visionary' thrown aside and intirely neglected."

vided he can obtain the concurrence of Mrs. Brownlow. Julius addresses himself by letter to his Mother, acquainting her with all those circumstances and soliciting her consent to his union with Sophia. I have already described Mrs. Brownlow to be a woman of Ambition. She doats on Julius, but regards his marriage not as a means of domestic felicity but as an instrument of advancement in his rank and fortunes. To make himself richer than he is at present and to allye himself to nobility she considers as the only purpose of his being, and [as] she herself never felt the inchantments of love, she imagines that they have no reality, and believes that every man is governed in the choice of his wife by motives of interest. She has therefore been for some time past, busily imployed in searching for a lady, who shall possess the requisite qualifications of youth, beauty, and wealth, and whom she shall think worthy to be presented to her Julius as his wife.

In the Neighbourhood of Keswick there resided a venerable nobleman whom I have denominated Lord Monthievers. His only daughter and the heiress of all his possessions was Caroline Monthievers: of the same age with Julietta, and as lovely and accomplished as her friend: for Caroline and Julietta, being within a small distance from each other are friends and visitants. Julius, on his return from Gottingen, was introduced to Caroline, and made an impression on her tender and susceptable heart, which gradually grew stronger. She frequently visited Julietta, and on these visits was treated by Julius with the utmost politeness and respect, but he felt no particular attachment to her, and was utterly a stranger to those emotions which his presence always excited in the bosom of Caroline. Her delicacy would not suffer her to make the first advances. Her condition, therefore, was hopeless; and her grief preying on her health and spirits, reduced her at length to a state of so much weakness, as greatly to alarm her father, whose life and happiness depended upon those of his daughter. Many fruitless efforts were made to discover the cause of her malady. At length however the drooping Caroline was prevailed upon to disclose. Parental fondness was superior to every other passion in the breast of Lord Monthievers, and the consideration of his daughter's life, which could not be other wise preserved, induced him to acquaint the mother of Julius with Caroline's situation and to declare his readiness to negotiate a marriage between their children. This offer was highly acceptable to that ambitious [mother]. She acknowledged the honour which his lordship intended her family in terms of unlimited gratitude, and imagining it impossible that her son should have the least objection to so advantageous an offer, the marriage was immediately determined upon. At this period Mrs. Brownlow was seized with a severe sickness, which disabled her from communicating the intelligence of those proceedings to Julius, under her own hand, and, while she was directing Julietta to write to her brother and inform him of those particulars, that letter from Julius was presented to her in which he explains his situation with respect to Sophia, mentions his intentions to make her his wife, and intreats her to approve of them. The effect of this unseasonable letter on Mrs. Brownlow may easily be conceived, she directs Julietta to acquaint her brother with her total disapprobation of his conduct: her utter and irreconcilable aversion to his union with Sophia. She commands him instantly to return home, to break off all connections with Miss Wentworth, and to prepare for the celebration of his nuptials with Caroline. She tells him also that she finds herself rapidly approaching her end, beseeches him to hasten his return that she may see him before she dies, bestow upon him her last blessing, and charge him with her last command. Julius is agitated with grief and dispair at the reception of this letter, explains to Mr. Wentworth the condition of his mother, and, after taking an affecting leave of Sophia, who acts on this, as on every other occasion, with heroic fortitude and magnanimity, he prepares for his departure from Glamorganshire. Mrs. Brownlow finding her death nearer than was expected, and hopeless of ever seeing her son, writes down, with difficulty, her sentiments with respect to Caroline and Sophia, solemnly adjuring him, by all sacred obligations of filial piety to forsake the one and wed the other. Julius arrives immediately after her decease. He is affected with the deepest Sorrow, is determined after many conflicts, which are copiously and minutely described in his letters to Sophia, he is determined to obey the dying injunctions of his mother. He writes to Caroline, informing her of all those circumstances, and offering himself to her acceptance. In this resolution Sophia generously endeavours to confirm him though at the expense of her own happiness. Caroline in answer refuses his proffered hand, since his heart is devoted to another. Caroline justifies and explains her refusal in letters to Julius and Julietta in answer describes the behaviour of Julius, her conversations with him, and her endeavours to persuade him to marry Sophia in opposition to his mother's exhortations. Julius is immovable in his resolution to obey his mother so far as obedience is in his power and is torn by all the violence of conflicting passions. He spends his hours in writing to Sophia, and in describing in strong colours his desperate condition. He wishes to die but will not hasten his death.[16] His health, however, rapidly decays, and, in compliance with the importunities of his sister and Caroline, he passes over to the Continent, intending to reside for the rest of his life, of which he knows the period is near, in Provence or Dauphine. He is taken sick in an unfrequented place in Picardy, is obliged to stop at a peasant's hut, and after writing pathetic letters to Julietta, Sophia, and Caroline —dies—

Such, my friend, was the plan of my performance, in writing which I had like to have undergone the fate of Julius, so violent were my emotions and so thoroughly did I feel all that I imputed to Julius: towards the conclusion, indeed, I grew absolutely sick with weeping, and was scarcely able to proceed to the Catastrophe.[17] All the incidents which I have related, their circumstances and effects are described with the utmost minuteness, in letters between the four principal personages, written, as it were, to the very moment.[18] Those events which happened previously to Julius' journey into Wales, at which period my performance opened, are occasionally and more particularly related in the Correspondence of which my Romance consists. From the arrival of Julius at Mangam till his death in Picardy I have

16. Brown's own letters are filled with Hamlet-like meditations on suicide. Invoking the "Angel of Destruction," in a letter to Bringhurst on May 5, 1792, the novelist begged, "Forbear to push me farther. . . . I overlook the precipice. What a turbulent and stormy sea! Darkness sits upon it. Shall I leap?" Later, in an undated letter to his friend (presumably in the summer of 1797), Brown wrote, "But it is, perhaps, of more importance to adopt a just opinion with regard to the lawfulness of suicide, than with respect to any other Subject. . . . I know that I was once on the very point of perpetrating this crime." Responding to Bringhurst's advice "to gaze at self destruction with abhorrence," the novelist was properly reassuring, "Do you fear that I shall ever kill myself *merely* because I *think* it justifiable? If this be your fear lay it aside because it is unreasonable."

17. Bringhurst, who was the beneficiary of a veritable correspondence course on the tender subject, needed no reminding of Brown's excessive sensibility. "My heart is open to divine and softening impressions," he was told in a letter on May 5, 1792. "I am soul all over. . . . I have often been in a graveyard at twelve . . . carried thither merely by the love of solitude and contemplation. . . ."

18. Richardson himself used the phrase, "to the moment," to describe the method of his new species of writing. The admiration Brown felt for *Clarissa* may have led him to employ the device of letters between the "four principal personages" to avoid the monotony of relying on only one major correspondent, a defect often objected to in *Pamela.*

supposed the busy and important interval to be no more than three months and ten days, and therefore though it be more voluminous than *Clarissa*, it occupies scarcely a fourth part of the time.[19]

So strong is the impression which the woes of Julius produced on my Imagination, that, to this hour, in lamenting the evils which have befallen myself, I frequently confound them with those which my invention heaped upon the head of Julius. As this work was written for the entertainment of Miss G—— to her it was piece meal delivered, and subsequent accidents have I fear rendered it irrecoverable. O my friend! how often were her bright eyes suffused with tears, at the perusal of it! how many sighs did it draw from the bottom of her heart! and did I rejoice at such affecting testimonials of its merit! The last Sheet was accompanied with an epistolary dedication to Henrietta, which (shall I venture to say it?) is a masterpiece if it be considered as the production of youth and inexperience. *This* I will shew to you, my friend, in due time.[20]

Did you ever observe the extraordinary influence of Imagination over the actions and sentiments of men? In assuming the persons or placing ourselves in the situations of others, we enjoy a new kind of existence, and think and act in a manner wonderfully befitting our assumed characters. I have often sat upon the rocks of Schuylkill, and shutting my eyes, imagined myself to be the identical Julius, to be transported to the vale of Keswick or the banks of Eden, to be seated within sight and hearing of the torrent, to have torn away from a rugged rock the moss with which it was covered, and to be employed in writing a letter to Lauder Allen, that young man so worthy to be called my friend: so remarkable for elevated ambition and towering

19. Bringhurst was forced to be content with a mere sketch. "I despair of ever having it in my power to shew you this performance," Brown wrote apologetically, ". . . and therefore have less scruples to describe to you the series of events and general tincture of the fable." Whether the "irrecoverable" manuscript allegedly read by Henrietta was actually "more voluminous than Clarissa" is doubtful, despite Brown's boast of having written "almost incessantly from sun rise to midnight for thirty days." In any event, unlike Richardson, Brown did not fret about the prodigious length of his story. The author of *Clarissa*, ashamed of his prolixity, contrived to reduce from eight to seven the volumes originally planned for the first edition by printing the last two volumes in smaller type.

20. This "epistolary dedication" to Henrietta appears to have been as "irrecoverable" as the lost manuscript itself. It was not included among Brown's papers printed in William Dunlap's *The Life of Charles Brockden Brown: together with Selections from the Rarest of His Printed Works, from his Original Letters, and from His Manuscripts before Unpublished* (Philadelphia, 1815).

genius, who is pursuing his studies at the Temple and treading in the steps of Murray and of Erskine—[21]

What! have I reached the bottom of the second sheet! I have put your patience to the test. I am almost ashamed of my prolixity. I have hitherto acted Julius, but next week must personate my good friend Allen, and apply myself indefatigably, for eight or ten days, to law, after which I will again metamorphose myself into Julius, and enjoy as much happiness as heaven permits.[22]

Farewell
C. B. B.

III

There is little in "The Story of Julius" to suggest that the sketch is anything more than one of Brown's early attempts to write a sentimental romance in epistolary form. It was not the first of such exercises sent to Bringhurst by the novelist. "I would willingly amuse my friend," Brown wrote, "and I think he derives amusement from my imperfect narratives, of fictitious adventures." On March 20, 1788, when he mailed the outline of an earlier narrative, based upon a sordid crime committed by a debauched husband, the author asked his friend, "What think you of this story. Would it not form the ground work of a noble tale. I will think more of it hereafter." Later, on August 16, 1793, in sending Bringhurst another germ for a story, Brown pondered the problem of the relation of fiction to truth. "I never met with in books, what I do not believe to be equally discoverable in nature," he remarked. "Richardson's fictions have, I doubt not, been a thousand times paralleled or exceeded by realities."

The sketch of "Julius," as it was communicated to Bringhurst, resembles a club sandwich with thin layers of narrative alternating with plans for its completion, which were never implemented, and

21. Since Allen was described as "the son of a Scottish Advocate," it was appropriate for him to study the treatises of his fellow countrymen, John Erskine (1695–1768), author of the celebrated *Institutes of the Law of Scotland*, and William Murray (1705–1793), whose *Outline of a Course In Legal Study* was admired in the period of Brown's own legal training in the office of Alexander Wilcox in Philadelphia in the early 1790's.

22. The ability "to personate" Allen was not sufficient to enable Brown to share his character's zeal for the law. He resigned from Wilcox's office in the summer of 1793. "The Story of Julius" was only one of several literary diversions to relieve the tedium of what the unhappy legal apprentice called "the rubbish of law," with "its endless tautologies, its impertinent circuities, its lying assertions, and hateful artifices."

problems of technique, which were never solved. Hardly more than a synopsis, with frequent shifts from past to present tense and back again, the story is fragile, tentative, and imperfect, and it foreshadows the weaknesses of Brown's major novels. The flat, one-dimensional characters are described rather than shown. The transcendent virtues of Julius, Sophia, and Julietta are not self-revealed, but imposed upon the reader who is told what to think of them. The leading figures are the familiar stereotypes of sentimental fiction: the ideal maiden, the generous friend, the benevolent rector, and the mercenary parent. The situations are the hackneyed ones of "the sacred obligations" of a death-bed promise, the tortuous conflict between love and duty, and the arrival of a fateful letter at the crucial juncture. The author's bungling use of the epistolary form in his later work suggests that if Brown had actually completed "The Story of Julius," the characters' letters would not have enabled them to speak for themselves without authorial intrusions. His failure to create the illusion of a genuine correspondence in *Wieland* compelled him to add an explanatory note. "It will be necessary to add," he wrote in the Advertisement of the novel, "that this narrative is addressed in epistolary form, by the Lady whose story it contains, to a small number of friends, whose curiosity in regard to it, had been greatly awakened.[23] And in *Jane Talbot* he was only mildly successful in accounting for the time and industry needed to produce the voluminous and frequent letters required to carry forward the narrative. "My desk is, of late, always open; my paper spread: my pen moist," declared the heroine, who felt some comment was necessary to explain how she contrived to write seven letters totalling more than twenty thousand words in four days.[24]

It is, of course, ungenerous to assume that Brown would not have avoided some of these defects in the projected "twenty duodecimo volumes" which he estimated were needed for the completion of his romance. Perhaps, if the novelist, contrary to his expectations, had succeeded in sending the "irrecoverable" manuscript to his friend, Bringhurst would have found in the full-bodied version that the letters of the principal characters possessed "the utmost minuteness" which Brown had promised. Nothing less than such detailed copiousness would have been required to satisfy the demands of the author's

23. C. B. Brown, *Wieland; or, The Transformation* (New York, 1798), p. [i].
24. C. B. Brown, *Jane Talbot: A Novel* (Philadelphia, 1801), p. 69.

time scheme, a period of "no more than three months and ten days," in which he predicted that the correspondence would fill a novel "more voluminous than *Clarissa* in "scarcely a fourth part of the time" elapsing in Richardson's work. And if Brown, as he intimated to Bringhurst, hoped to accomplish all this in the time snatched from his legal studies, the performance would have set a record even for one afflicted with a severe case of *cacoethes scribendi.*

Perhaps it is more charitable to assume that "The Story of Julius" never advanced beyond the outline and plan sent to Bringhurst for his amusement. If we are to believe in the existence of a flesh-and-blood Henrietta G———, who not only commanded her lover to write the narrative and suggested an appropriate literary method for its composition, but also sighed, wept over, and edited each successive installment, it is significant that their "correspondence" fails to mention it.[25] It is tempting to conclude that "Henrietta" had her habitation and name only in Brown's over-heated imagination. "My attachment to literature and my attachment to women are nothing but passions," the novelist confessed to his friend in a letter dated December 9, 1792. "There never was a more voluptious fancy than mine . . . . What an eventful romantic life has been mine."[26]

No reader of Charles Brockden Brown will be disposed to deny his claim to having lived a romantic life or having been possessed by an ardent fancy. "O my friend!" he exclaimed to Bringhurst. "How miserable should I be were I not rescued from the tedious or distressful present by an excessive imagination." Indeed, it was the blend of these qualities which confer upon "The Story of Julius" its curious distinction of being an unwritten epistolary romance, inspired by,

25. None of the circumstances attending the inception of the story or the slightest allusion to its composition is to be found in the "Henrietta Letters," which purport to be full transcripts of the originals and printed in Chapter III, "Love Among the Ruins," in David L. Clark, *Charles Brockden Brown*, pp. 53–107. The omission of any reference, either to "Henrietta" or the "letters," in the first biography of Brown begun by Paul Allen and completed by William Dunlap in 1815, is explained by Clark as the biographers' "deference to the wishes of the family." See Clark, p. 53.

26. One creation of his "voluptious fancy" with whom Brown fell in love was the "beautious Jacquelette," whose eyes beamed upon him with "mingled rays of love and devotion" while the ecstatic pair enjoyed the scenery of Lake Geneva in Switzerland. In a letter to Bringhurst postmarked from Philadelphia, June 1, 1792, but superscribed "Cuille Pays du Vaud," Brown wrote glowingly of his "*petite Espouse*." Another account of this imaginary lady also appears in a letter of the same date written to William Wilkins: "I am afraid, my friend, that my destiny is fixed . . . and that I shall live and die at the feet of Jacquelette . . . . What charms have innocence and beauty on a susceptible heart!" This letter to Wilkins is quoted by Clark, p. 30.

and dedicated to an idealized sentimental heroine who existed only in the gallery of Brown's other mythical lovers. But even in this shadowy world of eighteenth-century sensibility, "The Story of Julius" survives as a characteristic fantasy of a writer destined to become a child of the Enlightenment without ceasing to be an American Man of Feeling.

II. Periodical Publishing in America from Joseph Dennie to Thomas Wolfe

Randolph C. Randall

Joseph Dennie's Literary Attitudes in the Port Folio, *1801-1812*

Joseph Dennie, founder of the *Port Folio* in 1801 and its editor until his death in 1812, was in matters of literary taste the most influential American of the nineteenth century's first decade. Certainly his establishment of a magazine that went on after his death to an unheard of lifetime of twenty-seven years was an unparalleled American accomplishment. The achievement was all the more remarkable when one considers that as editor he represented a minority and fought against the prevailing democratic tide, for Dennie was a reactionary in a young republic awakening to laws and customs that contribute to the inequality of men. In the struggle he supported the upper class, took as editor the name Oliver Oldschool, Esq., and promoted the elegant simplicity of Joseph Addison and Oliver Goldsmith. He believed in a monarchy and an aristocracy. He abhorred democracy, and he deplored the American Revolution as a disaster.

He intended his new literary magazine to serve these political views. As he observed in the Prospectus of 1801 for the *Port Folio*, "It must be apparent to the most heedless observer, that it is the object of this undertaking to combine literature with politics, and attempt something of a more honorable destiny, than a meagre journal." He also made it clear that the politics of his magazine would be Federalist and reactionary. Known as the Federalist editor of the *Farmer's Museum* of Walpole, New Hampshire, between 1795 and 1799, and for a few months of 1800 as literary editor of the Federalist *Gazette of the United States* in Philadelphia, he had little need to say in the Prospectus for the *Port Folio*, "It must be understood that the Editor prohibits every thing Jacobinical."

As authoritarian in literature as in politics, he repeatedly dreamed of governing bodies for American letters. One form of the control that he envisioned was a cabinet of gentlemen, "avowed Partizans and Martinets in Religion, Politicks, and Literature," who would conduct a quarterly review in which they would announce "principles of the most lofty, intrepid, independent, high-toned, and decided character."

After having . . . promulgated the laws of legitimate composition, and exhibited the standard of correct principles, that luckless wight, who should in any publication deviate either from the one or the other should be treated like an audacious offender. The whole force of the confederacy should be exerted to render the hardened sinner contemptible. In the spirit of Romish anathema, his foolish or his flagitious page should be condemned by bell, book, and candle, and he should be interdicted from any approach to the empire of Learning or the purlieus of Wit."[1]

To Dennie there were two classes of men, the many and "the few." On the one hand there was an elite of the highly educated, the cultured, and usually the wealthy and their children; on the other was "the ignorant and giddy multitude." Lacking the faith that Franklin had had in the improvability of man, he put no emphasis on encouraging the common people to change their class through education and diligence. Although he favored a classical education for the rich and at times smiled upon the rudiments of schooling for the poor, he appears to have expected little movement from class to class. The *Port Folio* contended, in a column usually prepared by Dennie, that "differences in rank and subordination are . . . of God's appointment, and consequently essential to the well being of society."[2]

The trouble with democracy lay in the baseness of the great majority. With a blindness to his own advantage that is hard for a twentieth-century American to understand, he refused to flatter the common people. In the *Port Folio* he referred to "the multitude," who were, with the election of Jefferson in 1801, possessed of some political power, as "the vulgar," as "the *rascal rabble*," as "republican boors," who "have convened with a resolution to destroy culture" and "to form a general combination in favour of stupidity," and who have "a swinish sulkiness to every thing that looks like talents."[3] In the number for May 19, 1804, one class was described as "men of

1. "Polite Literature," *Port Folio*, Ser. 3, VI (Oct. 22, 1808), 264–265. This is a continuation of "Project of an Original Review," ibid., Oct. 15, pp. 251–253. For Dennie's other plans for a controlled literature, see III (Dec. 24, 1803), 415, and "New Prospectus for the Port Folio," Ser. 2, I (Jan. 11, 1806), 6–7. Unless otherwise indicated all subsequent periodical references are to the *Port Folio*.

2. IV (July 28, 1804), 239; III (April 30, Nov. 5, 1803), 143, 358.

3. IV (July 18, 1804), 239; I (July 4, 1801), 214.

genius, talents, principle, and property"; those of the other as "democrats, fanatics, knaves, and fools; *natural brute beasts*, as an impious, impudent, and savage gang, whom every man of genius and virtue is bound to meet with defiance on his brow and the horse-whip in his hand."[4] These shrill comments were apparently more than rhetorical flourishes designed only to please the Federalist patrons of the *Port Folio*. Writing to his Harvard classmate Roger Vose from Philadelphia on February 7, 1800, regarding his visit to Congress, Dennie said he thought well of some Congressmen from Connecticut and of "others of the Southern & Middle Interests who are able & active, but the brute mass, the men, who are told by the head, like all populace, are despicably mean, weak & miserable. Such is the filthiness of some of their persons, and such the stupidity of some of the faces in the lower house of your National Assembly that one would expect to see them following a dust cart or rising from a chimney and not even admitted into a scene of legislation."[5]

With practice, he gained in incisiveness. Democracy, he said, is "the most flagrant imposition ever practiced upon the credulity of mankind." "Republics," according to an editorial column, "are ever sure to be governed by the most wicked, ambitious, avaricious, and mischievous of mankind." One paragraph was so obnoxious to some of his fellow Philadelphians that they prosecuted him—though unsuccessfully—for seditious libel. Dennie wrote in the offensive passage:

> A democracy is scarcely tolerable at any period of national history. Its omens are always sinister, and its powers are unpropitious. With all the lights of experience blazing before our eyes, it is impossible not to discern the futility of this form of government. . . . It is on trial here, and the issue will be civil war, desolation, and anarchy. No wise man but discerns its imperfections, no good man but shudders at its miseries, no honest man but proclaims its fraud, and no brave man but draws his sword against its force.[6]

To his own country and its government he preferred the English monarch and the English people. "Had it not been for the *selfish* patriotism of that hoary traitor, [Samuel] Adams, and the bellowing

4. IV, 159.
5. Laura G. Pedder, ed., *The Letters of Joseph Dennie 1768–1812* (Orono, Maine, 1936), p. 180.
6. III (June 18, April 30, 23, 1803), 197, 143, 135.

of [William] Molineux . . . ," he wrote to his mother on April 26, 1797, "I might now, perhaps . . . [have] been in the service of my rightful king and instead of shivering in the bleakness of the United States, felt the genial sunshine of a court."[7] From Philadelphia on May 20, 1800, he wrote to his parents, "The English character, abstractly considered, is the most honest, the most generous, the most frank and liberal[,] and foul is that day in our Calendar, and bitterly are those *patriotic*, selfish and Indian traitors to be cursed who instigated the wretched populace to declare the 4th day of July 1776, a day of Independence."[8]

His sense of outrage betrayed him not only into admitting to the *Port Folio*'s pages, principally between 1802 and 1804, some fourteen anonymous poems slanderously insinuating that President Jefferson cohabited with a slave named Sally, but also into defending one such libel as "poetical, severe, and well deserved," and others (those of John Quincy Adams) as "worthy of the classic scholar, the elegant poet." While there is no defense of Dennie's transgression against the rules of decency, it can be recalled that the confiscation of property and the bloodshed at the guillotine in the French Revolution had so terrified some upper-class Americans that they felt no weapon was too savage to use against any democrat. Nor is it exonerating to note that such respectable anti-Jeffersonians as Thomas Green Fessenden, the son of a minister, and John Quincy Adams, the son of a President and later President himself, were among the authors of slanderous "Sally" poems. It is true that Dennie seems to have felt a growing revulsion against such scurrility, largely avoided it after 1804, and excluded political vituperation from his columns after 1807. The libellous "Sally" series remains the darkest stain on the pages of a usually refined journal.[9]

Dennie associated religious orthodoxy with sound politics. In his column "To Readers and Correspondents," he replied to a contributor, " 'Doubts' are written by a jacobinical hand. We will not taint

7. Pedder, p. 159.
8. Ibid., p. 186.
9. For the identification of Adams as the author of the verses, see my "Authors of the *Port Folio* Revealed by the Hall Files," *American Literature*, XI, (Jan., 1940), 386. Adams's burlesques of Jefferson are "Horace, Book II, Ode IV," and "Another Imitation of Horace, Book II, Ode IV," II (Oct. 30, 1804), 344. Fessenden is slanderous in Canto IV of *Democracy Unveiled* (Boston, 1805), pp. 99–125, 108. Dennie defended Fessenden's satire in Ser. 2, I (Jan. 18, 1806), 25; and Adams's verses, II (Nov. 13, 1802), 359; and the other author's, II (Dec. 18, 1802), 399–400.

our paper, or insult the faith of our readers, by giving currency to the dreams of scepticism."[10] The genuineness of his view is confirmed by a passage in the letter to his parents of May 20, 1800: "I go *conscientiously* to *Church*," he assured them, "and listen to a *perfect* liturgy and sound sermon from the lips of Bishop White. You will be happy to know," he continued, "what I can *truly* and *religiously* assert, that my long and assiduous habit of investigating the Sacred writings has ended with me . . . in a perfect and settled conviction of their Divine origin, and matchless utility to mankind. . . . The Bible is truly a blessed book, and happy and safe is that man, whose conduct, as far as mortal imbecillity [*sic*] will allow, comports with that most salutary doctrine contained in the Gospels." His views had been settled since his senior year at Harvard, for he had written to his classmate Roger Vose on May 24, 1790, "I have learned to make a just estimate of sceptics, and scepticism. I have learned that time is wholly lost, which is spent in tracing the intricacies of such authors."[11]

Though to our hindsight Dennie's struggle against the democratic tide seems to have been absurdly futile, it appeared to Dennie that the federal government was so weak that it might be "racked if not overthrown." He wrote to Vose that the ground was "sometimes in motion under our feet." Should the federal edifice fall, he thought it might be necessary to call in the British builders rejected in 1776 to repair the work, "perhaps lay the first stone of a new corner."[12] Coming less than a year after these predictions, the election of Jefferson on February 17, 1801, was a severe blow. Following Hamilton's reassurance to his party in May that the republican victory was only momentary, Dennie promised in the *Port Folio* of August 15, "The triumphing of Jefferson's party will be but short."[13]

Although his views were more conservative than those of many Federalists, he might have expressed them less stridently if there had been fewer stresses in his earlier life. When he was a child of three or four, his father at about the age of twenty-seven was so seized with physical illness and melancholia that he gave up his mercantile business in Boston and, in 1775, when his son was seven, retired to Lexington. Beginning about the time young Joseph was graduated from Harvard, his father became obsessed by the belief that he was being persecuted. He was sometimes deranged, and, his dementia increas-

10. I (Aug. 22, 1801), 272.
11. Pedder, pp. 183–184, 56.
12. Ibid., p. 180.
13. I (May 23, 1801), 162–163, 262–263.

ing in frequency and severity, he was confined to his house, and often to his bed, the remaining twenty years of his life.[14]

To the emotions raised in Joseph as a boy and young man by his father's collapse was added soon the dreadfulness of his own condition. Within a few months after his graduation he could no longer deny to himself or to his parents that he was in the grip of consumption and for the first time called the hated disease by its name. In the fierce winters of New Hampshire, where he was to spend the next eight years in the study of law and as a journalist, the disease tore at his body, periodically laid him low, and sometimes brought him close to death. He was racked also by agonizing headaches, and was subject to alternate fits of gaiety and despair as regular, he wrote to a college classmate, as the ebb and flow of the ocean. Perhaps in no letter to his parents does he fail to mention his precarious health, sometimes pitifully trying to cheer them and at others, with a perverse unfeelingness, reminding them that he had inherited his frail physique from them. He feared that his melancholia would turn into the dementia of his father. To a friend he wrote that he had "not many [hours] to enjoy."

More and more convinced of the "brevity and uncertainty of life," he determined to relish what he had. He became a convivial companion, described by his friends as charming. To his sense of the shortness of his time may be attributed a petulance, or what he called "the fierce impatience of my temper." His illness may have prevented, as it certainly hindered, prolonged study or analytical thought. He could not complete long or involved projects. His longest writings are essays of two or three pages, some of them later assembled as a volume entitled *The Lay Preacher*. Admitted to the bar in New Hampshire, he wrote to his parents that he would never be a profound lawyer and that his talents were superficial. Soon after he arrived in Philadelphia late in 1799, it seemed to him that his "feeble constitution" was "partially invigorated by the healing influences of a soft and southern sky," but in the *Port Folio* he frequently mentioned his illness as an explanation for the lateness of the journal's numbers, for his absence from his desk, or for his dissatisfaction with his performance.[15]

14. Harold M. Ellis, *Joseph Dennie and His Circle* (Austin, Texas, 1915), pp. 12–14.

15. For Dennie's comments on his health, see Pedder, pp. 38, 48, 59, 75, 123, 157, 172, 178, 179, 182.

Furthermore, because the cultural superiority of the upper class was assumed during the time of his editorship, it is likely that Dennie was acting out the authoritative role expected of him.[16] It was a time, as William Charvat observed of the period between 1810 and 1835, when "the privileged classes alone could afford the necessary higher education" and when literary criticism "was the work of a practically homogenous class which felt itself competent to legislate, culturally, for other classes."[17] Dennie addressed his Prospectus for the *Port Folio* with assurance "to Men of Affluence, Men of Liberality, and Men of Letters."

II

Dennie's literary comments in the *Port Folio* are brief. He expressed them in concise editorial headnotes and footnotes and in his columns "An Author's Evenings," "To Readers and Correspondents," "Literary Intelligence," and in some passages of "Miscellaneous Paragraphs." Usually his remarks about authors or their writings are contained in paragraphs of one, two, or three sentences. He wrote not more than perhaps a dozen reviews that are as long as a column or two and that approach anything like a sustained analysis. Sometimes repetitive and occasionally inconsistent, his remarks are usually vague and superficial. But if one assembles the comments he delivered on a given topic throughout his editorship, the pattern of his literary principles emerges. In this discussion I will pay some attention to Dennie's opinions regarding the American and English languages and then pursue with more thoroughness his treatment of Rousseau, Coleridge, Wordsworth, Addison, and Goldsmith. Dennie's remarks on the first three writers allow us to consider his views of Romantic authors; his comments on the last two present his attitude toward the elegant simplicity in English prose that he admired and steadily sought.

Although Dennie did not say that correct language was the mark of a Federalist, he did suggest that linguistic propriety and elegance were the characteristics of a gentleman, and he insisted that the language of democrats was impure and incorrect. He implied that

16. See, for instance, S. E. Morison, "Precedence at Harvard College in the Seventeenth Century," *Proceedings of the American Antiquarian Society*, n.s., XLII (Oct., 1932), 377.

17. *The Origins of American Critical Thought* (Philadelphia, 1936), p. 1.

though Thomas Jefferson reigned in the White House, the *Port Folio* held the bastion of correctness of language. He asserted that there was a close connection between false politics and false literature. "The republican faction not only think erroneously," he said, "but write incorrectly." "The effusions of every republican rascal and scribbler are *always* incorrect in expression."[18]

The crudities of the Republicans were the exaggeration and boastfulness of their language, their weak logic, and their innovations in words and pronunciations. In rebuking the author of a newspaper article for the use of bombastic expression in his account of the launching of a ship, Dennie protested that the harbor "was not *thronged*, nor choked," as the writer had said, and to write as he had done was to be guilty not only of lying but of bad taste.[19] Dennie found Independence Day oratory especially lacking in restraint. "Unsatisfied with *acting* like fools," he observed in a notice of the celebrations of July 4, 1801, "men begin to enlarge their schemes, and talk and write from the vocabulary of folly."[20] He scoffed at Noah Webster's American dictionary and derided Caleb Alexander's "Columbian dictionary" of the new republic's language as "a record of our imbecility." He was persistent in the struggle for elegance and purity. "To resist and ridicule absurd innovations in literature," he promised, "to cherish the classical and established forms of diction, and preserve the purity, and resort to the standards of English style is the constant aim of the editor."[21] He was not entirely consistent in what he considered absurd. He favored the use of certain American names— *intervale* instead of *dale*, *oak* and *elm* instead of *cypress* and *yew*—but condemned *likely* and *backwoodsman*.[22]

He felt little reverence for Jefferson's language in the Declaration of Independence. In the number for April 25, 1801, he urged an author who signed himself "Common Sense" to proceed with his analysis and to scrutinize the style of the Declaration. He promised that he would "cheerfully and promptly print, whatever will acutely detect the lurking gallicisms, *false* politics, *false* logic, and *false* metaphysics of a rambling declaration, whose language, like that of a huffing bully, supplies by hardihood, and audacity of assertion the

18. II (Nov. 6, 1802), 350; V (March 16, 1805), 73.
19. V (Aug. 17, 1805), 249–51.
20. I (July 11, 1801), 223.
21. II (June 5, 1802), 176; I (Aug. 1, Nov. 28, 1801), 245–248, 380.
22. I (March 14, 1801), 84; III (June 25, 1803), 207.

place of good manners, reason, and truth."[23] For the issue of August 15, 1801, Dr. James Kemp furnished a criticism of the Declaration's grammar and rhetoric. Dennie encouraged him in the paper for August 29: "We hope Busby [Dr. Kemp] will continue to brandish the critical rod. It is the terror of every truant from the rigid discipline of the English language." He thought Dr. Kemp's animadversions on the Declaration were "in no instance captious or unfounded. It is one of the most mysterious circumstances, in the history of public opinion, that the style of the Declaration, Notes on Virginia, &c. is viewed as a *model* by many, and pronounced correct by some. It would be easy to show that the style of the president is no less tinctured by French idioms, than his mind is tainted by French principles." Dennie regarded it as doubtful whether President Jefferson could write "one sentence of correct and classical English."[24]

To aspiring writers Dennie upheld as models the works of eighteenth-century masters of English prose. "The Editor," he said, "wishes to be skilled in no other choice or combination of words than those which we derived from the country of our ancestors, and which constitute the English style. He is satisfied with *Bolingbroke* and *Burke*, and with Addison and Goldsmith. Let others make a new language from the colloquies of our clowns, from the drawling cant of provincial idioms, and the turbid oratory of a Town meeting."[25] He complimented the youthful Thomas Sergeant for an article which analyzed the language of Swift and Addison and praised these authors for attempting to diffuse their opinions through all classes of society and for reforming English prose by adopting the conversational manner established by usage. "On every occasion," Dennie assured Sergeant, "we are most cordially disposed to animate every American writer, who is studious to emulate the diction of the finest authors in England."[26] In the number for November 7, 1807, Dennie informed his readers and correspondents that, at the beginning of that year he had "requested his Printers invariably to employ the orthography of Dr. JOHNSON, and in all doubtful cases, to consult that oracle, not as the responses are given in the common abridgment in 8vo. but according to the invaluable authority of the folio edition, with a careful attention to the authour's etymology, syntax, and apposite quotations."[27] Thenceforward the scrupulously proofread *Port*

23. I, 134–35.
24. I, 280, 271; II (Feb. 26, 1802), 39.
25. Ser. 2, I (April 19, 1806), 239.
26. V (Aug. 31, 1805), 265, 271.
27. Ser. 2, IV, 299.

Folio used the spellings *chuse*, *authour*, *critick*, and *cynick*, regardless of the author's original spelling.

Dennie frequently reminded his readers that the ultimate authority in letters was the method of the great writers of ancient Greece and Rome. To one would-be author he prescribed a longer and harder course than the one he had suggested to Sergeant. "The aspirers to literary renown," he informed the writer, "may be assured there is no little by path, no republican road to that sublime object. To write with energy, elegance, purity, and melody, they must patiently peruse the fine models bequeathed us by the Ancients." He frequently proved his own competence and the superior education of his upper-class readers by occasionally printing entire poems in Latin without any translation.[28]

Dennie tried to enlist the aid of other American authors in curbing political and linguistic change. In the *Port Folio* of December 24, 1803, observing that the French Revolution had been effected by men of letters, he proposed a union of writers for "the most salutary purposes" of combatting revolution in America, implying that American writers were then prevailingly conservative and that they could stave off revolution by the use of literary criticism. Later, in the prospectus for the *Port Folio* beginning in January, 1806, he again offered to lend his services to the formation of a confederacy of letters, "not exceeding in number that of the French academy." The members would be from the upper class—"men of fortune, of the fairest character, the staunchest principles, and the greatest intrepidity"—and the aim would be partly educational and partly prohibitive. It would, he wrote with probably more artlessness than arrogance, "revive classical discipline, create a passion for pure undefiled English, guide the taste and fortify the judgment of youth, multiply the editions of sterling authors, and absolutely eradicate every bad book in the country."[29]

III

Dennie appears to have regarded Rousseau as the writer largely responsible for liberating the host of democratic troubles in the world, especially for the republican appeal to the authority expressed in the

28. V (Aug. 17, 1805), 255. For poems in Latin, see I (Feb. 7, March 4, 1801), 47, 88; II (Sept. 11, 1802), 288.

29. III, 415; "Prospectus," pp. 6–7. For another proposal, see note 1, above.

Declaration as "the laws of Nature and of Nature's God." In some articles, the *Port Folio* questioned Rousseau's premises; in others, with less logic, it impugned the morality of Rousseau and of his principles. In five numbers of the *Port Folio* appearing over a period of eighteen months, the author of "Miscellaneous Paragraphs," almost certainly Dennie, challenged the validity of Rousseau's "Discourse on the Origin of Inequality" on the ground that Rousseau had improperly collected his "*facts*" from "an extensive perusal of voyages and accounts of remote nations."[30] He apparently objected to such dubious examples cited by Rousseau in Part I of his *Discourse* as "savages are strangers to almost every disease," the savages of America "tracked the Spaniards with their noses, to as great a degree of exactness, as the best dogs could have done," and unlike the civilized man, no savage was ever known "to have been so much as tempted to complain of life, and lay violent hands upon himself."[31] "The more I meditate," the author of "Miscellaneous Paragraphs" countered, "the more I am convinced that all speculations are illusory and unsatisfactory, unless they are established on prominent [*i.e.* obvious, undeniable] facts, which are to be first collected before we venture to indulge metaphysical disquisitions." In short, he considered Rousseau's methods unscientific and recommended the procedures of Machiavelli and Bacon: "The crafty Florentine, versed in the manners of princes, with sagacity equal to his genius, deduces all his reflections from those prominent facts, which passed under his eye, or which he collected from the records of instructive history. Lord Bacon introduced that wise philosophy which is only founded on experiments; the study of nature in her operations."[32] Perspicacious as Dennie was in the challenge of the premise, he did not explain—and perhaps did not discern—that Rousseau in his "Discourse on Inequality" attempted to weave a reasonable fabric for the hope of man's perfectibility and tried to show that, since the commoner had assented to being governed, it followed that he could revoke the contract.

In "Miscellaneous Paragraphs" of June 23, 1804, the author, using the words *nature* and *naturally* with a touch of irony, offered observations of his own that contradicted Rousseau's conclusions. Children,

30. III (Sept. 10, 1803), 295; IV (Feb. 11, March 24, June 23, 1804), 47, 197–198; V (April 6, 1805), 102.

31. *A Discourse upon the Origin and the Foundation of Inequality among Mankind*, Harvard Classics (New York, 1910), XXXIV, 175–176, 178, 198.

32. IV (March 24, 1804), 95.

he thought, begin among themselves with a democracy where every one is master. "Immediately and naturally quarreling with one another, they soon acquiesce in a Monarchy. One distinguishes himself from the rest either by greater genius, strength, or dexterity, in their little diversions. To him many submit, and hence an absolute, or energetic government." In the number for February 11, 1804, he ironically proposed that if Mr. Jefferson believed in the perfectibility of mankind, he might test his belief in the newly acquired territory of Louisiana, where the pupils would be "the children of nature, the savages of the forest, whose minds are unadulterated with the principles of civilized life, unshackeled [*sic*] with its useless restraints and 'unembarrassed with too much regulation.' "[33]

In the same column a year later, April 6, 1805, he reported some of his own observations of nature, though failing to inform his readers whether his facts were obvious. The nearer man approaches to a state of nature, he disclosed, the more dominant is man's cruelty. Children laugh at "the miseries which they inflict on every unfortunate animal which comes within their power; all savages are most ingenious in contriving, and happy in executing, the most exquisite tortures"; the common people are delighted with "bull baitings, prize fightings, executions, and all spectacles of cruelty and horror."[34] In "Miscellaneous Paragraphs" of June 23, 1804, there is an observation of even less authenticity. The modern French style of writing, the author believed, was totally different from those pure models of her early writers. "The new men of regicide *naturally* talk in the tone of butchers, shoe blacks, chimney sweepers, and lacqueys, because . . . [they] *must* use the gross gibberish, the mother tongue of every low bred rebel."[35]

Dennie's imputation of immorality and impiety to Rousseau may have been a more effective process of defamation with his readers than these observations of nature were. Dennie did not neglect to print Boswell's report of Dr. Johnson's opinion of Rousseau: "I think him one of the worst of men; a rascal who ought to be hunted out of society, as he has been."[36] One of the "Miscellaneous Paragraphs" describes him as "this sentimental scoundrel" and "the pagod of the French revolutionists." In "Literary Intelligence," Dennie labels him

33. IV, 47, 197.
34. V, 102.
35. IV (June 23, 1804), 198.
36. Ser. 2, I (April 5, 1806), 204.

"the eloquent lunatic, and splendid scoundrel."[37] A short story, "The Adventures of Crita" in the *Port Folio* for November 6, 1802, shows the callousness to morality that, the author implied, might be expected to result from following Rousseau's teaching. In the story, Crita had learned from Rousseau that love should not be restrained. She had had two love affairs and had borne two children in the second. Later, in Germany, she met a lady who invited Crita "to admit [her husband] to her affections and to share him between us." Crita stayed at the chateau for eighteen months, bore the man a child, "and experienced nothing but a calm, philosophical joy."[38] Apparently Dennie's opinion of Rousseau did not soften. In the August 16, 1806, number he reprinted an eight-year-old essay of *The Lay Preacher* in which he concluded, "From Rousseau down to his last imitator, if the whole race were restrained within a mad house[,] it would be fortunate for the tranquillity [*sic*] of mankind."[39]

Although "Politics, Essay IV, Equality," in the number for December 18, 1802, is a relatively dispassionate attempt to show that the "natural" man entering a cave has no rights, and although Dennie granted that Rousseau was one of the men of genius who had described Switzerland's rural wonders "with the finest flights of eloquence," the *Port Folio* did not reprint any of Rousseau's writings for its readers, publish any serious attempt to explain them impartially, or encourage readers to examine them. Thus Dennie failed to provide a rational consideration of some ideas of great pertinence to the American social experiment.[40]

IV

Dennie's antipathy to democracy is discernible in his treatment of Wordsworth. The first known American to publish a notice of him, Dennie reprinted his poems and praised him warmly for three years and then gradually turned against him, partly because he thought the language of Wordsworth's humble characters was without dignity. In the *Farmer's Museum* Dennie had shown enthusiasm for certain of Wordsworth's poems in the first edition of *Lyrical Ballads*

37. III (Sept. 10, 1803), 295; V (Aug. 10, 1805), 244.
38. II, 356–357.
39. Ser. 2, II, 82.
40. II, 395–396; I (April 25, 1801), 135–136.

(1798) as early as September 2, 1799, more than a year before the first number of the *Port Folio* appeared. In the *Port Folio* from 1801 to 1804 he reprinted from the first and second editions of *Lyrical Ballads* twelve of Wordsworth's poems: "Simon Lee," "The Thorn," "Strange Fits of Passion I Have Known," "Song" ("She dwelt among th' untrodden ways"), "Anecdote for Fathers," "The Mad Mother," "The Waterfall and the Eglantine," "Lucy Gray," "Andrew Jones," "The Fountain," "The Oak and the Broom," and "Written in Germany."[41] Dennie's selection of these poems may stem less from his belief in their intrinsic worth than in their sympathetic treatment illustrating the courage of creatures (human beings, an insect, plants) confronted with natural misfortune.

Dennie's comments on the new romantic poetry are disappointingly vague. For example, in the following typical criticism it is difficult to find any reason for Dennie's enthusiasm except Wordsworth's use of simple and natural language:

> The following delightful fable, and the subsequent poems, are from the magical pen of WILLIAM WORDSWORTH, a genuine poet, who judiciously employs the language of simplicity and NATURE, to express the tones of passion; who has forsaken the necromantic realms of German extravagance, and the torrid zone of Della Cruscan ardour, and has recalled erring readers "from sounds to things, from fancy to the heart."[42]

In any event, if we ignore the instance in which Dennie praised Wordsworth for a poem really Coleridge's, Dennie mentioned Wordsworth critically eleven times in the *Port Folio*.[43] In addition to his own comments, he reprinted a review of *Lyrical Ballads* from the *British Critic*, and in the number for March, 1809, he printed a brief discussion of Wordsworth, which he probably did not write.[44] All of Dennie's comments are brief, consisting of one, two, or three sentences. He cites simplicity as a merit in nine of the ten instances, using the word *simplicity* itself in seven, "thoughts in the simplest ex-

41. I (Jan. 17, March 21, June 13, July 18, Dec. 19, 1801), 24, 94–95, 188–190, 232, 408; III (Sept. 3, 1803), 288; IV (March 24, Oct. 27, 1804), 96, 342–343. Dennie's treatment of Wordsworth has been treated by Leon Howard, "Wordsworth in America," *Modern Language Notes*, XLVIII (June, 1933), 359–365. See also Lewis Leary, "Wordsworth in America: Addenda," ibid., LVIII (May, 1943), 391–393.

42. I (Dec. 19, 1801), 408.

43. I (Jan. 17, June 13, Dec. 19, 1801), 24, 191, 408; II (May 15, 1802), 152; III (Jan 1., Sept. 3, 1803), 8, 288; IV (March 17, 24, Aug. 19, 1804), 87, 96, 263; Ser. 2, IV (Nov. 14, 1807), 306; Ser. 3, III (May, 1810), 438. I believe Dennie was not the author of comments in Ser. 3, V (May, 1811), 46, or in VI (Oct., 1811), 463.

44. I (June 13, 1801), 189–190; Ser. 3, I, 256–258.

pression" in one, and "the familiar ballad style" in another. Other poetic virtues named but not defined are "genius," cited only once; "originality," named three times; "spirit," meaning liveliness, mentioned once; and "nature," apparently signifying naturalness of human action, specified twice. By "simplicity," the quality which excited him most, it may be that he meant the lack of complexity in the events of the poems, but he more likely referred to the meter of "the simple ballad style," the large proportion of one-syllable words, and the sentence order of conversation. Whatever he meant, he dilutes the value of his praise for simplicity as a new force in language by saying that Wordsworth "seems to follow GOLDSMITH in the easy and agreeable track of simplicity," and the term is somewhat blunted also by his use of it to describe the verse of Thomas Moore.

It may have been Dennie's enthusiasm that stimulated his friends in Philadelphia to imitate Wordsworth. In the *Port Folio* Dennie published between 1801 and 1803 at least three poems by admirers of the poet. Dr. John Stock's "Ballad," in the number for June 6, 1801, uses American characters and an American scene and follows the ballad form and the narrative outline of Wordsworth's pathetic "Lucy Gray."[45] Dennie praised Dr. Stock's "Ballad" ardently: "It is delightful to the editor to obtain original poetry of such merit as adorns the last page in his latest papers. The 'Ballad'... is alike faithful to truth, dear to humanity, and honourable to GENIUS."[46] Two other poems showing the influence of Wordsworth were by Samuel Ewing, "Reflections in Solitude," appearing January 20, 1802, and lines "Addressed to Her Who Best Understands It," in the number for January 1, 1803. The latter begins,

I saw a simple heedless child
  One fine May-morning roam,
In search of wild flowers in the wood,
  To blossom at his home.[47]

Dennie, recognizing that Wordsworth was Ewing's model, observed that Ewing's "stanzas . . . must be admired . . . by all who have a taste for that charming simplicity, with which a WORDSWORTH has taught us to believe, the most poetical ideas may be conveyed."

But there were in the *Port Folio* between 1801 and 1804 three verse parodies of Wordsworth's work, which suggest that Dennie was not

45. I, 184.
46. I (June 13, 1801), 191.
47. II, 32; III, 8.

completely captivated by Wordsworth as "a new voice" and which served to discourage the tendency of poets to follow him. These versifiers ridiculed the lack of dignity in the English poet's common people and in their language. Probably the most effective of the three burlesques was the first, the hitherto unnoticed "Jonathan to Jemima," in the number for May 15, 1802.[48] It was apparently written by a New Englander and, one is tempted to guess, by Royall Tyler. It is a telling attack, not only upon the diction of Wordsworth's rustic characters, but also upon the coarseness of "low and rustic life," which, as Wordsworth tells us in his Preface, "was generally chosen [as the subject of his poetry] because in that situation the essential passions of the heart find a better soil in which they can attain their maturity, are under less restraint, and speak a plainer and more emphatic language." The nature of the satire of Wordsworth's democratic proposition is set forth in the first five of the poem's seventeen stanzas:

JEMIMA, won't you let me sing
   A little song I have for you?
I love you so like any thing,
   I vow I don't know what to do.

      And yet I hate to let you know,
      It makes me feel all over so.

Don't you remember t'other day,
   When you was milking in the piggin,
You had a straw hat on your head,
   But on your neck there was no rigging.

      And yet &c.

Well, by a tree close to the fence
   I stood, and while you pull'd the teats,
I peep'd through a small knot hole there,
   Till I went almost into fits.

And when you twisted round your head,
   And turn'd your eyes towards the tree,
It made me feel amazing sham'd,
   So plaguy 'fraid that you would see.

I look'd right at your cheek and chin,
   And all from where your gown had fell,
It made me think of fifty things . . . .
   But you won't like it if I tell.

48. II, 152.

Dennie's disenchantment with Wordsworth's poetic principles is perceptible from his introduction to the poem: "Nothing, however exquisite or faultless in writing, but may be ludicrously parodied, or burlesqued. The following very characteristical lines seem to sneer at the charming simplicity of Wordsworth's 'Lyrical Ballads.' Whether this species of sarcasm, applied to the elegant work in question, be fair or not, the Editor will not now stay to settle; but will only add that the subsequent stanzas are very faithfully descriptive of *rustic* love in New-England; and though such a passion may be derided by the refinement of the city, yet it will cause no scornful smile in

> 'Many a youth and many a maid
> Dancing in the *checquer'd shade*.' "

The other two parodies, both written by Dr. Robert H. Rose, are "A Lyrical Ballad," in the *Port Folio* for August 18, 1804, and a caricature of "Written in Germany, on one of the coldest days of the century" in the number for October 27, 1804.[49] The latter is too far from the subject of Wordsworth's poem to be effective ridicule. "A Lyrical Ballad," however, mimics well the hesitant and repetitious language in some of Wordsworth's poems and makes their author seem foolishly indecisive.

The fitfulness with which Dennie reprinted the twelve poems from *Lyrical Ballads*, his mistake regarding the authorship of one of them, and his failure to print one of five that were successive in the original indicate that he was not a firm convert to Wordsworth's principles. The chronology of the appearance of the twelve poems in the *Port Folio* suggests his erratic and waning interest. He reprinted nine of the twelve in 1801, none in 1802, one in 1803, two in 1804, and none thereafter. On December 5, 1801, he reprinted for the second time "Strange Fits of Passion I Have Known," which had appeared in the *Port Folio* six months earlier as part of the review of *Lyrical Ballads* from the *British Critic*. It may be that he did not read this review very carefully, for as late as July 2, 1803, he reprinted Coleridge's "Love" from *Lyrical Ballads*,[50] attributed its authorship to Wordsworth, and praised him highly for it, even though Wordsworth states in the third paragraph of the Preface that the author was "a Friend" and even though that passage had been pointed out and "a Friend" had been identified as Coleridge in the *British Critic* review in the *Port Folio*

49. IV, 257, 342–343.

50. III (July 2, 1803), 209.

two years earlier. It may also be significant that, of five poems appearing successively in *Lyrical Ballads*, Dennie reprinted all but the fourth, "Lines Written in Early Spring," containing the stanza

> To her fair works did Nature link
>   The human soul that through me ran;
> And much it grieved my heart to think
>   What man has made of man.

Since it is the only one of the five expressing the belief that nature resides benevolently in man and motivates him toward brotherhood, it seems likely that antipathy to democracy, rather than accident, led Dennie to reject the poem.[51]

For an understanding of Dennie's literary attitudes, a list of the compositions in *Lyrical Ballads* that he did not reprint or mention may be more illuminating than a catalog of those he accepted. Notable poems usually included in modern anthologies but excluded from the *Port Folio* are "Lines, Left upon a Seat in a Yew-tree," "Lines Written in Early Spring," "Expostulation and Reply," "The Tables Turned," "Lines Written a Few Miles above Tintern Abbey," and, from the second edition of 1800, "Michael." Nor did Dennie quote from or mention the revolutionary Preface from the 1800 edition. The list reveals that he did not publish from either edition prose or poetry that directly declared the Wordsworthian and Romantic ideas of the pervasiveness of God in nature, of nature as a force for human morality, or of the dignity and worth of the emotions and language of the common man. It is possible that Dennie, like Francis Jeffrey, "fell far short of understanding [Wordsworth's] spiritual conception of nature." Yet Dennie could comprehend the idea of an ideal nature, whether he believed in it or not, as he once demonstrated in writing, with admirable precision, a footnote explaining Berkeley: "He taught the external universe has no existence, but an ideal one in the mind (or spirit) that perceives it."[52] It therefore seems more likely that Dennie was too orthodox as a churchman and too conservative as a Federalist to see throughout nature, as Wordsworth did, a motion and a spirit that impels all thinking things, all objects of all

51. The five are "Simon Lee," "Anecdote for Fathers," "We Are Seven" (in the *Gazette of the United States*; see Ellis, p. 13), "Lines Written in Early Spring," and "The Thorn."

52. II (March 27, 1802), 96n. For a discussion of Jeffrey's inability to understand Wordsworth, see J. V. Logan, *Wordsworthian Criticism: A Guide and a Bibliography* (Columbus, Ohio, 1961), pp. 5, 6, 7–12.

thought. Such views challenge established authority and they had led, as Dennie knew well, to phrases like "the Laws of Nature and of Nature's God" that Jefferson had used in the Declaration to justify revolution. Dennie appears to have believed that nature teaches man brutality,[53] not humanity, not "acts of kindness and of love," as Wordsworth taught. It is clear that Dennie deplored the democratic tendency of Wordsworth's Preface. A reader of Dennie, who continually alluded to common people as "the vulgar" or "the swinish multitude," can hardly conceive of his believing or wishing to propagate in his magazine the Preface's doctrine that the essential passions find "in low and rustic life" a better soil to mature in, or that the language of rustics "is a more permanent and a far more philosophical language" than that substituted for it by poets "who think that they are conferring honour upon themselves and their art in proportion as they separate themselves from the sympathies of men."[54]

Dennie, however, did not surrender at once to Wordsworth's detractors. As late as March 17, 1804, he asked his readers to find for him a copy of Wordsworth's first book, *Descriptive Sketches.*[55] But in the number for November 14, 1807, three years after he had ceased to reprint Wordsworth's poems, he declared that Scott's *The Lay of the Last Minstrel* was "the most beautiful poem that has appeared since the days of Goldsmith," and in the same column dismissed a new edition of Wordsworth's works with two terse sentences: "Wm. Wordsworth has published two volumes of poems. We hope that he does not *continue to strike the very base string of humility.*"[56] It is difficult to believe that he could have meant to convey by the italicized words anything but disgust for Wordsworth's belief in the dignity of low and rustic life. The quality for which he had admired Wordsworth most, simplicity of language, was a rhetorical ideal that had been accepted among educated men at least as early as 1783 when Hugh Blair published the lectures that he had been delivering since 1759 and that Wordsworth may have been acquainted with.[57] But by

53. V (April 6, 1805), 102.
54. R. L. Brett and A. R. Jones, eds., *Lyrical Ballads* (London, 1963), p. 239.
55. IV (March 17, 1804), 87.
56. Ser. 2, IV (Nov. 14, 1807), 306, 310.
57. *Lectures on Rhetoric and Belles Lettres* (Philadelphia, 1844). Blair discussed simplicity of language in Lecture XIX, pp. 205–215. It is probable that Wordsworth knew Blair's *Lectures* and that his writing was influenced by the work (E. C. Knowlton, "Wordsworth and Hugh Blair," *Philological Quarterly*, VI, July, 1927, 277–281). For a list of Harvard textbooks, see Ellis, p. 28.

March, 1809, Dennie had changed his mind enough about Wordsworth's language to admit to his pages an article declaring that "Wordsworth stands among the foremost of those English bards, who have mistaken silliness for simplicity; and, with a false and affected taste, filled their pages with the language of children and clowns." In fairness, one must add, the author of this notice, who seems not to have been Dennie, did say that in Wordsworth's poetry "we find flashes of a poetic imagination which excite our approbation."[58] But a year later Dennie himself returned to the question of language and, in introducing some doggerel in mockery of Wordsworth, deserted him entirely: "Some of Mr. Wordsworth's earlier effusions of poetical genius were certainly not unworthy of the muse. But, of late, he has extended so far his theory of simplicity in writing, that it degenerates into burlesque and puerility."[59] In short, Dennie could find no elegance in the simplicity of Wordsworth's common people.

It can hardly be said that Dennie's treatment of Wordsworth, viewed as a whole, did much to advance Wordsworth's popularity in America. The first American edition of Wordsworth's poems was *Lyrical Ballads*, published in Philadelphia in 1802. But there was no other American publication of a volume of Wordsworth until 1824. In England by that year no fewer than sixteen editions of his poetry had been published.[60]

V

During Dennie's editorship the *Port Folio*'s notices of Coleridge and his writings—frequent during the first year and a half, widely scattered thereafter—were marked more often than not by uneasiness about his politics. The three earliest notices were friendly. The first was "Foreign Literature" in the number for January 31, 1801, in which Dr. John Stock, drama critic for the *Port Folio*, reviewed Coleridge's translations of Schiller's plays *The Piccolomini* and *The Death of Wallenstein*.[61] The plays had been published less than nine months earlier, and Dr. Stock, believing that he had the only copy that had found its way to Philadelphia, devoted four columns to them.

58. Ser. 3, I (March, 1809), 286.
59. Ser. 3, III (May, 1810), 438.
60. Elsie Smith, *An Estimate of William Wordsworth by His Contemporaries, 1793–1822* (Oxford, 1932), pp. 365–367.
61. I, 37–38.

He saw in the dramas many passages of great beauty and quoted them liberally. "Some sentiments," he thought, "occasionally occur with a felicity almost Shakespearian," and he also commended warmly Coleridge's translation of the ballad from *The Piccolomini* beginning, "The cloud doth gather, the green-wood roar." But he adverted to the political question by citing some passages to refute the belief that the German dramatists constantly intended "the subversion of existing institutions, and from Wallenstein's speeches he quoted lines contrary to Coleridge's early political beliefs:

> The human being
> May not be trusted to self government;
> The clear and written law; the dry trod foot marks
> Of ancient custom, are all necessary
> To keep him in the road of faith and duty.[62]

Two months later, on March 21, Dennie included in his column "Literary Intelligence" Henri Caritat's announcement of his intention to publish under the editorship of John Davis "a Volume of Modern Poetry; forming a second volume of the London edition of Elegant Extracts in Verse."[63] It was to be a splendid work, "comprized in one thousand royal octavo pages." The volume was never published, but the advertisement is interesting because, in Davis's mind and probably Caritat's, Coleridge was then better known than Wordsworth. Coleridge was to be prominently represented in Davis's anthology with eleven compositions, all selected from the 1797 edition of his *Poems*. Of the many poets whose work was to be included, only two others were to be honored by the inclusion of so many works. Most of the authors listed by Davis are now forgotten, but he did intend to include poems by Cowper, Burns, Campbell, Southey, and Lamb. He omitted Wordsworth.

The *Port Folio* for June 13, 1801, contained the previously cited review of the 1800 edition of *Lyrical Ballads* copied from the *British Critic*.[64] This most favorable of the early reviews is believed to have been written by Francis Wrangham. A year earlier the same author had reviewed the first edition for the same journal and had there discussed "The Rime of the Ancient Mariner" with moderate praise and had attributed it—and with some hesitation all the other poems in the volume—to Coleridge. Since the second edition (1800) bore

62. Act III, Scene 2, ll. 34–38.
63. I, 90–92.
64. I, 188–189.

Wordsworth's name, but not Coleridge's, on the title page, the second review, reprinted in the *Port Folio*, dealt only briefly with Coleridge:

> In our review for October, 1799, we noticed, with considerable satisfaction, the first edition of this work, then comprised in one anonymous volume. It is now extended, by the addition of another volume; and the author has given his name to it, with the exception of the *Ancient Mariner*, the *Foster Mother's Tale*, the *Nightingale*, the *Dungeon*, and the poem entitled *Love*; all of which, as he informs us, are furnished by a friend, whose opinions, on the subject of poetry, agree almost entirely with his own. From this similarity of mind, and from some expressions in the advertisement prefixed to the first edition, we were then led to attribute the whole to Mr. Coleridge, the supposed author of the Ancient Mariner: we now, therefore, add to the list of our poets another name, no less likely to do it honour.

In the number for August 15, 1801, Dennie himself commented on Coleridge for the first time.[65] He had noticed in the preface to the second edition of *Poems* (1797) Coleridge's eloquent tribute to poetry, which he could not resist passing on to his readers:

> I expect neither profit nor general fame by my writings; and I consider myself as having been amply repaid without either. Poetry has been to me its own "exceeding great reward": it has soothed my afflictions; it has multiplied and refined my enjoyments; it has endeared solitude; and it has given me the habit of wishing to discover the Good and the Beautiful in all that meets and surrounds me.

But neither could Dennie refrain from letting his readers know that language of such beauty had come surprisingly from a politically tainted pen, and he introduced the passage by warning them, "In the preface to the last edition of his poems, a modern writer, Coleridge, who is more distinguished for the originality of his thoughts, than for the correctness of his opinions, and who is more obedient to the nine, than to the civil authority, makes the subsequent striking declaration."

Two weeks later, on August 29, 1801, Dennie referred to Coleridge in "An Author's Evenings," an article devoted entirely to a discussion of Southey's drama *Joan of Arc*.[66] In this brilliant essay Dennie undertook to state his objections not only to Southey's radical political views but to those of republicans generally and, in the process, to set forth the historical position of the political conservative. In doing so he revealed that, though his love for letters was great, he was preoc-

65. I, 263.

66. I (Aug. 29, 1801), 274.

cupied with fears of democracy, fears not only of loss of privilege, but also of the devastation of his culture.

"It appears that SOUTHEY and a Mr. Coleridge, another *democratic* poet," Dennie wrote, "were educated together and mutually inflamed with French liberty . . . . The poems of Southey and his companions are recited with *patriotic* emphasis, by the whole tribe of dissenters, innovators, wishers for parliamentary reform, and haters of church and king." Dennie did say, in a fifteenth of his essay that, "as a literary production, the epic of Southey is worthy of liberal commendation." But the political sentiments, he thought, were the "disjointed chat of a youthful dreamer." In Southey's view, he said, "what a glorious thing it would be for all the world to be of the same size, of the same strength, and to have purses and brains of *equal* fullness." It turned out, Dennie thought, that the idols that Southey wanted to destroy were the best features of our culture, "A grave and upright ruler; a pious teacher; a dignified gentleman; the founder of christianity; the virtues of chastity, mercy, and order." But the world was not as Southey, "with the fallacy of a dream and the madness of a Quixote," had described it. "In spite of R. SOUTHEY, and all his French crew," Dennie concluded, "as long as this world remains, Poverty, and all her brood of miseries, will *not* die; Oppression will *not* cease; Weakness will *not* be a match for Strength, and Folly will never rival Genius."

Six weeks later, in the number for October 10, 1801, he was again grumbling about the effects of wrong-headed politics on literature: "Cowper was not ashamed to learn a lesson from the *old* and admirable school of English sense and literature; and if the Southey's [*sic*] and Lambs and the Coleridge's [*sic*] of the day, would study in the same form, we should be relieved both from flimsy poetry, and abominable politics."[67]

In the number for July 17, 1802, Dennie inserted at the very end of his poetry page Coleridge's juvenile poem "Sonnet to My Love" with the heading, "From Coleridge's Poems."[68] There was no other comment upon this poem, which was said by Coleridge's biographer Lawrence Hanson to have been the author's first.[69] In the 1796 edition of Coleridge's poems, from which it must have been taken, it had the

67. I, 324.
68. II, 224.
69. *The Life of S. T. Coleridge* (New York, 1939), p. 19. The poem was originally entitled "Genevieve."

footnote, "This little poem was written when the Author was a boy."[70]

It was almost a year later that Dennie blundered into the previously noted mistake in attribution of authorship. In "An Author's Evenings" of July 2, 1803, he observed in introducing Coleridge's "Love," "Wordsworth is a favorite poet because, as Prior somewhere says, he talks like a *man of this world*. He is an intelligible and feeling writer. His description of the passion of Love, in the following Poem, is so exact, that it cannot fail to please, those, who admire the true, as well as the beautiful, and the two stanzas, preceding the last, will be remembered by all, who have been clasped to the bosom of Beauty."[71] The poem that follows this generous praise concerns Coleridge's and Sarah Hutchinson's discovery in November, 1799, of their pitiably hopeless attachment:

> Her Bosom heav'd—she stepp'd aside;
> As conscious of my Look, she stepp'd—
> Then suddenly with timorous eye
>   She fled to me and wept.
>
> She half inclosed me with her arms,
> She press'd me with a meek embrace;
> And bending back her head look'd up
>   And gaz'd upon my face.

Dennie had made a similar mistake in the *Gazette of the United States* for August 9, 1800, when he served that journal as literary editor. The error there was reversed: he reprinted Wordsworth's "We Are Seven," attributed the poem to Coleridge, and praised Coleridge for the "inimitable simplicity and tenderness" of the poem.[72] But the mistake of attributing "Love" to Wordsworth was a more flagrant instance of carelessness as a literary critic, for Dennie could have avoided it by attentive reading of the Preface to *Lyrical Ballads* or the *British Critic* review.

Yet there is a postscript. After Dennie's second confusion of Coleridge's poetry with Wordsworth's, the *Port Folio* was silent about Coleridge for six years and then mentioned him twice more. In the number for May, 1811, the later of the two remaining notices, a reviewer of Byron's *English Bards and Scotch Reviewers* participated

70. E. H. Coleridge, *The Complete Poetical Works of Samuel Taylor Coleridge* (Oxford, 1912), I, 19.

71. III, 209.

72. Ellis, p. 131.

in the derision as he noted that "the sighing and simpering Coleridge is thus brought in contact with his subject" in Byron's lines:

> "Yet none in lofty numbers can surpass
> The bard who soars to eulogize an ass;
> How well the subject suits his noble mind,
> A *fellow-feeling* makes us wondrous kind.[73]

But Dennie, chronically ill after 1807 and desperately so in 1811, did not write the review, and possibly never saw it.

It cannot be denied, however, that he was responsible for an earlier comment on Coleridge signed "Editor" and bearing other internal evidence of Dennie's authorship. Dennie reprinted the prospectus for Coleridge's *The Friend*, apparently from a journal published in London, in the *Port Folio* for August, 1809.[74] Probably in no other writing does Coleridge appear more humbly contrite for his uncompleted projects or does he so repeatedly and emphatically avow a moral purpose as he does in the prospectus. In a headnote to it, Dennie apparently assumes that Coleridge's intention of explaining in *The Friend* "the origin and growth of moral purposes" and "the true and sole ground of Morality" was a revulsion from his democratic beliefs:

> This journal [*The Friend*] is to be conducted by the celebrated Coleridge, already advantageously known to the republic of letters by many ingenious performances both in Poetry and Prose. With the utmost cheerfulness we insert his PROSPECTUS in The Port Folio, and this we do with the more alacrity, because it is plainly perceived that Time, Experience, and Observation, have totally changed the colour of this gentleman's mind, and that the reign of right principle is fully restored.
>
> The execution of this Prospectus, we think, falls rather below Mr. Coleridge's brilliant powers. It is manifestly a hasty production; and, in the awkward form of a fragment of a letter, has the guise of affected negligence, not to say slovenliness. Mr. Coleridge is unquestionably capable of much more glorious exertion, and, when we recollect that, with all an architect's ability, he is about to construct a magnificent Temple, we are not a little surprised that he has not been more studious of the elegance of its porch.

Dennie was justified in thinking the writing of the prospectus was slovenly. But while he shows in his headnote respect for Coleridge's "ingenious performances" and "brilliant powers," he was patronizing in doing so only after asserting that "the reign of right principle is fully restored" in Coleridge.

73. Ser. 3, V, 446.

74. Ser. 3, II, 104.

Commendatory as Dennie's remarks about Coleridge were in the headnote to the prospectus for *The Friend*, his overall treatment of Coleridge was unfavorable. The only poem of Coleridge's that he reprinted at his own instigation and with correct attribution of authorship to Coleridge was the juvenile "Sonnet to My Love" in 1802. The result of his repeated confusion of Coleridge's poetry with Wordsworth's, though unintentional, was uncomplimentary to Coleridge. He never mentioned "The Rime of the Ancient Mariner," the first and longest poem in *Lyrical Ballads*. This neglect and his expressed antipathy to Coleridge's politics reveal Dennie's biases and inevitably weaken his authority as a literary critic. The effect of his rebuffs is hard to assess, but except for the Philadelphia edition of *Lyrical Ballads* in 1802 there was no American edition of any of Coleridge's work before the publication of *Remorse* in New York in 1813; in Britain by that year there had been eighteen editions.[75]

VI

Inadequate as Dennie was as a critic of democratic and Romantic poets, his main enthusiasm was for searching out and holding up as models splendid pieces of elegant simplicity in prose. The best of these, he thought, were Addison's and Goldsmith's, but he reprinted in the *Port Folio* very little that Addison had written. In rejecting a contribution plagiarized from the *Spectator*, Dennie wrote, "If there be any book universally read, it is Addison's Spectator. Our readers would surely grumble, if we huckstered out those essays, which are to be found in every parlour window."[76] Passages from Addison's little-known essay on medals and his letter to his patron's wife rejecting the sexual favors she had offered him are the only pieces of any length that Dennie reproduced.[77]

Yet his critical comments and his own prose style demonstrate that he imitated Addison consciously. In introducing the first number of his essay series, "The Farrago," in 1792, long before the *Port Folio* began, Dennie, in justification of his own essays, had cited the immense value of the *Spectator* in the elevation of the morality and manners of the English-speaking peoples.[78] In the first volume of the

75. John L. Haney, *A Bibliography of Samuel Taylor Coleridge* (Philadelphia, 1903), pp. 1–9.
76. I (Feb. 28, 1801), 69.
77. Ser. 2, III (Jan. 31, 1807), 77; Ser. 2, I (May 31, 1806), 327.
78. Ellis, p. 229.

Port Folio he described his *The Lay Preacher* as "a series of essays, modelled after the designs of Addison, and the harmless and playful levity of Goldsmith." He referred to the English journal as "my laurelled predecessor, the Spectator." It was a standard of excellence to him as it had been to Franklin in Boston seventy-five years earlier. In 1803, Dennie observed in an introduction to a brief history of the *Spectator* and the *Tatler* that from his youth forward he had perused the periodical essayists and had tried to imitate them when, "with so much felicity, they select transient topics, and adorn them with such transcendent colours, [and] I have endeavoured to conform, with the most scrupulous care, to the purity of their standard."[79]

Whoever lays the first volumes of the original *Spectator* and of the *Port Folio* side by side is struck by the similarity of their appearance in spite of the ninety years that separates them. The two are similar also in spirit. Both editors forswear gossip and scandal; both pose as lounging observers of life; and both seek to entertain while they elevate their readers. In political purposes they differ sharply, the English journal promising to avoid "the Outrages of a Party," and the American averring that it will not be impartial.[80]

The only unfavorable mention of Addison in Dennie's *Port Folio* was that of the reviewer of his play *Cato*, performed at the theater in Philadelphia. The critic, possibly Dennie but probably Dr. John Stock, complained of the dullness of the whiggism in the drama.[81] But the *Port Folio* before 1807 honored no other writer of prose more often with affectionate enthusiasm. The author of "Miscellaneous Paragraphs," almost certainly Dennie, believed that Addison was the chief of the essayists because of the persona that he had created. "There is," he noted, "a *personal charm* in *the character* he has assumed . . . which is felt with such a gentle force, that one scarcely adverts to it. He has painted forth his little humours, and his individual feelings," with the result that the reader came away from reading Addison feeling that he had had a private conversation with him. Addison, he thought, "understood better than any other writer, the nature and province of true humour." There was nothing profane or impertinent in his mirth, he added, and "his smiles, like those of innocence, were irresistibly captivating."[82]

79. I (Jan. 3, July 25, 1801), 3, 236; III (Dec. 24, 1803), 410.
80. *Spectator*, No. 16, col. 3; *Port Folio*, "Prospectus," 1801.
81. I (April 4, 1801), 109–110.
82. IV (Jan. 21, 1804), 22.

Dennie believed that Addison's benefit to society had been immense. In New Hampshire in 1792, as noted earlier, he had applauded Addison in the first number of "The Farrago" series because he had "allured to the temples of wisdom and virtue" a host of readers who have not read or understood "the abstract reasonings of Locke or Bacon." Dennie believed that, by creating a prose that magnetized the entire literate public, Addison stood in the front rank of those writers "who, in the narrow compass of a sheet of paper, conveyed more useful knowledge to mankind than all the ponderous tomes of Aristotle."[83] The sentiment was repeated in the *Port Folio* in 1804: "If writing be good, in proportion as it is useful, and if its noblest use be, to improve the heart, refine the taste, and sweeten the temper, ADDISON is of all uninspired [secular] authours at least, in prose, the best, and the most delightful."[84]

Dennie did not explain the structure of Addison's prose, perhaps because he thought it had been sufficiently described in several chapters of Blair's *Lectures on Rhetoric and Belles Lettres*, Dennie's textbook at Harvard and the standard rhetoric of the period. He did welcome young Thomas Sergeant's study of Addison's prose for the *Port Folio* of August 24, 1805, but Dennie's comments are not helpfully specific.[85] Clear though Dennie's critical terminology may have been to his contemporaries, it seems ambiguous when he ascribes a "manly style" to both Addison and Fielding. In two other comments he alludes to but does not explain Addison's "elegance," his "beauties and graces," or tell us exactly how he was "always clear and harmonious, rational, manly, and interesting."[86]

VII

Dennie's admiration for Goldsmith increased until, in the late years of his life, he regarded him as the best of the English prose stylists. He constantly reminded his readers of his excellence. With the possible exception of the letters of Smollett which Dennie doled out in the *Port Folio* over a period of years, he reprinted and commented on more of Goldsmith's work than he did on the writing of any of the authors of England's Augustan age of prose. Goldsmith may have

83. Ellis, pp. 228–229.
84. IV (May 26, 1804), 165.
85. V, 257.
86. Ser. 2, III (Jan. 31, 1807), 65; IV (May 26, 1804), 165.

pleased Dennie partly because he once said, "Men are not born with equal talents," a statement that Dennie did not fail to copy in the *Port Folio*,[87] but he also felt a kinship with Goldsmith because he thought that, just as Ireland had not heaped rewards on the young Goldsmith so had Boston and the United States failed to appreciate his own talents. Dennie saw a parallel between the cultural and intellectual poverty of Ireland and that of his country and imagined that if Goldsmith, like him, had been set down in America among "deists, *new* philosophers, jacobins, convicts, swindlers, . . . buffoons," and "the robbers of his patrimony," he, too, would have thought of leaving his country.[88]

Dennie thought Goldsmith "deserves our love for the generosity of his nature" and for his "harmless and playful levity." He esteemed him for his sincerity, observing in his introduction to one of Goldsmith's letters that it was "a faithful journal of the honest emotions." He may have meant something similar when he wrote that Goldsmith was "faithful to truth and nature."[89] Dennie regarded him as a discerning critic, reprinted some of his essays on rhetoric, and often advised young writers to take him as a model.[90] He described his diction as "correct and elegant, and at the same time free from every species of affectation." He thought that "the judicious lover of that elegant simplicity that never wearies" in the works of great stylists like Xenophon and Addison will find that "every effusion from the pen of GOLDSMITH is eminently agreeable." He found his language pure, "the very reverse of that revolutionary jargon so much in vogue," and, in another instance, thought it "pure of ambitious conceits." Let the beginning writer "inspect the following passage from Goldsmith," Dennie once advised, "and, while he admires, remember that this is English *undefiled*; neither debased by foreign alloy; nor defaced by vulgar usage."[91]

Simplicity is the quality of Goldsmith's style that Dennie mentioned more than any other, especially if ease of expression be considered a part of the same quality. He regarded one of his letters as "a model of epistolary ease"; he reprinted a passage from another writing as a specimen of "pure and easy English." He declared that "his

87. V (June 1, 1805), 165.
88. III (March 19, 1803), 93, 93n.
89. V (June 29, 1805), 193; I (Jan. 3, 1801), 3; III (March 19, 1803), 93–94.
90. I (Jan. 24, 1801), 28; V (June 22, July 27, 1805), 191, 225.
91. III (March 19, Sept. 10, Dec. 3, 1803), 93, 294, 389; IV (Feb. 25, 1804), 58.

language flows from him without perceptible effort" and that "the classical ease of his manner has never been equalled," and he praised Wordsworth for following Goldsmith "in the easy and agreeable track of simplicity."[92] But Dennie did not mean to approve the easiness of conversational English, at least for his own use, as he demonstrated by the nice balances of his self-conscious sentences in the *Port Folio* of January 24, 1801: "The writings of Goldsmith are admirable models for him, who is serious of a style, easy, but not colloquial; free, but not wanton; and exact, though not elaborate. He certainly improved upon Addison, for he is never careless, or indistinct. His vivacity diverts the imagination, and his melody soothes the ear."[93]

In 1807 and 1808, apparently the last years that his health permitted anything like sustained good writing, Dennie became firmly convinced that Goldsmith, "the purest writer in the English language," was ideally suited to serve as the model for Americans tempted by fine writing and bombast.[94] He urged American booksellers to republish the British pocket-size edition of Goldsmith's works so that the volumes could be carried as constant companions. Such an edition "would do more to rectify that bad taste, and to purify that provincial diction, with which we are sometimes reproached, than all the reasonings of the philologer, than all the fastidiousness of Criticism, and all the sarcasm of Wit."[95]

VIII

Dennie's sense of a proper magazine becomes evident to us by contrast when for a period in 1809 Dennie was ill and "a confederacy of men of letters," temporary editors of the *Port Folio*, inserted articles on such topics as the construction of James Finley's chain bridge, sheep raising, and Betts's patent cheese press.[96] Nothing could have been farther from Dennie's intention. When he was in charge, the *Port Folio* was never homely, or practical, or provincial, but urbane and cosmopolitan. The American provincial who read Dennie's journal had a sense of belonging to the world of art and learning. He was informed of London's latest books and of the plays and actors at the Covent Garden and Drury Lane. Serialized accounts by American

92. III (March 19, Sept. 3, 10, 1803), 93, 287, 294.
93. I, 28.
94. Ser. 2, IV (Sept. 19, Nov. 14, 1807), 187, 312; Ser. 3, I (Jan., 1809), 13n.
95. Ser. 2, VI (Oct. 15, 22, 1808), 245n., 260–261.
96. Ser. 3, III (May, June, 1810), 401, 441; Ser. 3, IV (Dec., 1810), 565–572.

travelers—like John Quincy Adams's "Journal of a Tour through Silesia," and Francis Kinloch's "Letters from Geneva and France"—kept the reader aware of European history and manners.[97] Above all, he was steadily reminded that his cultural home was eighteenth-century Europe.

"The Conductor of this Journal apprizes the publick," Dennie wrote for the *Port Folio* of October 31, 1807, "that a constant regard to elegant and useful literature will always be a distinguishing feature of this publication."[98] He printed with pride the long list of Scottish, French, and English periodicals which he received[99] and from which he copied articles for the *Port Folio*: translations of Schiller's plays, of a tale by Florian, of the fables of Gellert, and of the memoirs of Marmontel; brief essays by Richard Cumberland, Goldsmith, and Dr. Johnson; and critical essays on Sterne, Smollett, and Fielding. Throughout his editorship Dennie published brief biographies of classic eighteenth-century authors: Thomas Gray, Colley Cibber, Richardson, Goldsmith, Defoe, Boileau, La Bruyère, Racine, and Le Sage. "We are entirely of opinion," Dennie wrote in the number for September 12, 1807, "that by a series of such biographical sketches, interspersed with enlightened Criticism, Polite Literature may be . . . most extensively disseminated among the reading classes of the community; the taste and intelligence of the nation may be greatly improved; our notions of excellence may be enlarged and corrected."[100]

He was especially fond of printing the letters of elegant writers for the improvement of the taste and literary style of his readers. Some of Smollett's letters which had not then been published in America appeared through much of 1801 and 1802, and those of William Cowper during 1805. When one of his friends protested the copying of Cowper's published letters in the *Port Folio*, Dennie replied that at the time "he could exhibit nothing more new, interesting and elegant. The epistles of Cowper," he said, "challenge a decided superiority over every other effort in that walk in the English language."[101] He was assiduous in searching out for the *Port Folio* fugitive letters by or about eminent authors of the eighteenth century. In introducing to his readers a lost letter of Edmund Burke's he confided, "As we knew that this neglected letter was extant somewhere, our admiration

97. The Adams *Journal* ran through 1801; Kinloch's *Letters* from Ser. 2, V (Jan. 30, 1808), 97–99, through 1808 and into 1809.

98. Ser. 2, IV, 286.

99. V (April 20, 1805), 118.

100. Ser. 2, IV, 175.

101. Ser. 2, III (Jan. 3, 1807), 15.

for its wise and eloquent authour has induced us for many years to search for it as for *hidden treasure*." He rejoiced in finding the document "in the shop of Mr. Patrick Byrne, formerly an eminent bookseller in Dublin, and since fully established in Philadelphia."[102] One of Dennie's brightest pages resulted from his persuading the Reverend James Abercrombie, his friend in Philadelphia, to allow him to publish for the first time Dr. Benjamin Rush's letter of April 22, 1793, describing the guests and the conversation at a dinner in London at Sir Joshua Reynolds's, where Rush had had the good fortune to be seated between Goldsmith and Dr. Johnson.[103]

Though Dennie believed the modern form of classical elegance resided in the best writings, particularly those in prose, of the eighteenth century, he thought one could hardly emulate them without a thorough acquaintance with the literature of ancient Greece and Rome. He began to publish his contributors' translations of Juvenal and Horace in the volume for 1801. These were followed by numerous versions of Anacreon's odes. In 1807, he inserted biographical sketches of Livy, Plautus, Terence, and Seneca. In August of that year Dennie announced his inheritance of the papers, including the lectures on classical literature, of his intimate friend Dr. Charles Nisbet, formerly a clergyman of Montrose in Scotland, and for many years principal of Carlisle College in Pennsylvania. "To our great joy," Dennie reported, "we have at length obtained what we have long anxiously desired." Under the title "Classical Learning," Dennie published in late 1807 and early 1808 Dr. Nisbet's lectures on the life and works of Vergil, Ovid, Horace, Plato, Xenophon, and Aeschylus. Through his publication of the lectures, he predicted, "the rising geniuses of Columbia, the gentlemen and the cavaliers, all the ambitious, all the aspiring, will *unfold Plato* and Tully by the bright reflection of the CLASSICAL LAMP; and, leaving the vile trash of literature to be devoured by the *swinish multitude*, will fervently echo our wish that the enchanting waters of antiquity may be studied in every age by the side of the gentle Thames and the romantic Schuylkill."[104]

In his conduct of the *Port Folio* Dennie aimed at nothing less than the development of literary elegance in the writing of his American friends and admirers—housewives, students, young women, lawyers, doctors, businessmen, and clergymen—who were contributors to his

102. Ser. 2, V (April 30, 1808), 281.
103. IV (Dec. 15, 1804), 393.
104. Ser. 2, IV (Aug. 8, 1807), 94.

journal. Although outstanding American writers of the decade—Charles Brockden Brown, Royall Tyler, Thomas Green Fessenden, Irving, and Freneau—were represented in his magazine, two thirds of his writers were Philadelphia friends and neighbors whom he attracted to his pages through his conversations with them at the meetings of the Tuesday Club, at teas and dinners, the theater, and concerts.[105] But the main attraction was the personal character he gave to the magazine in his polished columns "An Author's Evenings," "Literary Intelligence," and especially "To Readers and Correspondents," which through its intensity and intimacy instigated a remarkable enthusiasm for writing. In one of his early numbers, that for March 7, 1801, Dennie wrote, "The Editor will exercise great tenderness and lenity toward all who tempt the dangerous *ocean of ink*. The literary offspring of youthful and trembling authors shall, if possible, be fostered."[106]

A special example of his cultivation of new talent was his encouragement of the writing of women. In one of his rare liberal moments he declared, "In a large portion of this country, women *have been* disgraced and degraded in consequence of the neglect, indifference, or tyranny of man. It is within our remembrance when a girl of the brightest talents had no other discipline than what the narrowest school could bestow. They were thus systematically shut out of Minerva's Temple." What, he asked, "has been the genuine classification and description of any individual of the sex, but that of a washing, baking, brewing, spinning, sewing, darning and child-producing *animal*?"[107] "The editor," he said, "is anxious . . . to give the most liberal encouragement to the genius, talents, and virtue of the ladies."[108] "The influence of women over the fate and fortune of this paper is much greater than that of statesmen."[109]

By no means all the contributions that Dennie received were fit to print, and he was rarely able to say that an entire number consisted of original writing. As a teacher of composition, he was often compelled to rebuke his eager contributors, particularly for their offerings in verse, which were, he noted, ten times more frequent than those in prose. Great heaps of the verse, he thought, was scarcely less offensive than piles of manure, but sometimes he found a jewel in it, and "Every

105. See my "Authors of the *Port Folio* Revealed by the Hall Files," *American Literature*, XI (Jan., 1940) 379–416, including notes.

106. I, 79.

107. Ser. 3, IV (July, 1810), 85.

108. IV (June 2, 1804), 175.

109. V (Jan. 19, 1805), 14.

article so precious," he said, "is preserved with a sort of religious care."[110] Doubtless his authors dreaded rebukes like the one in his column for September 19, 1801: "The pastoral dialogue between two *shepherds of Schuylkill,* we are obliged to reject . . . nothing can be more insipid. . . . The 'oaten reed' and the 'skipping lamb,' the 'brawling brook,' and the 'whispering breeze,' are images of egregious triteness."[111] Usually he was gentler, and sometimes awarded high praise, as he did to Jaques (Samuel Ewing) for the "refinement and tenderness in his melancholy not unlike that discernible in the poems of COLLINS."[112]

By 1807 Dennie had succeeded in making the *Port Folio* an authority on literary excellence. One Bostonian wrote of the journal's admirers "who were in the habit of looking up to The Port Folio, as the criterion of their taste in most matters of literature,"[113] and Senator Uriah Tracy of Connecticut, recommending the magazine to his daughters said, with some exaggeration perhaps, that "what is called style in writing . . . is better exhibited in the Port Folio than in any modern books, of this, or any other country."[114] The magazine's success was due to Dennie's ability to excite a love for elegance. His friends agreed that his enthusiasm was infectious. John Elihu Hall, in youth Dennie's disciple and friend, remembered, "Such a spirit of literature prevailed among his associates, and the young men generally of that period, that his table abounded with contributions for the Port Folio."[115] Another contributor and friend, Gertrude Meredith, wrote fifteen years after Dennie's death that Dennie was the one "who excited the first love of letters among us," and his light "illumines the path of all who direct their steps toward elegant and classical learning."[116] Nicholas Biddle, founder of the Pennsylvania Academy of the Fine Arts and Dennie's associate and successor as editor, observed, "His example had a magical power, not only over the circle who were influenced by attachment to his person, but on all who had the slightest tincture of learning. The attention of the people was

110. Ser. 3, II (Dec., 1809), 579.
111. I, 303.
112. I (Feb. 28, 1801), 70.
113. Ser. 2, IV (Nov. 7, 1807), 295–296, 299.
114. John T. Queenan, "The *Port Folio*: A Study of the History and Significance of an Early American Magazine," doctoral dissertation, University of Pennsylvania, 1955, p. 231.
115. John E. Hall, ed. *The Philadelphia Souvenir* (Philadelphia, 1826), p. 89.
116. Queenan, p. 53.

excited by his brilliancy—the purest scholars of the country flocked to his standard, and the nation was seduced at once into the luxury of literature."[117]

117. Ser. 3, VII (Feb., 1812), 187

Charles R. Anderson

Thoreau and The Dial: *The Apprentice Years*

America's first "little magazine" was *The Dial* (1840–1844), deliberately founded as an organ to encourage new ideas, experimental writing, and young unknown authors. Sponsored by the Transcendental Club, it drew upon that richly talented group for its editors and chief contributors: Emerson, Margaret Fuller, Thoreau, Alcott, the Channings, J. F. Clarke, C. P. Cranch, F. H. Hedge, Elizabeth Peabody, Theodore Parker, the Ripleys, and others. At the time it began publication, July, 1840, Emerson was only thirty-seven years old and Thoreau twenty-three, most of the others being thirty or younger. The first editor, Margaret Fuller, clearly regarded it as an experiment, declaring in a letter of March 22, 1840: "It were much if a periodical could be kept open . . . merely to afford an avenue for what of liberal and calm thought might be originated among us, by the wants of individual minds."[1] Emerson, writing the Address to Readers in the first number, described its contributors as those "spirits which are withdrawing from old forms, and seeking in all that is new somewhat to meet their inappeasable longings." What chiefly induced him to devote time and money to it was his hope that it would afford an outlet for the writings of his young protégés, Ellery Channing and Henry Thoreau.

Even when supporters of *The Dial* were critical, this was evidence of how high they wanted their journal to aim. For example Ripley, though admitting that the opening number had produced a decided sensation, complained: "It was not *prononcé* enough. [The best

Just forty years ago, when Prof. Gohdes and I were sharing an apartment as young instructors at Duke University, I was helping him correct the proof sheets of his dissertation, *The Periodicals of American Transcendentalism*. This essay provides a footnote to that scholarly book, and another leaf to the album of an old friendship.

1. G. W. Cooke, *An Historical and Biographical Introduction to Accompany The Dial*, 2 vols. (Cleveland, 1902), I, 63. The other quotations in this paragraph and the next are from pp. 70, 75, 78.

judges] expected hoofs and horns, while it proved as gentle as any sucking dove." Parker thought it did not have "fire and flame" enough. Alcott wrote to an English friend: " 'The Dial' partakes of our vices, it consults the mood and is awed somewhat by the bearing of existing orders, yet is superior to our other literary organs, and satisfies in part the hunger of youth. It satisfies me not, nor Emerson. It measures not the meridian, but the morning ray; the nations wait for the gnomon that shall mark the broad noon." Concord's celebrated idealist, who had given the journal its name, was quick to indicate just how lofty a pointer (gnomon) he had had in mind for this new kind of sundial.

The Dial lasted for only four years and never had a circulation of more than a few hundred, but it had an influence far beyond what such statistics can suggest. The significance of its role in American cultural history was established many years ago by the researches of George Willis Cooke, published in 1902 as an introduction to the Rowfant Club reprint of the magazine. His summary comment is pertinent here: " 'The Dial' was . . . a journal of youth, filled with the high hope and dreams of those who had not tested themselves by long experience or severe trial. This youthfulness gave it the freshness and the courage that made it a new beginning in literature."[2] Cooke's conclusion invites a shift from his general commentary on *The Dial* to a particular consideration of its most important young contributor. The same scholar identified all of Thoreau's contributions and gave a biographical account of his connections with the magazine. But the present essay is the first attempt at a close reading of these apprentice writings for the purpose of evaluating Thoreau's achievement as a literary artist during the years prior to publication of his first book, *A Week on the Concord and Merrimack Rivers* (1849).[3]

All told, Thoreau contributed to *The Dial* sixteen poems, six essays, four translations from the Greek classics, and five articles made up of selections from the Oriental scriptures—a total exceeded only by Emerson, Fuller, and Channing. Yet Thoreau made a very small showing in the first two volumes, 1840–1842. He had responded

2. Ibid., I, 67. The historical facts in the next few pages are taken from the same source, unless otherwise indicated.

3. Sherman Paul, *The Shores of America: Thoreau's Inward Exploration* (Urbana, Ill., 1958), has made detailed analyses of two of these early writings, "Natural History of Massachusetts" and "A Winter Walk." But his study is focussed on Thoreau's intellectual development and so is complementary to my own, which is concerned with his art rather than his mind.

eagerly to the advent of the new journal, seeing in it a medium through which the Transcendentalists could communicate with each other. He sent in his subscription at once, only to have his money refunded on the grounds that he was expected to be a regular contributor. Acting on this he submitted a poem, "Sympathy," and a brief critique of the Roman satirist Persius, both of which were accepted (at Emerson's urging) and appeared in the first number—the former undistinguished, the latter little more than a college essay. Then two more poems were submitted, but one was rejected and the other returned for revision. Margaret Fuller, the editor, did not look favorably on Thoreau's writings, and her next rejection had a cooling effect on his ardor. By July, 1840, Thoreau had written his first ambitious essay, "The Service," an attempt to bring together all his principal themes to date—Friendship, Self-Reliance, the Brave and "Spheral" Man in opposition to Society—which he sent off to *The Dial.* Miss Fuller kept it for five months before finally returning it with a curious letter of rejection. She complained chiefly of its want of order and its arrogant tone, then concluded: "I cannot read it through without *pain.* I never once feel myself in a stream of thought, but seem to hear the grating of tools on the mosaic."[4] The essay was a literary failure, as Thoreau himself might have been willing to admit later on; it was abstract, fragmentary, and bookish in its imagery. But what probably pained the young writer was having the editorial finger placed right on his most vulnerable spot, his lifelong difficulty with creating a unified form. He sent two more poems to Miss Fuller, but it was not until she resigned as editor, a year and a half later, that he submitted another important composition.

The largest number of Thoreau's contributions to *The Dial* came in Volume III (1842–1843), after Emerson took over the editorship—eighteen items of poetry and prose. The sequence began with "Natural History of Massachusetts." Ostensibly a review of four books on the plants, insects, quadrupeds, and fishes-reptiles-birds of the state, actually it turned out to be Thoreau's first major essay, drawn largely from his own *Journal.*[5] His authorship was not indicated by name or

4. Carl Bode and Walter Harding, eds., *The Correspondence of Henry David Thoreau* (New York, 1958), pp. 41–42. See also Harding, *The Days of Henry Thoreau* (New York, 1965), pp. 113–115.

5. Paul, *Shores,* p. 102, suggests that had it not been for Emerson's prompting, in sending him these books for review, Thoreau might have continued writing abstract essays on Transcendental themes: "Emerson apprised him of the literary value of natural facts and introduced him to the hidden ore of his own *Journals.*"

initial, but many readers probably guessed it from the "Preliminary Note" affixed to it by *The Dial*'s editor:

> We were thinking how we might best celebrate the good deed which the State of Massachusetts has done, in procuring the Scientific Survey of the Commonwealth, whose result is recorded in these volumes [listed beneath Thoreau's title], when we found a near neighbor and friend of ours, dear also to the Muses, a native and an inhabitant of the town of Concord, who readily undertook to give us such comments as he had made on these books, and, better still, notes of his own conversation with nature in the woods and waters of this town. With all thankfulness we begged our friend to lay down the oar and fishing line, which none can handle better, and assume the pen, that Isaak Walton and White of Selborne might not want a successor, nor the fair meadows, to which we also have owed a home and the happiness of many years, their poet.[6]

Emerson's paragraph alerted readers not only to the identity of the author, but also to the kind of writing that might be expected from his pen.

The only part of this essay that resembles a "review" is its last page. There Thoreau observed, by way of summary, that the volume on fishes and reptiles was of great value because of the research that had gone into it; the one on quadrupeds should have been more definitive; those on plants and birds were inferior to treatises already existing. He concluded with an apology for the unavoidable dullness of such surveys, saying that we should not complain if the pioneer raises no flowers with his first crop. In this context he added a sentence that seems prophetic of his goal as a writer: "Let us not underrate the value of a fact; it will one day flower in a truth" (III, 39). Certainly his purpose in the "Natural History" essay was to make fact flower into truth. Thoreau was interested in the facts of nature only if they had been lived with and assimilated into the mind. He was actually defining not a scientist but himself as an artist when he said: "The true man of science will know nature better by his finer organization; he will smell, taste, see, hear, feel better than other men. His will be a deeper and finer experience" (III, 40).

Pedestrian as the books under review were, they had a double appeal for Thoreau. They dealt with the local scene, to which he was dedicated, and their instrument for seeing was science, on which the young poet had placed so much hope. They were only factual surveys,

6. *The Dial* (Cleveland, 1902), III, 19. Volume and page references to this edition are given in parentheses at the end of succeeding quotations.

of course, but the barest list of this sort could trigger his imagination. "It appears that we have eight kinds of tortoises, twelve snakes,— but one of which is venomous,— nine frogs and toads, nine salamanders, and one lizzard, for our neighbors," he wrote, with his finger on one of the reports. Then he made his own contribution: "I am particularly attracted by the motions of the serpent tribe. They make our hands and feet, the wings of the bird, and the fins of the fish seem very superfluous, as if nature had only indulged her fancy in making them" (III, 34). Again, taking off from the report on insects:

> Entomology extends the limits of being in a new direction, so that I walk in nature with a sense of greater space and freedom. It suggests besides, that the universe is not rough-hewn, but perfect in its details. Nature will bear the closest inspection; she invites us to lay our eye level with the smallest leaf, and take an insect view of its plain. She has no interstices; every part is full of life. I explore, too, with pleasure, the sources of the myriad sounds which crowd the summer noon, and which seem the very grain and stuff of which eternity is made. Who does not remember the shrill roll-call of the harvest fly? There were ears for these sounds in Greece long ago, as Anacreon's ode will show. [III, 22]

(Then he quoted the classic poet's lines on the cicada—though most of the verse that interlards the prose is Thoreau's own.)

This style holds up throughout, so that the review makes good reading as a literary essay, and it is as such, rather than as a scientific critique, that it claims attention. It shows great improvement stylistically over "The Service" but shares one fault with that rejected essay, again failure to achieve a unified structure. Instead of being one sustained essay, "Natural History" breaks down into a series of short ones. For example, in the section dealing with birds there is a paragraph on the Great Northern Diver (p. 27) that seems like a first draft of the famous loon-chase in *Walden* (at the end of Chapter XII, "Brute Neighbors"), though it is not lifted up into myth. Somewhat longer are the account of running a fox (p. 30), a spear-fishing episode (pp. 33–34), and a vignette on frost-work (pp. 36–38)—similar to three of the "Miniatures from the *Journal*" selected by the present writer for inclusion in *Thoreau's World*, strictly on the basis of literary excellence.[7]

The separate parts of Thoreau's essay are interesting in themselves, some being of high quality, but they are only loosely related in that all

7. See my book, *Thoreau's World* (Englewood Cliffs, N. J., 1971), pp. 66, 146, 274.

are aspects of the natural history of Massachusetts. Perhaps the one thing that holds the essay together, if anything does, is the sharp polarity of Thoreau's attitudes toward nature and society. It is surprising to find that this crucial point of view was adopted so early in his career, by the age of twenty-five:

> In society you will not find health, but in nature. Unless our feet at least stood in the midst of nature, all our faces would be pale and livid. Society is always diseased, and the best is the most so. There is no scent in it so wholesome as that of the pines, nor any fragrance so penetrating and restorative as the life-everlasting in high pastures. I would keep some book of natural history always by me as a sort of elixir, the reading of which would restore the tone of the system. . . . Surely joy is the condition of life. Think of the young fry that leap in ponds, the myriads of insects ushered into being on a summer evening, the incessant note of the hyla with which the woods ring in the spring, the nonchalance of the butterfly carrying accident and change painted in a thousand hues upon its wings, or the brook minnow stoutly stemming the current, the lustre of whose scales worn bright by the attrition is reflected upon the bank.
>
> We fancy that this din of religion, literature, and philosophy, which is heard in pulpits, lyceums, and parlors, vibrates through the universe, and is as catholic a sound as the creaking of the earth's axle; but if a man sleep soundly, he will forget it all between sunset and dawn. [III, 20–21]

Here is one of the central themes of *Walden*—with something of its precise observations of the natural world, its language modes of wit and metaphor, but not its final touch of distinction—in a *Dial* essay that appeared more than a decade before the book.[8]

If Emerson launched Thoreau's essay with an editorial note of praise, another older contemporary, Hawthorne, left a record of his pleasure in reading it. On the occasion of a day-long visit from Thoreau, the novelist made a full entry in his *Notebook*, under date of September 1, 1842, about this "young man with much of wild original nature left in him." After a brief description and a sketch of his life, he declared that Thoreau was "a keen and delicate observer of nature—a genuine observer, which, I suspect, is almost as rare a character as even an original poet." Sandwiched between two paragraphs devoted to admiration of his extraordinary skills and his intimate knowledge of the natural world comes the passage relevant to this study:

8. Paul, *Shores*, pp. 120–124, calls attention to a number of other themes later elaborated in *A Week* and *Walden* that are foreshadowed here: nature's flux, the cycle of rebirth, pond and river as symbols.

With all this he has more than a tincture of literature—a deep and true taste for poetry, especially the elder poets, although more exclusive than is desirable, like all other Transcendentalists, so far as I am acquainted with them. He is a good writer—at least, he has written one good article, a rambling disquisition on Natural History in the last Dial,—which, he says, was chiefly made up from journals of his own observations. Methinks this article gives a very fair image of his mind and character—so true, minute, and literal in observation, yet giving the spirit as well as letter of what he sees, even as a lake reflects its wooded banks, showing every leaf, yet giving the wild beauty of the whole scene;—then there are passages in the article of cloudy and dreamy metaphysics, partly affected, and partly the natural exhalations of his intellect;—and also passages where his thoughts seem to measure and attune themselves into spontaneous verse, as they rightfully may, since there is real poetry in him. There is a basis of good sense and moral truth, too, throughout the article, which also is a reflection of his character; for he is not unwise to think and feel, however imperfect in his own mode of action. On the whole, I find him a healthy and wholesome man to know.[9]

The reactions of other contemporaries are not known, but they may well have been mixed, favorable for the passages on natural history, unfavorable for the attacks on society. Indeed Thoreau's main thesis is put forward so positively and aggressively—his preference for nature being so exclusive as to entail social renunciation—that it disturbed even his Transcendental friends, according to Sherman Paul; the final satiric thrust at "this din of religion, literature, and philosophy, which is heard in pulpits, lyceums, and parlors," he declares, was a virtual repudiation of Emerson, Alcott, and *The Dial* itself.[10] However this may be, Thoreau's essay was clear enough in its stance and sufficiently novel in its style to have made an immediate impact. With this small publication he had established his relation to nature as the proper place for the re-creation of man, rendering his thesis in language that revealed the joy of that way of life. Alert readers of *The Dial* must have recognized a new writer of originality and force.

The poems Thoreau contributed, though numerous, did little to augment this impression. For the most part they are like notes to his prose pieces, not grace notes—since meter and rhyme crippled him instead of giving him wings—but mere appendages. Those in the first two volumes of *The Dial*, and a few in the third, are verse renderings of themes from his rejected essay, "The Service": definitions of friend-

9. Nathaniel Hawthorne, *The American Notebooks*, ed. Randall Stewart (New Haven, 1932), pp. 166–168.

10. Paul, *Shores*, pp. 106–107.

ship, explorations of the self, praise of the brave man.[11] After he had written the "Natural History of Massachusetts" it is not surprising to find him turning to nature for themes for his poems also, but these are disappointing on the whole, mediocre or derivative. One of them, "The Inward Morning," is of some interest because it extends a theme only touched on in the essay, that natural facts are the expression of spiritual facts: "Packed in my mind lie all the clothes / Which outward nature wears." Some lines in the *Journal* version a year earlier (omitted in the published poem) underscore this note of subjective idealism: "My eyes look inward, not without, / And I but hear myself."[12]

Of the sixteen poems Thoreau published in *The Dial* only two deserve serious attention from the student of literature. Printed together under the rubric "Orphics," they too are nature poems but in a new and very un-Wordsworthian sense. One of them, "Haze," is like the hymns ascribed to Orpheus only in a limited way, chiefly in that it consists of a long series of epithetical descriptions of the particular natural phenomenon being addressed: haze is called "etherial gauze . . . Visible heat . . . sun-dust . . . Fine summer spray on inland seas," and so on. The concluding one is particularly effective:

> Bird of the sun, transparent-winged, . . .
> From heath or stubble rising without song;
> Establish thy serenity o'er the fields. [III, 506]

The other paired poem is much closer in form and content to the so-called hymns of Orpheus, several of which Thoreau was copying down in his Literary Notebook during this very year.[13] "Smoke" is one of the very few successful poems he ever wrote. It is striking enough in its own right, as it appeared in *The Dial* of April 1843:

> Light-winged smoke, Icarian bird,
> Melting thy pinions in thy upward flight,

11. See "Sic Vita" and "Friendship" (II, 81, 204); "Sympathy" and "Stanzas" (I, 71, 314); "Metrical Prayer," "The Black Knight," and "Free Love" (III, 79, 180, 199).

12. "The Inward Morning," III, 198; cf. Thoreau's *Journal*, I, 291. Paul, *Shores*, p. 119, says in this connection that the essay itself was less a "Natural History of Massachusetts" than a natural history of Thoreau.

The other nature poems are "The Moon," "The Summer Rain," and "To a Stray Fowl" (III, 222, 224, 505); two more combine nature with vague idealizations: "Rumors from an Aeolian Harp" and "To a Maiden in the East" (III, 200, 222).

13. See my discussion in *The Magic Circle of Walden* (New York, 1968), pp. 248–249, 297. Barbara Carson's forthcoming book, *Orpheus in New England*, discusses the analogy in some detail.

Lark without song, and messenger of dawn,
Circling above the hamlets as thy nest;
Or else, departing dream, and shadowy form
Of midnight vision, gathering up thy skirts;
By night star-veiling, and by day
Darkening the light and blotting out the sun;
Go thou my incense upward from this hearth,
And ask the gods to pardon this clear flame. [III, 505–506]

It was greatly enhanced in meaning a decade later when it appeared in *Walden* (where most readers today have become acquainted with it), enriched by the context of "House-Warming." Thoreau's ostensible subject in this chapter is the building of his chimney, part of the "economy" of the Walden experiment, as cold weather came on; and since he was helped in this project by a friend, who stayed on to take part in celebrating its completion, he was able to give his title a double meaning. The passage describing the construction ends with a metaphor that evokes the chapter's real theme: "The chimney is to some extent an independent structure, standing on the ground, and rising through the house to the heavens."

The poem "Smoke," reprinted in *Walden* from *The Dial*, becomes an elaborate extension of this metaphor. The sentence that launches it is part of its new meaning: "When the villagers were lighting their fires beyond the horizon, I too gave notice to the various wild inhabitants of Walden vale, by a smoky streamer from my chimney, that I was awake." The woodland solitude makes an appropriate setting for Thoreau's morning ritual of kindling a fire, his ever fresh renewal of purpose; "awake" is his recurrent term for being alive, the "dead" being those who are always asleep. The sentence following the poem is also a gloss on it. Referring to his cabin in the woods he said: "It was I and Fire that lived there." "Fire" has a dual meaning, representing the vital heat for sustaining life through the winter and the "flame" of his thought or inner self. Its use in the poem proves this.

If the chimney is only indirectly a symbol for Thoreau, the smoke is made directly so: "Go thou *my* incense upward from this hearth." Not quite his prayer, but his fragrant burnt offering that might stand for it, and offered quite safely in a Christian land to the plural "gods," without specifying which ones. But why does he ask the gods "to *pardon* this clear flame"? The last line is the crux of the poem, and one must circle back to the first to clarify its meaning by asking why he calls the smoke "Icarian bird"? The allusion brings in the legend of

Icarus, the arrogant demi-god who defied the laws of nature (and hence the gods) by trying to fly on man-made wings, came too near heaven and, burned by the sun's heat, fell to his death in the sea. Thoreau's smoke, in its "upward flight" like a bird, also challenges heaven and might seem to risk a similar fate—except that it is quickly transformed through a series of images into a lark, dawn's messenger, a dream, a vision. Still the "clear flame" of his spirit burns so brightly that its smoke "blots out the sun," and needs a plea for pardon to keep him from verging on hubris. "Smoke" is almost like a prayer from one god to another, from an earthly Apollo to the heavenly one.[14]

Thoreau's favorite image for the poet was Apollo, and often in his writings he likens himself to this god of light and song. He was also acquainted with Orphism, the religious reformation in Greece that tried to mediate between the cults of Apollo and Dionysus, both of whom were worshipped at the same Oracle of Delphi, though at different seasons of the year. Feeling that the heavenly aspiration of the former was too austere and the orgiastic ecstasies of the latter should be modified, priests of the new religion attempted a synthesis better suited to the dualism of man's nature. Thoreau, by putting his Orphic Hymn in the chapter immediately following the discussion of his own duality of wildness and spirituality in "Higher Laws," and his rejection of both extremes, indicates that he has chosen the middle way.[15] This final meaning of "Smoke" is clearer in the *Walden* context, but it was probably suspected by some of the Transcendental readers of *The Dial* in 1843; Alcott had just returned from England with a number of volumes by the Neo-Platonist Thomas Taylor, containing references to the religion of Orphism, and these were being passed around the Concord "inner circle."[16] What is remarkable is that Thoreau was only twenty-five years old when he took his most characteristic stance, choosing the Orphic Way: man should aspire toward heaven, sending his incense steadily upward, though he is compelled to kindle his flame on an earthly hearth.

Greece plays another part in Thoreau's contributions to *The Dial*, but one with little relevance to him as a creative writer: his transla-

14. My explication of "Smoke" first appeared in *The Magic Circle*, pp. 274–276.

15. See *Walden*, Chaps. X–XII, "Baker Farm," "Higher Laws," "Brute Neighbors," and my interpretation of them in *The Magic Circle*, pp. 131–212.

16. K. W. Cameron, *The Transcendentalists and Minerva* (Hartford, 1958), III, 803–807, "The Library at Fruitlands (1843)." See also I, 303, 308, 368, for books relating to Orphism read by Thoreau, 1841–1843.

tions of *Prometheus Bound* by Aeschylus (III, 363–386), some lyrics of Anacreon (III, 484–490), and fragments of Pindar's odes (IV, 379–390, 513–514). These apprized contemporaries that his classical studies did not end with graduation from Harvard. That his translations were read and appreciated is proved by an editorial note prefixed to the third article: "Some of our correspondents, who found aid and comfort in Mr. Thoreau's literal prose translations of Anacreon and Aeschylus, have requested him to give versions of the Olympic and Nemaean Odes." As a matter of fact, he was the best Latin and Greek scholar among the New England literary figures of that day, according to a specialist in the field.[17] In his own prefatory note to the Anacreontics he gives a clue to the nature of his response to these ancient literatures that takes us out of the realm of scholarship into that of poetry: "We know of no studies so composing as those of the classical scholar. . . . In serene hours we contemplate the tour of the Greek and Latin authors with more pleasure than the traveller does the fairest scenery of Greece or Italy. . . . Reading the classics . . . is like walking amid the stars and constellations, a high and by-way serene to travel." In such ways his study and translating did become a part of Thoreau the author.

Another kind of reading, quite different and more directly influential on his own writing, furnished Thoreau with several *Dial* contributions—namely, his studies of Oriental scriptures. In the July, 1842, issue Emerson had started a series of extracts from the oldest religious books by making four pages of selections from the *Heetopadees of Veeshnoo Sarma*, the great book of Indian fables. The next January Thoreau continued the series with a much longer selection from *The Laws of Menu* (III, 331–340), also of India, and in the April issue with two pages from the *Sayings of Confucius* (pp. 493–494); he followed these in Volume IV with selections from *Chinese Four Books* (pp. 205–210), *White Lotus of the Good Law* ["The Preaching of Buddha"] (pp. 391–401), the *Divine Pymander of Hermes Trismegistus* and the *Gulistan* of Saadi (pp. 402–404). Egypt, Persia, India, Nepal, China—a much more far-flung tour than that of the Greek and Latin authors mentioned above! The man who boasted "I have travelled a good deal in Concord" was not referring just to his endless nature rambles. He was indeed a world-traveller, in the realms of literature. Thoreau's only "contribution" in these five arti-

17. Ethel Seybold, *Thoreau: The Quest and the Classics* (1951), pp. 14–26.

cles was to choose the books to be read, then make the selections. But these were neither space-fillers supplied by an assistant editor from his casual reading nor pretentious samplings from esoteric books to impress subscribers to *The Dial.* A number of the Transcendentalists were seriously reading the Oriental scriptures about this time, looking for confirmation of their Idealism and their ascetic tendencies. Thoreau read as widely as any, and his selections are quite revealing because these scriptures entered significantly into his own creative writing, as a few examples will prove.

The austerity of his life at the pond, as recounted in *Walden*, is foreshadowed in one of the *Sayings of Confucius* he had selected for *The Dial* a decade before: "Coarse rice for food, water to drink, and the bended arm for a pillow—happiness may be enjoyed even in these" (III, 493). The rituals Thoreau says he underwent for purification—bathing every morning in Walden Pond, purging himself of all the conventions of society so he could front only the "essential facts of life"—are prefigured in *The Laws of Menu*: "Bodies are cleansed by water; the mind is purified by truth; the vital spirit, by theology and devotion; the understanding, by clear knowledge" (III, 332). At one of the cruxes of *Walden* these two Oriental philosophers seem to converge. The narrator in the guise of a *Hermit*, coming back to earth after his Ideal aspirations in "Higher Laws," has just had his trance-like meditations interrupted by a *Poet* (his alter ego) who wants to go fishing. Then we read: "*Hermit alone.* Let me see; where was I? . . . I was as near being resolved into the essence of things as ever I was in my life. . . . I will just try these three sentences of Confut-see; they may fetch that state about again."[18] Of the sentences Thoreau had selected from *Sayings of Confucius* the ones most pertinent to the *Hermit's* situation are:

> Silence is absolutely necessary to the wise man. . . . Heaven speaks, but what language does it use to preach to men, that there is a sovereign principle from which all things depend; a sovereign principle which makes them to act and move? Its motion is its language. . . . This silence is eloquent. [III, 494]

But the *Hermit* really had lost his train of thought when the *Poet* interrupted his meditation. He was probably not reading Confucius at all but *The Laws of Menu.* Three sentences from that truly mystical

18. *Walden* (Boston, 1906), pp. 248, 249. See *The Magic Circle*, pp. 179–181, for a fuller discussion of this passage.

ascetic, as transcribed in *The Dial*, could much more easily have induced Thoreau's near state of trance in the *Walden* chapter. They deal with the ultimate stage of the Brahman's retirement to the forest for a life of solitude "in the haunts of pious hermits":

> Alone, in some solitary place, let him constantly meditate on the divine nature of the soul; for, by such meditation, he will obtain happiness. . . .
>
> Let him reflect also, with exclusive application of mind, on the subtil, indivisible essence of the supreme spirit, and its complete existence in all beings. . . .
>
> Thus, having gradually abandoned all earthly attachments . . . he remains absorbed in the divine essence. [III, 337, 338]

A final example relates to that cryptic symbol of what the narrator of *Walden* says he is still in quest of, "a hound, a bay horse, and a turtle-dove" that he lost long ago, one of a cluster of images for the poet's vocation, which has called forth numerous interpretations. Perhaps the most likely source for this celebrated passage is the saying of Mencius, selected by Thoreau from *Chinese Four Books* and published in *The Dial*: "If a man lose his fowls or his dogs, he knows how to seek them. There are those who lose their hearts and know not how to seek them. The duty of the student is no other than to seek his lost heart" (IV, 206). As Sherman Paul points out, Mencius meant by "heart" man's innate goodness, lost by his contact with the world.[19] Thoreau's reading in the Oriental scriptures prepared the way in many respects for his Walden experiment and the famous book that came out of it.

A third kind of literature, that in his native tongue, furnished Thoreau with a single *Dial* contribution, his essay on Chaucer. It takes off from a few pages in praise of the epic poetry of Homer and Ossian. (Like many others, he was completely taken in by the Ossianic hoax.) The result of this contrast is a diminished view of the Father of English Poetry: "The bard has lost the dignity and sacredness of his office. . . . No hero stands at the door prepared to break forth into song or heroic action, but we have instead a homely Englishman, who cultivates the art of poetry. We see the pleasant fireside, and hear the crackling faggots in all the verse" (IV, 297). This preference for the vatic genius as against the mere artist was a typical Romantic posture, so that there is nothing original in Thoreau's approach. In the body of the essay that follows he shows a sensitive

19. Paul, *Shores*, p. 321, was the first to call attention to this analogy.

appreciation of Chaucer, yet fails to say anything new or significant, even when writing at his best, as for example:

> He is fresh and modern still, and no dust settles on his true passages. It lightens along the line, and we are reminded that flowers have bloomed, and birds sung, and hearts beaten, in England. Before the earnest gaze of the reader the rust and moss of time gradually drop off, and the original green life is revealed. He was a homely and domestic man, and did quite breathe as modern men do. [IV, 300]

There are felicitous phrasings here, but it is clear that literary criticism is not Thoreau's forte. And since the poetry of Chaucer bears little if any relation to his later career as a literary artist, this essay lacks importance both intrinsically and by association.

His remaining contributions, three essays, are much more interesting to students of Thoreau. The one appearing in the final number of *The Dial* (April, 1844) belongs with that minor but impressive stream of his writings in which he took a bold stand on the most burning issue of the day. It lacks the effectiveness of "Civil Disobedience" and "A Plea for Captain John Brown," which had the great advantage of being centered on a dramatic episode and a dramatic personality, respectively. In fact "Herald of Freedom" (IV, 507–512) is scarcely an essay at all, consisting merely of fiery quotations from an antislavery journal of that name interspersed with eulogistic comments by the radical young assistant editor of *The Dial*. It is chiefly interesting as evidence of how early Thoreau struck out against slavery.

The other two essays, one short and one full-scale, belong in the mainstream of his work. Along with "Natural History of Massachusetts" and "Smoke," they are the best of his apprentice writings. "Dark Ages" is an excellent example of those miniature essays Thoreau experimented with throughout his career and brought to a high degree of excellence. Though he wrote nearly a thousand of them, this is the only one that found its way into print. In the seventeenth century there would have been no difficulty in getting the best of them published, for this was an accepted genre in that era. But in the nineteenth century there was no market for pieces of such brevity. *The Dial*, with its openness to experimental forms as well as to new ideas, was the only magazine that would have accepted such an unorthodox composition as "Dark Ages." It would certainly have been included in my volume, *Thoreau's World: Miniatures from His*

Journal,[20] except that the *Journal* version includes only the first half of it and thus lacks wholeness and unity, two of my criteria for inclusion. The *Dial* version has these merits and others besides, since the last half gives a new dimension of meaning to the first. What is unfortunate is that such a fine miniature was not included in the collected *Writings of Thoreau* (1906, 20 volumes) as a separate essay, and apparently has never been reprinted as such.[21] Consequently it has received no critical attention.

Its radical thesis, wit, and poetic use of language make this brief essay worthy of rediscovery. Fortunately it is brief enough to be reproduced here in its entirety:

DARK AGES

We should read history as little critically as we consider the landscape, and be more interested by the atmospheric tints, and various lights and shades which the intervening spaces create, than by its groundwork and composition. It is the morning now turned evening and seen in the west, —the same sun, but a new light and atmosphere. Its beauty is like the sunset; not a fresco painting on a wall, flat and bounded, but atmospheric and roving or free. In reality history fluctuates as the face of the landscape from morning to evening. What is of moment is its hue and color. Time hides no treasures; we want not its *then* but its *now*. We do not complain that the mountains in the horizon are blue and indistinct; they are the more like the heavens.

Of what moment are facts that can be lost,—which need to be commemorated? The monument of death will outlast the memory of the dead. The pyramids do not tell the tale that was confided to them; the living fact commemorates itself. Why look in the dark for light? Strictly speaking, the historical societies have not recovered one fact from oblivion, but are themselves instead of the fact that [which] is lost. The researcher is more memorable than the researched. The crowd stood admiring the mist, and the dim outline of the trees seen through it, when one of their number advanced to explore the phenomenon, and with fresh admiration, all eyes were turned on his dimly retreating figure. It is astonishing with how little co-

20. *Thoreau's World* contains 245 miniatures, winnowed from nearly 1,000 in the *Journal*, strictly on the basis of literary excellence. Items Thoreau used in his essays and books were excluded. The first half of "Dark Ages" may be found in the *Journal*, I, 268–269.

21. The four paragraphs from *The Dial* were incorporated in the "Monday" chapter of *A Week* (Boston, 1906), pp. 161–164, as part of a long disquisition on history, mythology, and ancient literatures—almost verbatim but without the title "Dark Ages", so that its identity as a separate essay was lost. This explains both why it was not printed as such in the collected *Writings of Thoreau* and the resultant critical neglect.

öperation of the societies, the past is remembered. Its story has indeed had a different muse than has been assigned it. There is a good instance of the manner in which all history began, in Alwákidi's Arabian Chronicle. "I was informed by *Ahmed Almatın Aljorhami*, who had it from *Rephâa Ebn Kais Alâmiri*, who had it from *Saiph Ebn Fabalah Alchâtquarmi*, who had it from *Thabet Ebn Alkamah*, who said he was present at the action." These fathers of history were not anxious to preserve, but to learn the fact; and hence it was not forgotten. Critical acumen is exerted in vain to uncover the past; the *past* cannot be *presented*; we cannot know what we are not. But one veil hangs over past, present, and future, and it is the province of the historian to find out not what was, but what is. Where a battle has been fought, you will find nothing but the bones of men and beasts; where a battle is being fought there are hearts beating. We will sit on a mound and muse, and not try to make these skeletons stand on their legs again. Does nature remember, think you, that they were men, or not rather that they are bones?

Ancient history has an air of antiquity; it should be more modern. It is written as if the spectator should be thinking of the backside of the picture on the wall, or as if the author expected the dead would be his readers, and wished to detail to them their own experience. Men seem anxious to accomplish an orderly retreat through the centuries, earnestly rebuilding the works behind, as they are battered down by the encroachments of time; but while they loiter, they and their works both fall a prey to the arch enemy. It has neither the venerableness of antiquity, nor the freshness of the modern. It does as if it would go to the beginning of things, which natural history might with reason assume to do; but consider the Universal History, and then tell us—when did burdock and plantain sprout first? It has been so written for the most part, that the times it describes are with remarkable propriety called *dark ages*. They are dark, as one has observed, because we are so in the dark about them. The sun rarely shines in history, what with the dust and confusion; and when we meet with any cheering fact which implies the presence of this luminary, we excerpt and modernize it. As when we read in the history of the Saxons, that Edwin of Northumbria "caused stakes to be fixed in the highways where he had seen a clear spring," and "brazen dishes were chained to them, to refresh the weary sojourner, whose fatigues Edwin had himself experienced." This is worth all Arthur's twelve battles.

But it is fit the past should be dark; though the darkness is not so much a quality of the past, as of tradition. It is not a distance of time but a distance of relation, which makes thus dusky its memorials. What is near to the heart of this generation is fair and bright still. Greece lies outspread fair and sunshiny in floods of light, for there is the sun and day-light in her literature and art, Homer does not allow us to forget that the sun shone—nor Phidias, nor the Parthenon. Yet no era has been wholly dark, nor will we too hastily submit to the historian, and congratulate ourselves on a blaze of light. If we could pierce the obscurity of those remote years we should find it light enough; only there is not our day.—Some creatures are made to see in the dark.—There has always been the same amount of light in the world. The new and missing stars, the comets and eclipses do not affect the general illumination, for only our glasses appreciate them. The eyes of the oldest fossil remains, they tell us, indicate that the same laws of light prevailed then as now. Always the laws of light are the same, but the modes and degrees of seeing vary. The gods are partial to no era, but steadily shines their light in the heavens, while the eye of the beholder is turned to stone. There was but the eye and the sun from the first. The ages have not added a new ray to the one, nor altered a fibre of the other. [III, 527–529]

"Dark Ages" is studded with aphorisms, paradoxes, puns—those distinctive traits of Thoreau's mature style that could on occasion degenerate into decorative mannerism. Here they are so integrated into the texture of the essay that, besides giving color and verve to individual sentences, they enhance the thematic unity with a rhetorical one. The control of language and the compositional skill are such as to tempt one to explicate it like a poem. Note the symbolic maneuvering of key terms, for example, "light" and "dark." The theme is highly original, sufficiently so to be a challenge to the imaginative historian. Time and place are matters of indifference, Thoreau proposes, since the basic conditions of life and man's experience of it are the same everywhere and at all times; put more succinctly, What *are* the uses of history?[22] Though "Dark Ages" is a miniature essay in the history of ideas, its abstractions are effectively tied down by concrete illustrations, for example, the passages on the battlefield and on Greece (in the second and fourth paragraphs). The latter reference—identifying the land with its literature, so that any other history is unnecessary—makes a link back to Thoreau's account of the rewards of classical scholarship: "In serene hours we contemplate the tour of the Greek and Latin authors with more pleasure than the traveller does the fairest scenery of Greece or Italy." Earlier in "Dark Ages" he illustrates an unorthodox view of history by quoting from Alwákidi's Arabian Chronicle—another example of assimilation from an Oriental classic into his own writing. Finally in this brief essay, at the end of volume three of *The Dial*, there is an interesting link back to "Natural History of Massachusetts," the long essay he had contributed

22. Paul, *Shores*, p. 111, says in reference to the incomplete *Journal* version: "Thoreau used history to verify his experience, and he used his experience to verify the record of history." Paul makes no comment on the finished essay in *The Dial.*

to the first number. Universal History pretends to go back to the beginning of things, Thoreau declares, but can it tell us "when did burdock and plantain sprout first?" as natural history might attempt to do. This is what is meant by the statement above that "Dark Ages" is in the mainstream of Thoreau's work. There is a remarkable continuity and interrelatedness in his major writings. Travel and history, nature and art—filtered through the consciousness of man-at-the-center—all are integrated into Thoreau's view of the world as presented in his most characteristic essays and books.

The other and much longer essay, "A Winter Walk" (IV, 211–226), one of Thoreau's last contributions to *The Dial*, was his first significant use of the "excursion" as a compositional mode. Hitting on this thematic and structural device was a happy stroke. It came naturally to Thoreau, growing out of his experience. The daily nature rambles constituted his way of life; the longer journeys became symbolic of his never-ending quest for meaning. The great value of the "excursion" for him as a creative writer was in solving the recurring problem of how to shape his highly original but discrete observations into unified wholes. It later provided the form for his best essays ("Autumnal Tints," "Walking," "Wild Apples") and for all his books (*A Week, Cape Cod, The Maine Woods—Walden* itself being a kind of journey through the seasons). His use of it in "A Winter Walk," published during his apprentice period (October, 1843), was only partially successful.

This essay gets off to an inauspicious start. The opening sentence is marred by trite phrasing—the wind "gently murmured" and "sighed like a summer zephyr"—and there are similar lapses here and there. The fault is soon redeemed by fresher language from precisely observed details, though some of the lines that first catch the eye are not entirely original. Looking out of his bedroom window early one winter morning, Thoreau says in his second paragraph:

> We see the roofs stand under their snow burden. From the eaves and fences hang stalactites of snow, and in the yard stand stalagmites covering some concealed core. The trees and shrubs rear white arms to the sky on every side, and where were walls and fences, we see fantastic forms stretching in frolic gambols across the dusky landscape, as if nature had strewn her fresh designs over the fields by night as models for man's art. [III, 211]

Readers of *The Dial* with good memories may have felt that what Thoreau saw was not the landscape outside his window but Emerson's "Snow-Storm," which had appeared in that magazine less than three years before (January, 1841). Here are the pertinent lines:

> . . . Come see the north-wind's masonry.
> Out of an unseen quarry evermore
> Furnished with tile, the fierce artificer
> Curves his white bastions with projected roof
> Round every windward stake, or tree, or door. . . .
> On coop or kennel he hangs Parian wreaths;
> A swan-like form invests the hidden thorn;
> Fills up the farmer's lane from wall to wall. . . .
> Leaves, when the sun appears, astonished Art
> To mimic in slow structures, stone by stone,
> Built in an age, the mad wind's night-work,
> The frolic architecture of the snow. [I, 339]

The echo is only a faint one, to be sure, but it is equally true that the authentic quality of the master's voice is only faintly reproduced.

It was because of occasional similarities like this that Lowell in *A Fable for Critics* (1848) tagged Thoreau as a second-hand Emerson. After nearly a hundred lines of praise-blame devoted to the Sage of Concord, the satirist declared "He has imitators in scores," then proceeded to tick off two of them, Channing and Thoreau, in a few lines each. Though they were not actually named, contemporaries had no difficulty filling in the blanks:

> There comes ———, for instance, to see him's rare sport,
> Tread in Emerson's tracks with legs painfully short; . . .
> Fie, for shame, brother bard; with good fruit of your own,
> Can't you let Neighbor Emerson's orchards alone?
> Besides, 'tis no use, you'll not find e'en a core,—
> ——— has picked up all the windfalls before. . . .
> When they send him a dishful, and ask him to try 'em,
> He never suspects how the sly rogues came by 'em. . . .[23]

Light-hearted satire should not be taken seriously, of course, but the labels stuck. Both young men were known to be protégés of Emerson. Thoreau, who had been living in Emerson's house during much of this period, 1841–1843 and 1847, would have been especially thought of as a disciple. Ellery Channing never became a writer of any distinction. But the other charge of imitation, coming just before Henry Thoreau's claim to originality was clearly established by publication

23. *Lowell's Complete Poetical Works* (Cambridge Edition, 1896), p. 128.

of his first book (*A Week*, 1849), gave an unjust twist to his reputation for years to come.

Borrowing from another author is one thing, echoing oneself is something quite different. The very next paragraph of "A Winter Walk" ends with twenty-six lines of blank verse that immediately bring to mind the ten-line poem "Smoke" Thoreau had published in *The Dial* only six months before (April, 1843). Comparison is inevitable because of the similar subject matter: smoke ascending from distant chimneys early on a winter morning, that picturesque feature of the rural landscape a century ago. In all other respects they are utterly different, and readers then, as now, must have felt that Thoreau's development as a poet was going downhill. Here was a mere diffuse sequence of verses as compared with the earlier compact Orphic, clichés instead of novel imagery and verbal surprise, a picturesque subject but unenriched by thematic ambiguity. Lacking a theme, it has no real beginning or end and could just as well have gone on for another twenty-six lines. Its trite poetic diction and awkward inversions can be illustrated by a random sample:

> The sluggish smoke curls up from some deep dell,
> The stiffened air exploring in the dawn, . . .
> The while the chopper goes with step direct,
> And mind intent to swing the early axe. . . . [IV, 212]

It is unfair to dwell so long on the faults of "A Winter Walk." But it seems necessary to point out that the disciplined control of language and the easy mastery of materials that mark the mature Thoreau did not come all at once, though they are remarkably present in two of his apprentice pieces, the short poem "Smoke" and the miniature essay "Dark Ages." Extending these skills to longer compositions took some years more of arduous practice.

"A Winter Walk" has its own very real merits, however. For one thing its prose style is quite superior to that in the verse (sampled above). It is competent throughout, and at times rings with a true Thoreauvian accent:

> The ground is sonorous, like seasoned wood. . . . There is the least possible moisture in the atmosphere, all being dried up, or congealed, and it is of such extreme tenuity and elasticity, that it becomes a source of delight. The withdrawn and tense sky seems groined like the aisles of a cathedral. . . . All things beside seem to be called in for shelter, and what stays out must be part of the original frame of the universe, and of such valor as God himself. [IV, 213, 214]

Examples of such fresh and vigorous writing could be multiplied. Also there is some effective use of paradox in this essay. Of the occasion celebrated in his winter walk he says: "The day is but a Scandinavian night. The winter is an arctic summer" (p. 216). There was apparently much more of this in his first draft, but it was pruned away by Emerson. When accepting "A Winter Walk" for publication in *The Dial*, he wrote to Thoreau:

I had some hesitation about it, notwithstanding its faithful observation and its fine sketches of the pickerel-fisher and of the wood-chopper, on account of *mannerism*, an old charge of mine,— . . . for example, to call a cold place sultry, a solitude public, a wilderness *domestic* (a favorite word), and in the woods to insult over cities ["insult cities" or "exult over cities"?], whilst the woods, again, are dignified by comparing them to cities, armies, etc. By pretty free omissions, however, I have removed my principal objections.[24]

In the privacy of his *Journals* he was more outspokenly critical:

Henry Thoreau sends me a paper with the old fault of unlimited contradiction. The trick of his rhetoric is soon learned: it consists in substituting for the obvious word and thought its diametrical antagonist. He praises . . . villagers and woodchoppers for their urbanity, and the wilderness for resembling Rome and Paris. . . . It makes me nervous and wretched to read it.[25]

As a young contributor Thoreau knuckled under to his editor, but this does not mean that he gave up the use of paradox. Instead, he developed it into a principal characteristic of his mature style, one that gives distinction to *Walden*.[26]

Since the first draft of "A Winter Walk" has not survived, it is only by reference to Emerson's examples of *mannerism* that one can conjecture what the deleted paradoxes were. Traces of one survive in Thoreau's description of a woodland nook, despite the editorial pruning:

The sun rises as proudly over such a glen, as over the valley of the Seine or the Tiber, and it seems the residence of a pure and self-subsistent valor, such as they never witnessed; which never knew defeat nor fear. Here reign the simplicity and purity of a primitive age, and a health and hope far remote from towns and cities. Standing quite alone, far in the forest,

24. Letter of Sept. 8, 1843, reprinted in *Correspondence of Thoreau*, p. 137. Emerson is said to have removed "two pages or so" from the essay (see p. 138n).

25. *The Journals of Ralph Waldo Emerson*, ed. E. W. Emerson and W. E. Forbes (Boston, 1909–1914), VI, 440.

26. See my discussion in *The Magic Circle*, pp. 54–56.

while the wind is shaking down snow from the trees, and leaving the only human tracks behind us, we find our reflections of a richer variety than the life of cities. The chicadee and nuthatch are more inspiring society than the statesmen and philosophers, and we shall return to these last, as to more vulgar companions. In this lonely glen . . . our lives are more serene and worthy to contemplate. [pp. 216–217]

This passage picks up the most belligerent theme of "Natural History" (his first important contribution to *The Dial*) and extends it by the rhetorical irritant of paradox, to prove the superiority of nature to civilization. If Emerson was made "wretched" by Thoreau's new mannerism, other contemporaries were no doubt equally offended by it, just as they had been by the extravagant language of the earlier essay.

There are fragments of a kindred paradox in "A Winter Walk" that escaped the editor's blue pencil even in that sketch of a wood-chopper he had singled out for praise on other grounds. It is framed by paradoxical statements of Thoreau's preference for solitude over cities, which Emerson deplored, but its three paragraphs constitute a miniature which he could not help admiring. Perhaps both aspects of this "interior essay" can be represented by the following extracts:

Let us go into this deserted woodman's hut, and see how he has passed the long winter nights and the short and stormy days. For here man has lived under this south hill-side, and it seems a civilized and public spot. We have such associations as when the traveller stands by the ruins of Palmyra on Hecatompolis. . . . But he has not been here this season, for the phoebes built their nest upon this shelf last summer. I find some embers left, as if he had but just gone out, where he baked his pot of beans, and while at evening he smoked his pipe, whose stemless bowl lies in the ashes. . . .

See how many traces from which we may learn the chopper's history. From this stump we may guess the sharpness of his axe, and from the slope of the stroke, on which side he stood, and whether he cut down the tree without going around it or changing hands; and from the flexure of the splinters we may know which way it fell. This one chip contains inscribed on it the whole history of the wood-chopper and of the world. On this scrap of paper, which held his sugar or salt, perchance, or was the wadding of his gun, sitting on a log in the forest, with what interest we read the tattle of cities, of those larger huts, empty and to let, like this, in High-streets, and Broad-ways. . . .

After two seasons, this rude dwelling does not deform the scene. . . . Thus, for a long time, nature overlooks the encroachment and profanity of man. The wood still cheerfully and unsuspiciously echoes the strokes of the axe that fells it, and while they are few and seldom they enhance its wildness, and all the elements strive to naturalize the sound. [pp. 217–218]

The quality of the writing here places this essay with the best of Thoreau's apprentice work.

What should not be missed, above all, is the unique turn these paragraphs give to the aggressive theme of "Natural History." Readers now had proof of the depth and sincerity of his dedication to nature, and sufficient evidence that his attacks on society were not so much symptoms of his perversity as they were negative statements of his preference, needed for emphasis. In this sketch of the woodman Thoreau is trying for the first time to formulate one of his central positions about the relation of man to the world, a position he continued to clarify in his life and writings to the very end. The two aspects of it can be illustrated by declarations late in his career. A *Journal* entry for 1857, previously overlooked, makes a basic point: "Let men tread gently through nature."[27] The other is longer and better known, having been given wide currency by furnishing the title for a handsome book of photographs recently published by the Sierra Club.[28] It comes from an essay Thoreau prepared for posthumous publication under the title of "Walking," though the subject is actually "Wildness," the title used when he gave it as a lecture during the 1850's. "I wish to speak a word for Nature, for absolute freedom and wildness," he begins in the bold introductory paragraph: "I wish to make an extreme statement, if so I may make an emphatic one, for there are enough champions of civilization." Then in the middle of his longest essay (his best one, *me judice*) comes the startling pronouncement: "What I have been preparing to say is, that in Wildness is the Preservation of the World."[29] All of this is implicit in the closing lines of his sketch of the woodman, published in the fall of 1843.

One may also see in this miniature essay a prefiguration of Thoreau's own experiment of living alone in the woods, which began in the spring of 1845. This hunch is confirmed on the very next page by a striking vignette. His winter walk has culminated at Walden

27. Thoreau, *Journal*, IX, 344.

28. *In Wildness Is the Preservation of the World* (San Francisco, 1962). Selections and Photographs by Eliot Porter.

29. *The Writings of Thoreau* (Boston, 1906), V, 205, 224.

Pond, though he conceals its name as a poet might that of his mistress:

> And now we descend again to the brink of this woodland lake, which lies in a hollow of the hills. . . . Without outlet or inlet to the eye, it still has its history, in the lapse of its waves, in the rounded pebbles on its shore, and in the pines which grow down to its brink. It has not been idle, though sedentary, but, like Abu Musa, teaches that "sitting still at home is the heavenly way; the going out is the way of the world." . . . In summer it is the earth's liquid eye; a mirror in the breast of nature. The sins of the wood are washed out in it. See how the woods form an amphitheatre about it, and it is an arena for all the genialness of nature. All trees direct the traveller to its brink, birds fly to it, quadrupeds flee to it, and the very ground inclines toward it. [p. 219]

The last three sentences (some of whose phrases reappear in the central chapter of *Walden*, "The Ponds") were drawn from a *Journal* entry of December 4, 1840. One other sentence in that original draft, omitted from the published essay, not only identifies the pond but underscores the yearning for it that sustained Thoreau through the years of waiting: "The thought of Walden in the woods yonder makes me supple jointed and limber for the duties of the day. Sometimes I thirst for it."[30] By the summer of 1843, when "A Winter Walk" was being written, the yearning was increased by homesickness for Concord and its environs, since Thoreau had gone to New York in a futile effort to find a paying market for his writings. This explains the otherwise cryptic sentence he added to his essay at that time (third in the quotation above): The woodland lake, "like Abu Musa [an isle in the Persian Gulf], teaches that 'sitting still at home is the heavenly way; the going out is the way of the world.' "[31] Before another two years passed he was trying the heavenly way.

"A Winter Walk" is interesting not only for its evidence of Thoreau's developing prose style and for the thematic links back and forward to his other writings, but also because it is the first sign of his progress toward achieving form in his longer compositions. There are fine miniatures here too, as in "Natural History," but now the essay as a whole is more than just a capsule to hold them loosely

30. Thoreau's "Lost Journal", ed. Perry Miller as *Consciousness in Concord* (Boston, 1958), pp. 185–186.

31. This sounds like a quotation from Saadi, whom Thoreau was reading at the time, but I have been unable to find it in either the *Gulistan* or the *Bustan*.

together. To return briefly to a consideration of the "excursion" as an organizational device, the first two paragraphs of "A Winter Walk" are preliminary to the walk itself: an imagined account of the snowstorm that took place while he was asleep and a description of the white landscape at dawn outside his bedroom window (with its Emersonian borrowings, as pointed out). Then the reader is launched into the wintry world: "Silently we unlatch the door, letting the drift fall in, and step abroad to face the cutting air" (p. 211). The next two paragraphs report the sights and sounds that greet the traveller as he makes his way through the village and the farms beyond, followed by two given over to meditations on the health afforded by nature, as the sun rises (pp. 212–214). The walk is then resumed through the woods, the fields, and the swamps. Everywhere he finds "a slumbering subterranean fire in nature which never goes out"; this is matched by a slumbering fire "in each man's breast" if "summer is in his heart" (pp. 214–215)—thus rounding out the previous meditation: "if our lives were more conformed to nature, we should not need to defend ourselves against her heats and colds" (p. 213). At this point the essay begins to wander from its excursion framework, but only for four brief paragraphs of general observations (pp. 215–216). When the walk is resumed it becomes a journey in time as well as in space ("As the day advances," and so on), giving an added dimension to the structure. There follow in rapid succession those vignettes and sketches, already discussed, that form the effective center of the essay—forest glen, wood-chopper's hut, woodland lake (pp. 217–220).

The sequence continues, after the interruption of another mediocre poem, with two more fine miniatures that take the narrative into the afternoon: a vignette ("Before night we will take a journey on skates along the course of this meandering river") and a character sketch ("Far over the ice, between the hemlock woods and the snow-clad hills, stands the pickerel fisher"). In addition to their intrinsic worth, these offer a suggestion of that more complex kind of structure Thoreau achieved in *Walden*—a network of images to render a unifying theme, here the theme of wildness. It is first touched on near the beginning of the essay, when the walker reaches the woods: "It seems to us that no traveller has ever explored them" (p. 214). Now, near the end, skating brings another perspective: "The river flows in the rear of towns, and we see all things from a new and wilder side" (p. 222). Then the pickerel fisher, "with dull, snowy, fishy thoughts, himself a finless fish, separated a few inches from his race"; he symbolizes the possible merger of man in nature: "He does not make the scenery less wild . . . but stands there as a part of it" (p. 224). The theme of wildness finds its fullest expression in the central woodchopper episode (pp. 217–218), as already pointed out. These echoes of it go a long way toward making it dominant throughout the essay, though falling short of that subtle unifying effect it gives to the structure of "Walking" many years later. The most obvious unity in "A Winter Walk" comes from adopting the mode of an excursion. It is a simple form, certainly, but it does grow organically out of the material, the kind of form preferred by Transcendentalists to any that could be imposed from without. So, the essay concludes as naturally as it began: "The surly night-wind rustles through the wood, and warns us to retrace our steps." Another snowstorm has come up, obliterating the landscape and forcing the walker to end his wintry journey: "With so little effort does nature reassert her rule, and blot out the traces of men" (pp. 224–225).

In one of the verses he contributed to *The Dial*, "The Poet's Delay," Thoreau apologized for his slowness in maturing:

> The birds have sung their summer out,
> But still my spring does not begin. [III, 200]

He was just twenty-five at the time, to be sure, but many lyric poets hit full stride by such an early age, notably the great Romantics of the preceding generation. Thoreau, on the other hand, had published only a handful of poems, all in *The Dial* and all mediocre but two ("Haze" and "Smoke"). Although he had written a great many more, the years of his greatest poetic activity being 1840–1842, when he submitted them to the magazine, they were turned down or subjected to heavy revision. Finally, about 1843, he destroyed many of his verses because Emerson "did not praise them," and composed only a few thereafter.[32] Thoreau's poetic "spring" never did begin. But by the time of his last contribution to *The Dial*, April, 1844, he had established himself as a prose writer of considerable promise. In his essays there was clear evidence of his mature style, his major themes, his characteristic stance with relation to nature and society. In the

32. Carl Bode, introduction, *Collected Poems of Henry Thoreau* (Baltimore, 1964), pp. vii, x.

translations and selections he had set up two of the chief areas of reference that lend universality to his special brand of New England Transcendentalism—the classics of Greece and of Asia. *The Dial* had given him a public and, more important, confidence in himself as a writer. His connection with it was also prophetic of the fact that his audience was always to be a limited one, however sympathetic, and that neither editors nor publishers would pay for the kind of writing he had to offer.

Meanwhile Thoreau had gone to New York during the last half of 1843, at the behest of Emerson, to see if he could make a paying vocation of authorship. With the aid of Horace Greeley, editor of the *Tribune*, he besieged the periodicals of that city with his writings, but to little avail. Two essays which he "wrote to sell," by his own admission, were published in the *Democratic Review* for October and November, 1843, but there is no evidence that he was ever paid for them.[33] Earlier that year another one had appeared in the *Boston Miscellany* for January, but that magazine reneged on its promise of payment though Thoreau continued his requests for nearly a year.[34] His frustration comes out in a letter to Emerson, September 14, 1843, telling how he had tried half-a-dozen other New York magazines in vain: "Literature comes to a poor market here, and even the little that I write is more than will sell."[35] A year and a half later he had moved out to Walden Pond to try his famous experiment, how to be a non-selling author and survive. While there he made one more effort to find a paying market. Greeley, this time acting specifically as Thoreau's literary agent, managed to sell a long essay to *Graham's Magazine*, where it appeared in two installments during the spring of 1847, but the author did not receive his pay ($75.00) until May, 1848, when Greeley in desperation drew a draft on the publisher.[36] In a letter that same month Thoreau's response to the proposal in Boston to start a new magazine shows he had given up hope of finding that kind of outlet for his writings. "I am more interested in the private journal than the public one," he punned. Then he added: "Men talk as if you couldn't get good things printed, but I *think* as if you couldn't get them written. That at least is the whole difficulty with

33. *Correspondence of Thoreau*, pp. 142–143.
34. Ibid., pp. 113, 126, 134.
35. Ibid., p. 139.
36. Walter Harding, *A Thoreau Handbook* (New York, 1959), p. 49.

me."[37] With as much zeal as if he had an assured audience and a remunerative market, he was at this very time writing "good things" daily in his "private journal"—putting the finishing touches on *A Week* and completing the first draft of *Walden.*

Since *The Dial* could not afford to pay its contributors, the editor had feared they would send in only what they had been unable to sell to commercial magaines. But at least one of them, Thoreau, gave it the best of what he had to offer. The scattered apprentice pieces he published elsewhere deserve brief mention, however, since each one is interesting in its own way. Two of those mentioned in the preceding paragraph were deliberately written for the market, and as a result they seem contrived rather than expressions welling up from some inner compulsion. "The Landlord," a short essay, was his unsuccessful effort to find a tone and a kind of humor by which he could reach a wider audience for his serious themes—the landlord being a transcendental exemplum of the whole or "spheral" man—but it is notable as his first wholesale use of punning, later with discipline to become a superb adjunct of his serious style. The longer piece, "Paradise (To Be) Regained," was an extended book review, a critique of one of those grandiose utopian tracts that appeared from time to time during the period of Brook Farm, Fruitlands, and other idealistic communities. Thoreau here ridicules with heavy-handed mockery what he termed "transcendentalism in mechanics," collective reform as opposed to his own program of self-reform, and in contrasting the two he employs the device of paradox. Though the essay has some interest as the negative aspect of his own experiment in Utopia, it is an entirely theoretical argument without the concreteness of actual experience that gave both style and form to *Walden.*

The best of these "outside" essays in terms of literary art was "A Walk to Wachusett," his first attempt to use the excursion as a device to give shape to his experiences in the world of nature. As such it was a kind of trial run for "A Winter Walk," written a few months later, which carried the form far beyond the simple journey-narrative. The longest piece, and the only one for which he is known to have been paid, was a discerning appreciation of "Thomas Carlyle and His Works." This is Thoreau's acknowledgement of a debt to the author who taught him the art of exaggeration, a third important element

37. *Correspondence of Thoreau,* p. 226.

in his developing style. When after praising Carlyle for giving England what it needs (the hero as reformer, presented with strident humor), he points out the author's failure to provide what America needs (poets who will write scripture), Thoreau is giving us what has been called "a disguised preface to his own work."[38]

In comparison with these essays published in other magazines, Thoreau's contributions to *The Dial* are clearly superior in quality and variety, as well as in quantity. The "little magazine" of the Transcendental Club served as the real vehicle of his apprenticeship. In it he found the freedom to develop experimentally the themes and the methods for his whole career as a writer. It is interesting to note that all of his early publications came within the brief period of *The Dial*'s flourishing, 1840–1844, except for the long piece on Carlyle in 1847. By the time Thoreau's next essay was published the apprentice years were over. "Civil Disobedience" appeared, without remuneration, in Elizabeth Peabody's *Aesthetic Papers* for May, 1849.[39] The same month saw publication of *A Week on the Concord and Merrimack Rivers*. Both book and essay belong to Thoreau's maturity.

38. Paul, *Shores*, p. 207.
39. Harding, *Handbook*, pp. 50, 52.

Kimball King

Local Color and the Rise of the American Magazine

The emergence of the American magazine after the Civil War provided for many young writers access to the reading public and afforded them the opportunity and encouragement necessary for their development. Also the more established authors were in a better position to negotiate publication of separate full-length, hard-back books after their works had found an audience in the journals. Yet authors paid a price for magazine publication: compromises were extracted from those who chose this route to literary fame. The taste and expectations of the average magazine reader and the editor's philosophy imposed restrictions upon an artist's development. In turn a writer might unwittingly accustom his public to certain reassuring fictional attitudes or formulae which they would expect in his subsequent publications. It became difficult for some authors to mature because their initial writings had burdened them with an image which they were frequently hesitant to jeopardize.

American magazines have at various times created markets for literary genres which they have later felt bound to perpetuate. A case in point is the local color movement which was encouraged by post–Civil War literary journals and which was an integral part of the American family magazine's development. Local color writers expressed the optimism of a war-weary nation eager to suppress an awareness of social realities and nourished the growing cultural ambitions of an aspiring middle class. Capitalizing on the national yearning for self-improvement and social harmony, magazine editors fostered a romantic literary tradition which continued to exist even after interest in regional writing began to wane, and local color writers either became more national in their interests or faded into obscurity.

The "magazine revolution," as it has been called, established a bourgeois ethic in American journalism which continues in some degree to the present time. Always, of course, there is an interesting reciprocal relationship between what the media offer and what the public demands. Magazine editors, for example, claim to provide the public with the quality, quantity, and type of entertainment the reader seeks; yet it often has appeared that the public accepts the offerings of a medium simply because it is not provided with alternatives, and the hard economic facts of publishing tend to make the publishers cynical. They blame subliterature on the pedestrian yearnings of an uncultivated and uninformed public. Or they assume that the public necessarily shares their prejudices and inhibitions.

In fairness it must be acknowledged that many readers do expect editors to exercise some form of censorship and guidance. There is a longstanding strain of prudery in American readers who have on occasion responded vindictively to "indelicate" disclosures in their magazines. For example, James C. Austin reveals that an article by Harriet Beecher Stowe called "The True Story of Lady Byron's Life" so distressed a large number of the *Atlantic's* readers in 1861 that circulation plummeted.[1] It took the journal several years to recover from its losses. The essay's inflammatory passage described Byron's incestuous relationship with his sister as a "secret adulterous intrigue with a blood relation so near in consanguinity that discovery must have been utter ruin and expulsion from civilized society."[2] This decorously phrased accusation was responsible for a public outcry.

But for the most part it was the publishers, considering themselves the custodians of public morality, who consistently imposed a genteel tradition. No matter how puritanical and unsophisticated they considered their public, publishers nevertheless viewed their growing number of readers in America with enthusiasm.

The rapidly increasing market for family magazines reflected the technological, economic and social changes of that period and was welcomed by aspiring young editors as well as writers. Advances in printing and in the reproduction of illustrations by using half-tones made it possible to assemble attractive journals at a modest cost. Publishers and congressmen had worked together to have the postal rates for second class mail reduced from three cents per pound in

1. James C. Austin, *Fields of the Atlantic Monthly: Letters to an Editor, 1861–1870* (San Marino, Calif., 1953), p. 298.
2. Austin, p. 295.

1874 to two cents in 1879, and finally to one cent in 1885. Within a burgeoning capitalistic system, businesses were discovering the possibilities of marketing and advertising in magazines. Merle Curti has suggested that certain social attitudes also played their role in the public's new interest in magazines. Essentially the "popularization" of culture, as Curti calls it, continued to broaden the base of an educated reading public, which began before the Civil War with the expansion of academies and colleges and the distribution of penny newspapers and inexpensive books.[3] Curti has credited Edward Youman with the popularization of natural science by making available to the public the most significant studies of European scientists and by keeping Americans up to date on the latest scientific ideas, such as the theory of evolution, in his *Popular Science Monthly*. The public library movement and the growth of adult education seminars, such as those at Chautauqua Lake, were equally important. This was the heyday, too, of authors' reading tours. Mark Twain, George W. Cable, Thomas Nelson Page—in fact, most major writers of the period—supplemented their incomes by reading favorite stories, poems, and essays on the lecture platform. Inexpensive books were made possible by innovations in printing and publishing methods, and mail-order houses like Sears, Roebuck, and Company often were responsible for distributing them. A growing political awareness, perhaps stimulated by the Civil War, assured reform-minded, muckraking periodicals like *McClure's* of interested readers. The American cult of self-improvement flourished in this era of Horatio Alger and the robber barons, and the public was ready for the thinly disguised history and geography lessons upon which early local color sketches and stories were based. People were reading to be educated and measured in part the literary merit of a work by the information it provided. Not surprisingly, magazine editors saw themselves in the role of educators and arbiters of taste.

Thus, R. W. Gilder, assistant editor of *Scribner's Monthly* from 1870 to 1881 and editor of the *Century* from 1881 to 1909, writing to Hamlin Garland in 1890, outlined the obligations of the journalist:

> People who are trying to bring up their children with refinement, and to keep their own and their children's language pure and clean, very naturally are jealous of the influence of the magazine—especially of the *Century*

3. Merle Curti, *The Growth of American Thought*, 3rd ed. (New York, 1964), pp. 576–587.

Magazine—in this respect. Here is really a predicament, and feeling the predicament, we at least think a dialect story—especially . . . where "yup" is used for yes, for instance, and where all sorts of vulgarisms occur,—should very strongly recommend itself before being sent into almost every cultivated household in the United States!" [4]

Here Gilder appeared to view writers and editors as cultural missionaries. He and other magazine editors wished to cement the ties of the union, reaffirm federalism and the democracy, and encourage public acceptance of free enterprise, optimism, and national pride. Within the local color movement there were dramatically opposed philosophies, but these individual philosophies tended to be translated, altered, or absorbed into a bland mixture of platitudes acceptable to purposes of an editorial campaign intended to "shape" the thinking of the American middle class. The magazine was the proper medium for reaching the masses, and local color was felt to be the literary movement best suited to an audience inexperienced but eager to learn. As early as 1870 Thomas Wentworth Higginson argued the benefits of local color in an article called "Americanism in Literature." Higginson stated that American writers would do well to follow Emerson's example and "make allusions to natural objects" (such as the "humblebee"), and he explained that a writer seeking worldwide recognition ought not to omit everything "occasional and temporary" from his work but "make this local coloring forever classic through the fascination of the dream it tells."[5]

Some critics, Claude Simpson among them, believe that local color had already begun with frontier humor in the early nineteenth century, first acquired respectability with the publication of Longstreet's *Georgia Scenes* (1835) and J. J. Hooper's *Adventures of Captain Simon Suggs* (1835), and eventually transcended sporadic newspaper publication to become the staple of family magazines.[6] Bret Harte provided the model for the local color short story in 1868 with "The Luck of Roaring Camp," and during the next twenty-five years the reading public was surfeited with this new literary subgenre.

The dominant political and social philosophy of the post–Civil War

4. Herbert F. Smith, *Richard Watson Gilder* (Twayne series) (New York, 1970), p. 95.

5. *Atlantic Monthly*, XXV (Jan., 1870), 58–63.

6. Claude Simpson, ed., *The Local Colorists: American Short Stories, 1857–1900* (New York, 1960), p. 3.

years was nationalism. The war had forced Americans in all parts of the country to reevaluate their commitment to the Union. The westward movement introduced new experiences and attitudes, impressing upon everyone the variety and heterogeneity of American life. A pride in regional differences was found to be compatible with an overall faith in democracy. In fact, readers learning about the geographical and cultural peculiarities of a Louisiana or California community took pride in discovering the uniqueness of their fellow countrymen. Such a spirit of friendly discovery, however, was not conducive to sober investigations of troublesome social or economic problems. The racial injustices of a southern city like New Orleans which continued after the Civil War were overlooked in favor of its exotic atmosphere and rich, foreign traditions. The hardiness and perseverance of the Westerner and the rough beauty of his terrain overshadowed the frequent lawlessness and brutality of pioneer life.

The continued rise of a middle class also played its part in the acceptance of local color since the emphasis in this literature was on simple people who were proud of their provincial heritage. Average men and women took delight in stories they could understand and gained some satisfaction from knowing that Boston's influence on the national culture was waning and that stories by and about the Eastern intelligentsia were encountering fierce competition from neglected segments of the country.

As a literary form local color fiction represented a gentle initiation into realism. It was a blend of romanticism and realism, and Helen McMahon, writing on the popularity of regional fiction in the *Atlantic*, has noted that in "dealing with regions far enough removed from every-day experience to offer a certain romantic charm and with the recent past rather than with the immediate present local color offered a gradual transition to realism which undoubtedly made that movement more palatable to many readers."[7] She draws attention to a review by William Dean Howells of some local color stories by Stowe, De Forest and Eggleston in which the editor praises a magical blend of social "narrowness and intolerance" and "lurking pathos" with the "charm of romance in their transitory aspects."[8] Howells

7. Helen McMahon, *Criticism of Fiction: A Study of Trends in the Atlantic Monthly, 1857–1898* (New York, 1952), p. 15.
8. McMahon, p. 16.

suggested here that since public enlightenment is inevitable, an amused tolerance toward past wrongs in fiction softens the edge of the author's social realism.

Writers from the South, in particular, worried their editors when they spoke too candidly about secession, the Civil War, or carpet-bagging. A Southerner who was defensive about his region's past, like Thomas Nelson Page, or one who saw himself as a reformer and champion of civil rights, like George Cable, could be equally tactless and challenge the new sense of national harmony. For example, a lingering belligerence toward the North frequently had to be toned down in Page's works. One editor at *Scribner's*, Mary Mapes Dodge, wrote to Page that he must disguise his obvious approval of the rebel's cause in "Meh Lady" or the story would not be the "olive branch" he intended.[9] "Meh Lady" is an archetypal formula story of the local color era, since it focuses on the marriage of a Southern girl to a Yankee. Anecdotes about intersectional marriages were popular after the war, and some specific incidents may have influenced the author in developing the plot of "Meh Lady." The theme, however, was suggested to Page by Robert Underwood Johnson, then an editor of *Century Magazine*, who had seen a performance of Lessing's *Minna Von Barnhelm* in New York and wrote to Page that he might profitably adapt the play to a Southern setting. Page, never a deeply imaginative writer, was grateful for the idea and used it; in this way, a Northern editor influenced the literary image of a reunited nation.

Sometimes editorial changes were so careless as to disrupt a narrative's logical development. Page created a violent tale in "No Haid Pawn," a story which contained an attack on abolitionists and a savage beheading by slaves. But *Scribner's* E. L. Burlingame urged Page to modify the horror in the story and stress the exotic local color atmosphere instead. He wrote Page on January 8, 1887, that "it seemed to me that one incident—the severing of the head at the hanging—was unnecessarily repellent without increasing the force of the story." Page acquiesced to Burlingame's judgment and emphasized the mysterious rather than the macabre in his story. Clearly *Scribner's* was not ready for the gothic horrors of twentieth-century Southern fiction. But in the magazine's desire to remove the possibility of anything offensive to their readers, the symbolism of "No Haid Pawn"

9. Harriet Holman, "The Literary Career of Thomas Nelson Page: 1884–1910," doctoral dissertation, Duke University, 1948, p. 64.

became pointless, and the plot was rendered hopelessly confusing. Harriet Holman has discovered in Page's correspondence with *Scribner's* and *Century* countless examples of editorial interference, and always with the purpose of avoiding confrontation with social or moral issues or of toning down the author's prejudices. Obviously his editors intended him to pass as a reconstructed Southerner, epitomizing the best of the old and new Souths.

George Cable was similarly plagued by editorial interference, as Arlin Turner and Louis Rubin have often noted. In fact, Cable's work in many ways illustrates most clearly the detrimental effect of editors who refused to accept a local colorist's attempt to transcend a genre they favored. Cable's first story "Bibi," which dealt with the Creoles' barbarous treatment of a slave prince, was rejected by the *Atlantic* on the grounds that its total effect was "unmitigatingly distressful."[10] The Scribners also rejected "Bibi" in 1873 although they accepted "'Sieur George" at the same time. It was the local color aspects of Cable's writing that appealed most to the editors at *Scribner's*; they seem to have been somewhat insensitive to the subtler nuances of his stories. They encouraged Cable to be more like Bret Harte, making clear their interest in well-plotted, suspenseful stories with clear-cut resolutions of them.

From the beginning Cable's manuscripts were closely supervised by Gilder, from submitted copy to page proof. Gilder was a benevolent editor with a genuine interest in literature, but he was not a man of vision. He wanted to make Cable acceptable to the majority of readers at a time when the author's dissenting views were certain to be unpopular. Arlin Turner believes that Gilder was "cautious and over-sensitive to the limitations a family magazine such as *Scribner's* must impose on its authors."[11] As publishers, the Scribners had always promoted the idea of reconciliation, and elements in an author's work which might reopen old wounds were deleted—as they were, for different reasons, from the works of Page. Cable's harsh indictment of slavery and his provocative questions about the dilemma of the freedman threatened the illusion of national harmony.

Despite pressure from the men at *Scribner's*, however, Cable continued to write about thorny and embarassing issues. His reforming purpose was probably encouraged by the opposition he received, and

10. Arlin Turner, *George W. Cable* (Durham, N.C., 1956), p. 54.
11. Turner, pp. 66–67.

he politely refused the advice of those who told him to abandon what they considered didacticism. What Cable could not ignore, however, were the occasional charges that his work contained immodest or indecorous elements. He was distressed at the thought of appearing vulgar, offensive, or immoral. Gilder rejected Cable's humorous story "Posson Jone' " in 1875, although *Scribner's* published the story with its sequel under the title *Posson Jone' and Pere Raphael* as a separate book in 1909. R. U. Johnson believed that Gilder later regretted the initial decision to refuse publication of this story, but at the time he feared the depiction of a drunken clergyman might offend Dr. Holland, then the editor of *Scribner's Monthly*. After the New York *Times*, the *Galaxy*, and *Harper's Magazine* also rejected the story, "Posson Jone' " was accepted by *Appleton's Journal* for publication in 1876. Despite its final acceptance, Cable did not again attempt to write an essentially earthy tale. His comic touch may have been inhibited by the rebuff from *Scribner's*.

Gilder continued to exert what he felt was a refining influence on Cable's work, as Turner has noted:

> Though Gilder did not say . . . that a story must be pleasant he repeatedly urged Cable to avoid the unpleasant. He found a figure of speech in " 'Tite Poulette" unpleasant; he would print "Cafe des Exiles" if he could "omit a touch or two of horror," and he added, "Write something intensely interesting—but without the terrible suggestion you so often make use of."[12]

Gilder didn't specify what particular "terrible suggestion" he had in mind, but Johnson implied in his autobiography that an acceptable topic must be "short of disgusting," adding that death and alcoholism, a topic which Cable later treated in "Gregory's Island," were two subjects which could be edifying if "treated from the right point of view and with the right tone."[13] Later in Cable's career Gilder and other editors expressed despair at Cable's excessive moralizing, little realizing that their own attempts to suppress controversial aspects of his work were partly responsible.

The Grandissimes had been published serially by *Scribner's* in 1879, as were Page's novels, and fortunately Gilder had decided that despite its emphasis on racial unrest in Louisiana, the book was essentially conciliatory. He wrote Cable that the novel would help "to bring about the days of a better understanding and a more cordial

12. Turner, p. 67.

13. Turner, p. 291.

feeling."[14] It is inexplicable that Cable's bold dissection of the deep South should have received the same praise from Gilder as Page's "Marse Chan." Possibly the relatively happy conclusion of *The Grandissimes* was supposed to mitigate the effect of the novel's social protest.

Cable's later books, however, with the exception of *The Cavalier*, were not as popular as *The Grandissimes* and the early stories collected in *Old Creole Days*. Johnson found frequent cause at this time to warn Cable about his "tendency to leave the novel and go pamphleteering."[15] The public looked to Cable for more stories with a local color flavor, and instead he gave them novels increasingly centered on social reform. Perhaps he had listened too carefully to his editors and had become somewhat self-conscious about his style and choice of materials. His spirit was essentially more rebellious than Page's, and his views were frequently more radical than his editors desired. He insisted on advocating in his fiction civil rights for the Negro, education for the masses, revision of the penal system, and denounced his own society for passively accepting poverty, ignorance, and injustice.

Although Gilder was personally opposed to segregation and published three articles which Cable later collected in *The Negro Question*, the controversy which these essays engendered convinced Gilder that continuing involvement with civil rights would decrease rather than augment national unity. When Cable's friend, Charles Chesnutt, offered his essay, "The Negro's Answer to the Negro Question," to Gilder, the editor politely declined to accept it, claiming it was "a timely political paper. So timely, in fact so partisan—that we cannot handle it. It should appear at once somewhere."[16] Gilder grew increasingly hostile toward any literature he considered polemical, especially when it dealt with racial problems, and was so thoroughly disgusted with the manuscript of Cable's reconstruction novel, *John March, Southerner*, that he told him, "I could weep with disappointment."[17]

Garland's stories of the midwest also were criticized by Gilder for being too polemical. When Gilder refused to publish Garland's story, "A Prairie Heroine," he warned the author to "present things concretely. Let others find the preaching."[18] Even a Garland story, such

14. Turner, p. 95.
15. Turner, p. 98.
16. Smith, p. 71.
17. Turner, p. 291.
18. Smith, p. 92.

as "A Girl of Modern Tyre," which Gilder reluctantly accepted, distressed him because it contained a social viewpoint which he distrusted. The hero of the story, Albert Lohr, gives up college and his desire for a career in politics and law in order to get married. Garland implies that the young man's emotional needs combined with social pressures ended his chances for personal fulfillment. Gilder rejected any such notion of determinism and confessed he found the young man's capitulation pointless. In his correspondence with Garland, Gilder consistently strove to eliminate controversial elements from the author's fiction. He asked him to suppress allusions to the democratic politician, James Gillespie Blaine, because they would conjure up "violent and disagreeable controversies," and he asked the author to substitute Vanderbilt as an example of an American tycoon in place of Jay Gould, a man Gilder considered "a live thief whom we would rather not honor, even in that way."[19]

In his biography of Gilder, Herbert Smith comments that the editor was never comfortable with Garland's starkly realistic pictures of midwestern life, and that he preferred writers like Edward Eggleston who shared his own optimism about American society. Gilder, according to Smith, found it "easier to accept the softer, more sentimental view of Eggleston than he did the more socially oriented, bleaker 'veritism' of Hamlin Garland."[20] Smith adds in the same passage that Gilder could never approve those writings of Garland such as "A Prairie Heroine" or *Jason Edwards* "in which the degradation of life in the West is clearly stated and the social causes are made evident."

It may be unrealistic to assume that any writer whose career was jointly linked to the local color movement and the American family magazine could forge an independent literary identity. Considering the torrent of bland literature offered by the popular journals at the turn of the twentieth century, one finds it difficult to believe that the works of James, Howells, Crane, and Dreiser also were available. Only a small number of readers, however, were ready for realism or naturalism. Perhaps the dichotomy between the general reading public and the educated reading public already had begun. The former appeared to expect—and usually got—conservative attitudes and sentimental events in their fiction. And the popularity and subsequent financial success of a work had a declining relationship to the acclaim

19. Smith, p. 97.

20. Smith, p. 102.

it received from professional critics and scholars. The concept of the "bestseller" had evolved, and the idea of giving the public "what it wanted" resulted in a pandering to unsophisticated tastes.

A brief look at the commercially successful fiction from the late 1890's until the First World War reveals that romance, especially with an historical setting, was a predominant form and that areas used by local color writers, such as the antebellum South, were still considered an ideal backdrop for tales of chivalry and love. Readers who had been conditioned to formulaic local color fiction could identify with the nostalgic, orderly world of Page's *Red Rock*, a best seller of 1898, or they could revel in the glamorous pseudo-history of Mary Johnston's *To Have and to Hold*, which was the best seller of 1900. Similarly, drawing on the local color aspects of colonial America, New Hampshire-born Winston Churchill wrote *Richard Carvel* (1899), then turned to the Civil War scene in *The Crisis* (1901). In Indiana Booth Tarkington's first and best-selling novel, *The Gentleman from Indiana* (1899) blended romance and local color, while his fellow Hoosiers Maurice Thompson and Charles Major were presenting George Rogers Clark in *Alice of Old Vincennes* (1900) and glamorizing the Middle Ages in *When Knighthood Was in Flower* (1898). Churchill's Civil War novel capitalized on the romantic aspects of the conflict between the states and emphasized the adventurous spirit of the time, much as Page had done. Page's *Gordon Keith* and *John Marvel, Assistant* were published during the first decade of the new century, and they projected in a modern setting the same romantic characters and values of the author's Tidewater fiction. Cable's *The Cavalier*, a bestseller in 1901, dealt directly with the Civil War. Both this novel and the play adapted from it offered the public melodrama in a Southern setting. The climactic moment of the play's New York production was actress Julia Marlowe's singing of the Star-Spangled Banner to a dying Union soldier. The fact that the play was an enormous success helps us gauge the pervasive acceptance of romantic historical backgrounds in this era.

The fundamental values which the majority of local colorists had supported in the years immediately following the war had been respect for authority, a rather static vision of social order, and affirmation of charity, self-sacrifice, and a stoical and emotional acceptance of life's vicissitudes. The same scheme of values underlies the era of sentimental fiction. There is generally an avoidance of unpleasant sociological analysis in such fiction, and characters tend to develop or mature in these works in so far as they are able to reconcile themselves to their environment without excessive expectations of improving their lot. The gift of romantic love is usually considered sufficient compensation for thwarted personal freedom or ambitions.

Just as the monthly magazines had been acceptable reading for the whole family, the popular novel was suitable fare for all ages. Much of the best known fiction contained children as protagonists or at least in crucial, respected roles. Gentleness of temperament, patience, and self-sacrifice were the most apparent virtues of these oddly unchildlike young people. Frances Hodgson Burnett's *Little Lord Fauntleroy* (1886) has become a notorious example of this genre. In 1903 John Fox's *Little Shepherd of Kingdom Come* vied for popularity with another children's tale, Kate Douglas Wiggin's *Rebecca of Sunnybrook Farm.* The maudlin sentimentality of Wiggin's fiction was defended by Gilder, who described her work and that of other writers in the same sentimental tradition as representative of the "genial" in fiction: "In the rush and strain of modern life is the genial especially valued. The romantic has been of late warmly welcomed, by contrast to straining modern conditions, but the genial seems now, in America, to be living up promisingly to its claims."[21] The aging editor's alarmed observation of rapidly changing social and literary trends contributed to his defense of a fiction which compensated for its literary deficiencies by reaffirming traditionalism. Traditional bourgeois values form the core of Gene Stratton Porter's *Laddie,* which was introduced serially by *Scribner's* in 1913 as a "true blue story" and was followed by *Freckles* in 1917, a story of a one-armed boy who overcame adversity with stoicism and gentleness. *Harper's* claimed another popular sentimentalist in the first two decades of the new century, Mary Heaton Vorse. She penned a number of unusually vapid love stories such as "Awkward Question" and "The Case of Carolinda."

It would be unfair, however, to denigrate all the major journals because they contained sentimental stories of minimal literary value. *Scribner's*, the *Century*, the *Atlantic, Harper's* and *McClure's* among others published major authors such as Howells, Dreiser, Crane, Wharton and some sophisticated nonfiction articles on important political and social questions. The quality of their publications was

21. Smith, p. 144.

uneven, but essentially they raised the level of national culture and provided entertainment and education for millions of readers. These journals promoted first the local color movement and later encouraged the continuation of the style and ethical values of this movement in the sentimental popular fiction of the years preceding the first World War. It is difficult to say whether or not the journals were merely satisfying the demands of their newly acquired, eager-to-be-informed readers or whether they were in fact molding American values according to the principles of their editors. Most probably editorial enthusiasm and general public acceptance mutually combined to create a market for popular fiction which fulfilled the expectations of the journal's circulation department and the readers' dreams of educational but soothing literature. Wedged somewhere in between these two factions were the writers themselves. The exceptionally gifted could forge a separate literary identity but the majority were, to borrow James's phrase, "ground into the very mill of the conventional." Courted by an easily pleased magazine audience in their youth, many young writers of promise prospered as long as their fiction reflected the complacency and optimism of their age, but they discovered as mature and wiser men that they were only valued as purveyors of a dream world which their editors and readers tenaciously refused to outgrow.

Rayburn S. Moore

Paul Hamilton Hayne and Northern Magazines, 1866-1886

Shortly after the end of the Civil War, Paul Hamilton Hayne (1830–1886), poet, editor, and a lifelong resident of Charleston, South Carolina, left his ruined home, went to Augusta, Georgia, and took a job on the *Constitutionalist*, a local newspaper. Discovering after a few months that his frail constitution could not stand the ten-hour day, Hayne resigned, bought Copse Hill, a small tract of land sixteen miles away, and settled into a career as magazinist and man of letters.[1]

Before the war Hayne had in the 1850's written three books of poetry; contributed to the *Southern Literary Messenger*, *Graham's Magazine*, and the *Atlantic Monthly*; and edited the *Southern Literary Gazette* and *Russell's Magazine*. After Appomattox, Hayne, like Poe and Simms before him, turned more and more to the periodicals and served in various editorial capacities and also as a contributor to many Southern newspapers and magazines. He was literary editor of the *Southern Opinion* (1867–1869), a Richmond weekly, and of *Southern Society* (1867–1868), a Baltimore journal, and he wrote essays, reviews, and notices for periodicals in Atlanta, Augusta, Rome, Charleston, Columbia, Raleigh, Wilmington, Richmond, and New Orleans, to name only a few.

He had contacts everywhere in the Southern press, but he was also eager to contribute again to the Northern magazines. Consequently, in April, 1865, he began to explore the possibilities of selling his verse to Northern periodicals. He enlisted the aid of a former friend, Richard Henry Stoddard, a fellow poet and an editorial assistant on the *Round Table* at the time, and Stoddard managed to place some of Hayne's poems with his weekly and with the *Old Guard*, another

1. For a more complete account of Hayne's life and career, see Jay B. Hubbell, *The South in American Literature* (Durham, N.C., 1954), pp. 743–757, and my "Paul Hamilton Hayne," *Georgia Review*, XXII (Spring, 1968), 106–124, a slightly expanded version of the first chapter of my book on Hayne in the Twayne series (1972).

New York magazine which accepted Southern contributions. Neither journal paid very well, but Hayne could not yet expect to be welcomed in the *Atlantic* or *Harper's Monthly*. Nevertheless, things soon improved, for the *Galaxy* was established in 1866, *Lippincott's Magazine* in 1868, and *Appletons' Journal* in 1869, and all were hospitable to Southern writers. Hayne lost no time in contributing to these magazines, and by 1870 he had also sold verse to the newly founded *Scribner's Monthly*, and by 1872 to the *Atlantic* again and to *Harper's Monthly*. It is his relations with four of these periodicals—*Lippincott's*, *Scribner's-Century*, *Harper's*, and the *Atlantic*—which I wish to examine in this essay.[2]

I

Lippincott's Magazine was inaugurated in January, 1868, and was praised by Hayne himself in an April issue of *Southern Opinion* as "the only really impartial literary periodical published at the North." Hayne's own first contribution, "From the Woods," appeared in May, apparently through the good offices of George Henry Boker, the Philadelphia poet and a friend to both Hayne and Simms. Thereafter Hayne's work appeared sporadically—his most important offering being "Under the Pine: To the Memory of Henry Timrod," an elegy published a year after Timrod's death in October, 1867—and when John Foster Kirk, the historian, became editor in 1870, Hayne continued to contribute but with varied success.

During Kirk's sixteen-year tenure, Hayne managed to get sixteen poems accepted, but for the period between the early fall of 1871 and the summer of 1877 he failed to appear in the magazine. He could not understand the editor's rejections. Finally, after having a number of his longer poems returned, Hayne wrote Kirk on March 21, 1874, asking if he had room for "brief poems." To this inquiry Kirk presumably answered in the affirmative, for Hayne on April 10, 1877, informed Mrs. Margaret J. Preston, the Virginia poet and an old friend, that Kirk "eschewed poems of any length."[3] In discussing the

2. Since *Appletons'* was a weekly until 1876, became an "eclectic" (reprint magazine) in 1879, and folded in 1881, and the *Galaxy* was a semi-monthly until May, 1867, and was absorbed by the *Atlantic* in February, 1878, I am concentrating on the four monthlies (the *Century*, for all practical purposes, is an extension of *Scribner's Monthly*) whose pages were open to Hayne throughout most of his postwar career.

3. This letter (and all others quoted herein, unless otherwise noted) is in the Hayne Papers, Perkins Library, Duke University. I am grateful to Dr. Mattie Russell,

rejection of some of his own longer verse, Hayne added somewhat bitterly: "Considering that *Lippincott's* has been crowded during the last twelvemonth by elaborate poems of Lanier, Miss Lazarus etc., I could not fail to admire the *exquisite candor* of the excuse." "As a poet," he concluded, "Kirk seems to despise me!"

Kirk, however, had no prejudice against the poet, and a few months later in June, 1877, he began accepting Hayne's poems again. Caught by surprise, Hayne expressed his "amazement" in a note to Mrs. Preston: "Would you credit it? Kirk . . . after turning the cold shoulder upon me for years has lately grown amiable, accepting poem after poem. He took (to my utter amazement) a prodigious fancy to 'Consummatum Est.' I can't make it out."

Nevertheless, given the quality of some of Hayne's contributions and the usual problems of magazine publishing, the poet should not have been surprised by some of the editor's rejections, though in one or two cases, especially in that of "Forest Pictures," a good nature study which Howells printed in the *Atlantic* in December, 1872, Kirk's judgment was surely faulty. The exigencies of editing a national monthly—a large backlog of contributions and the vagaries of editorial taste (Hayne thought Kirk an "Addisonian in prose" and a "Popite in verse"), to say nothing of other considerations—undoubtedly accounted for some of Hayne's difficulties in getting his pieces accepted, but he frequently made his own troubles by sending in too many contributions and sometimes without properly polishing them. He was writing for a livelihood, of course, and his aesthetic standards occasionally bowed to other demands, as he ruefully acknowledged to Mrs. Preston on March 30, 1875: "I am *forced* to write, *too often forced* to write for 'bread'; and the consequence is that 'Pegasus' unwillingly weighted with harness, plays me many a wretched prank."

Despite the truth of these remarks, Hayne had few difficulties after 1877 in publishing his work in *Lippincott's*, and continued to contribute verse until his death in the summer of 1886. Many of these contributions deal with various aspects of nature from a romantic point of view, though even when his topics and treatment are conventional, the result may be striking or pleasing, as, for example, in the sonnet "A Morning After Storm" (March, 1880) or in "The Mocking-Bird"

Curator of Manuscripts, for gracious hospitality and for permission to use this fine collection and to quote from it.

(July, 1878). The latter in many ways is the best poem of the 19th century (those by Richard Henry Wilde and Sidney Lanier notwithstanding) about the so-called Southern nightingale.

> Lo! from a neighboring glade,
> Flashed through the drifts of moonshine,
> swiftly came
> A fairy shape of flame.
> It rose in dazzling spirals overhead,
> Whence to wild sweetness wed,
> Poured marvellous melodies, silvery trill
> on trill;
> The very leaves grew still
> On the charmed trees to hearken . . . .

"Consummatum Est," on the other hand, expresses a cynical outlook not usual with Hayne (and perhaps for that reason the poem appealed to Kirk, whose "scarcely repressible current of cynicism" had been a topic with the poet and one of his correspondents in 1875), but it nevertheless forms a healthy contrast to some of his more conventional work. His last poems for *Lippincott's*—particularly "Closing In" (August, 1882) and "Shadows All" (September, 1885)—disclose his thoughts on ever-approaching death and emphasize indirectly his courageous spirit in the face of the unequal contest he was waging against disease in his last years.

Altogether, Hayne managed in his poems for *Lippincott's* to maintain a standard of performance which, in view of his poor health and need to keep the pot boiling, is very respectable; and his verses are generally several cuts above the average quality of the other poetic contributions to the magazine.

II

In November, 1870, almost three years after the initial appearance of *Lippincott's*, the first issue of *Scribner's Monthly* came out, and Hayne's first poem was accepted in the following month, though because of a tremendous backlog of verse (Hayne's manuscript, according to Josiah Gilbert Holland, the editor, was numbered 392) this contribution did not appear in print until 1876. The delay in publication did not delay payment, nor did it prevent Holland from accepting more poetry, and in the following decade Hayne published a total of eight poems in the magazine. He was not always successful, however, for the editor turned down three poems and an essay on Arthur Hugh Clough.

Hayne's first appearance in *Scribner's* was not the piece Holland had bought in 1870. It was rather "The Awakening" (August, 1875), a short lyric which Howells had refused for the *Atlantic* in February and which Holland had accepted in March, 1875. The poem that Hayne had sold the magazine in 1870 probably was "Choice and Chance" (September, 1876). His most interesting and important offering, however, was "Unveiled" (January, 1878), a long, irregular ode expressing a somewhat Wordsworthian view of nature and dedicated to William Cullen Bryant, which earned a check for fifty dollars and a note of praise from Dr. Holland on December 10, 1877: "This is much the best, largest, most strongly and evenly sustained piece of work I have ever seen from your hand." And though he thought it too long for the magazine, Holland could not refuse the poem. Bryant also congratulated Hayne on it and accepted "with pleasure" the dedication. Bayard Taylor, on the other hand, thought that "Unveiled" contained the "substance" of a fine poem but that the "keystone" of the arch was lacking. Hayne was distressed by Taylor's opinion, but E. C. Stedman, Mrs. Preston, and others assured him the poem was one of his best; and by 1884 he considered it his "highest water mark."[4]

The only piece with a Southern setting, "Forest Quiet (In the South)" (July, 1877), presents a variation in the regular *terza rima* rhyme scheme and a conventional romantic treatment of nature, but, generally speaking, Hayne's contributions to *Scribner's*, or the *Century* for that matter, include little to indicate the condition of his homeland and seldom express his opinions on political or contemporary problems.

Hayne's convictions on such matters, among other things, gradually

4. Hayne wrote Andrew Adgate Lipscomb on November 14, 1884: "In 'Unveiled,' I gained, *me judice*, my highest water mark!, for I do think, at least I *hope* that therein (to borrow your own exquisite phraseology) 'the two ideals of the spirit & the sense have come together like the dust of Paradise in Adam's body & the breath of God.' " Lipscomb responded on November 18: ". . . I find it uppermost among all your poems as to the individuation of Nature's power over the spiritual senses and the entire subserviency of sense-impressions to the higher subjectiveness. It is a very subtle and profound reading of Nature's meaning as the counterpart of the soul, and a wonderful collocation of the mediation of eye and ear as avenues to the mystical beyond the symbolism of the two great senses." For Taylor's criticism, see *The Correspondence of Bayard Taylor and Paul Hamilton Hayne*, ed. Charles Duffy (Baton Rouge, La., 1945), p. 92.

cooled his friendly relations with the magazine and the editor after almost a decade of cordiality. As early as November, 1871, for example, Hayne had written Holland that he was one of the periodical's "*staunchest friends at the South*" and was doing his "utmost to extend its circulation in this Section." This testimonial he hastened to put into print a few weeks later in the Augusta *Constitutionalist* for December 12, 1871:

> In three particulars it excels, we think, all of its rivals and contemporaries. We allude, firstly, to the brilliant *variety* of the articles . . . ; secondly, to the vigor, fidelity and richness of the wood engravings, which are of unrivalled talent; and thirdly, to the high, moral, conservative tone of the *editorial* department the entire content of which, under the supervision of Dr. J. G. Holland, is in striking contrast with the loose thought and tone of moral and spiritual *bouleversement*, which characterizes too many of the periodical issues of our day.
>
> *Scribner's*, too, is free from sectionalism, and may be safely patronized by the public of the South.

Six years later Hayne still thought highly of the monthly. On October 30, 1877, he wrote Mrs. Preston that it was a "noble mag*n*—the most catholic—in a *large artistic sense* perhaps, of all our American periodicals." Thereafter, however, his opinion began to change. He was annoyed by the rejection of his brief lyrical tribute to the late Sidney Lanier (later published in *Harper's Monthly*) in the fall of 1881, and after the *Century* succeeded *Scribner's* in November of that year, Hayne was convinced that the new staff nursed an "*animus*" against those who upheld the traditions of the Old South.

Most of Hayne's dealings with *Scribner's* were with Holland, who put Hayne on the magazine's free list; encouraged him to contribute; accepted his poems frequently (and when he rejected them, did so tactfully); printed reviews of his books; and wrote him frankly about political matters. A letter of December, 1876, discusses the Negro problem in the South and concludes: "At any rate, you and I will not quarrel. There will be no schisms in the republic of letters." Hayne responded in kind. He praised the magazine (and the editor) in the Southern press and in letters to friends, and offered it some of his best verse of this period.

Late in the seventies, however, Hayne's good opinion of Holland changed. The editor had, for example, refused to allow the poet to use in his forthcoming "collected edition" (*Poems*, 1882) some cuts printed in *Scribner's* as illustrations for one of his poems originally published there. On October 24, 1881, less than two weeks after Holland's death, Hayne penned an appraisal of him in a letter to Mrs. Preston: "Once I liked him as a personal correspondent, & as an Editor likewise, but somewhat previous to his decease, he turned so *violently* & *unreasonably* against the South; & displayed a temper at once so bitter, & narrowly mean that I could no longer respect the man." Still, he acknowledged, "disease perhaps was responsible for this."

With the editor's death and the coincidental change of *Scribner's* into the *Century*, Hayne's relations with the magazine may be said, for all practical purposes, to have come to an end. Though Holland had shortly before his death written Hayne commending to him his successor, Richard Watson Gilder, the Southern poet and the new editor did not become friends, and Hayne contributed to the *Century* only once.[5]

This contribution, a double sonnet entitled "The Decline of Faith," had been accepted in the early spring of 1882, set up for publication in June, but "crowded out" from issue to issue, according to Hayne, until it appeared in January, 1883. Such treatment irritated and discouraged the touchy poet and typified for him the attitude of Gilder and his staff towards his work. Many of his letters of the 1880's contain caustic and irascible comments on the *Century's* reception of his contributions and on its attitude towards the Old South. Holland's effort to inaugurate cordial relations between Hayne and Gilder had been in vain. Less than a year after Holland's death, for example, Hayne wrote Hamilton W. Mabie, a member of the editorial staff of the *Christian Union*, that Gilder was neglecting him, and three years later matters had changed only for the worse. Hayne described the situation in a letter of February 26, 1886, to Charles Gayarré, the Louisiana historian and a warm friend: "I pledge you my honor, that ever since this magazine passed out of 'Scribner's' hands, the 'Century' people have systematically rejected every article I offered them; — well! — I recently tried them once more, and in a *decisive* manner they showed themselves true to their hostility; and now it is plain as a pikestaff, that *nothing* with *my* name attached, is ever to be pub-

5. It should be noted that Hayne's difficulties with the *Century* were not shared by his son, who was also a poet. William Hamilton Hayne published eight brief lyrics in the magazine in the 1880's.

lished by them! No 'backing,' no influence at least in the South, could avail!"

There were of course other reasons why Hayne published only once in the *Century*. During the 1880's, for example, his poetic production in all the major Northern monthlies declined. From November, 1881, the date of the *Century's* first number, to his death in July, 1886, he contributed only five poems to *Harper's*, three to *Lippincott's*, and two to the *Atlantic*. At the same time, he was contributing the bulk of his output to other periodicals which frequently paid him better than the more prestigious Northern magazines. *Home and Farm*, the Louisville weekly, usually gave fifty dollars for a moderately long poem, and the *Southern Bivouac*, another Louisville journal, offered five dollars a page for prose. Moreover, for a good part of this period he was in ill health, and spent much of his dwindling time and energy on the publication of a collected edition of his poems, a labor consummated late in 1882. Finally, Hayne, like other poets, was squeezed out of the *Century's* columns by its Battles and Leaders Series and was forced to compete with local-color fiction in its heyday, a fact which inevitably led to a decline of editorial interest in poetry. If, however, he had contributed dialect verse in the style of Irwin Russell, had written dialect tales with the skill of Harris or Page or Cable, or had known one of the new editors as well as he had known Holland, more of his work might have appeared in the *Century*.

III

Hayne's experience with *Harper's Monthly* is not unlike that of his career with *Scribner's-Century*. Although a contributor to *Harper's Weekly* and *Harper's Bazar* after the war, Hayne did not break into print with *Harper's Monthly* until January, 1873, long after his poems had appeared in *Lippincott's*, almost a year after the *Atlantic* had brought one out, and over two years after *Scribner's* had accepted a lyric from his hand. Then, within a month in the fall of 1872, he sold Henry Mills Alden, *Harper's* editor, three poems for a total of fifty dollars. For one whose contributions in prose and verse had been consistently turned down since March, 1866, Hayne was naturally elated. He continued to contribute thereafter, and by the time of his death in 1886 had published twenty-one poems in *Harper's*, including "Muscadines," "The Snow-Messengers," "The Battle of King's Mountain," "In Harbor," and "Face to Face," some of the best poems he ever wrote.

"Muscadines" (December, 1876), a sensuous ode which offers a "beaker full of the warm South" and recalls Keats in other ways as well, had been declined by Howells, but Alden liked the piece and published it immediately. Maurice Thompson and Edgar Fawcett, fellow poets and friendly correspondents, and Moses Coit Tyler, teacher, literary historian, and a warm friend to Hayne, also thought highly of it. Tyler, indeed, always referred to it in his letters as the "immortal 'Muscadines.' "

"The Snow-Messengers" (March, 1880), on the other hand, is an open-hearted tribute to Longfellow and Whittier, old friends and mentors, whom he had visited in 1879. (He lunched on several occasions with Longfellow and spent five days with Whittier at Oak Knoll.) Not only is the poem worthy of consideration on its own merits, but as a gesture of reconciliation from the "representative" Southern poet and laureate of his section to leading New England spokesmen, it is significant. Both Longfellow and Whittier were touched by the compliment and acknowledged their gratitude in letters of appreciation.

Like "Snow-Messengers," "The Battle of King's Mountain" (November, 1880) is another laureate statement but a more official one in that it was occasioned by the centennial of the Revolutionary engagement and was commissioned by the executive committee of the King's Mountain Centennial. Hayne's tribute to the New England poets, on the contrary, had been his own idea and spontaneous, though in it he is no less aware of his position as a speaker for the South. Indeed, the ballad-like account of the fighting at King's Mountain (thereafter one of Hayne's own favorite poems) contained some sentiments which were omitted from the text in *Harper's*, but were restored in 1882 in the Complete Edition of Hayne's poems:

> There are some wrongs so blackly base, the
>   tiger strain that runs,
> And sometimes maddens thro' the veins, of
>   Adam's fallen sons,
> Must mount and mount to furious height,
>   which only blood can quell,
> Who smite with hellish hate must look for
>   hate as hot from hell!

Finally, "In Harbor" (July, 1882) and "Face to Face" (May, 1886) are both valedictory statements and, despite the four-year interval between them, express Hayne's serenity of spirit in the face of approaching death. In their manifestation of faith in the future and in sureness of artistic control, each poem is in the tradition of Emerson's "Terminus" and Browning's "Epilogue" to *Asolando*, and each deserves to rank among the best lyrics of Hayne's mature output.

During the summer following the appearance of Hayne's first contribution to *Harper's* in January, 1873, he met Alden and Joseph W. Harper, Jr., one of the Harper Brothers, in New York. While there he injured his ankle seriously enough to have two "surgical operations," and some of his new friends—Harper among them—lent him money to take care of his unanticipated expenses. He was pleased, he wrote his wife, at his reception in New York: "The welcome I have had from the literary people here actually astonished me. Editor after editor called personally, and my own visit to the Harpers and elsewhere, was like an ovation!" And he was equally touched by the generosity of the new friends who came to his rescue. Joseph Harper, for example, wrote a "charming letter" in the following December in which he "retired" Hayne's "note."

Meanwhile, Hayne continued to send contributions, some of which, including "The Mountain of the Lovers," a long narrative which became the titlepiece of his next volume in 1875, were rejected, but his good opinion of Alden and the periodical lasted well into the 1880's. By 1885, however, he was disappointed and disgruntled by the reception of his work in the *Harper's* editorial office. He expressed himself frankly in a letter of March 9 to Andrew Adgate Lipscomb, former chancellor of the University of Georgia and also a contributor to the magazine: "*Entre nous*, Alden . . . (who professes to be a *friend*) has accepted *one* out of about 6 or 7 pieces contributed by me during the last year!" The following fall he wrote Charles Gayarré that *Harper's* and some of the other chief Northern periodicals were "closed practically" to him. He perhaps had some cause for grumbling about Alden's treatment, for the editor had failed to publish any of his poems for over three years. In the last months of Hayne's life Alden made slight amends for his rejections by bringing out two more lyrics, but, despite the fact that by the mid-eighties *Harper's* was in many ways the most hospitable to the South of all the great Northern monthlies, Hayne closed out his account with the magazine in much the same way he had with the *Century* and, to a lesser extent, with *Lippincott's*—convinced that he was not receiving fair treatment from the editors.

IV

Similarly with the *Atlantic Monthly*, Hayne's relations followed the pattern of initial acceptance and cordiality and subsequent rejection and antipathy. He had contributed to the *Atlantic* before the war, and though he agreed with his friend John Esten Cooke that the Boston journal was a "New England coterie affair," Hayne also recognized its literary merits, as he clearly demonstrates in the Augusta *Constitutionalist* for February 17, 1867: "This magazine originated in the enterprise of a literary clique, has been supported by the talents of a clique, and will live and die a cliquish affair altogether .... But this unquestionable fact . . . does not blind us to another fact, quite as potent, namely, the splendid ability of the writers who form the charmed circle of its contributors."

Despite his awareness of the *Atlantic's* so-called cliquishness, Hayne had sought soon after the war to join the "charmed circle" again. In March, 1866, he sent a sonnet to James T. Fields, editor of the magazine and publisher before the war of two of Hayne's books, but this poem and others as well were rejected by Fields and his successor, William Dean Howells. Finally, however, in March, 1872, after Hayne's work had appeared in most of the Northern monthlies except *Harper's*, Howells accepted "Aspects of the Pines" (September, 1872), the first of nine nature pieces to capture his fancy. These lyrics (and others published elsewhere during this period) show that Hayne was taking a close look at his own Copse Hill surroundings and infusing romantically conceived and styled poems with local color and personal observation.

Hayne, of course, was delighted with this reception and offered the *Atlantic* some of his best work of the period; and though Howells liked some of Hayne's poems (he not only purchased them, but he also said complimentary things in letters and in reviews of *Legends and Lyrics* and of *The Mountain of the Lovers*), he declined at least two of Hayne's best poems—"Cambyses and the Macrobian Bow" and "Muscadines"—rejections which the poet could not understand.

"Cambyses," a terse and vivid account in blank verse of an incident ultimately derived from Herodotus, is stark and grim in manner, and

Howells, the future high priest of realism, thought it too strong for the *Atlantic*. Hayne expressed his displeasure to Mrs. Preston on December 23, 1873: "He [Howells] was unaffectedly struck by what he called its 'dramatic vigor,' but he nevertheless rejected it! And why? Because, oh! ye Gods! — because the subject was *too painful*, & the 'strong picturesque treatment' only made it the more *agonizingly 'impressive'* ! ! ! What idea must [we] form thus, of the moral & artistic 'grit' of Mr. Howells' readers? Why, they must be soft as pancakes, fit to 'die of a rose in aromatic pain.'"

Hayne was equally nonplussed by Howells's rejection of "Muscadines," a lyric, in his opinion, "of pure imagination & picturesque effects." On January 10, 1878, two years after Howells had declined to publish the poem, Hayne wrote F. B. Stanford, an editor of *Sunday School Times* and a regular correspondent: "I almost exhausted myself in making it as perfect a work of art as possible. Having been previously admitted to the columns of '*The Atlantic*,' I offered this production to Howells. He never even answered my note enclosed with the 'MS' and the said 'MS' was *never* returned. And yet my *name* was on his 'regular' list of contributors."[6]

These rejections were not warranted, but Hayne was even more surprised and disgruntled when he failed to place a single contribution with the monthly from the summer of 1876 to the fall of 1884. He had been aware of Howells's editorial "crotchets," as he observed in a letter of April 1, 1876, to A. H. Dooley, an Indiana book seller and a frequent correspondent: "The truth is that Howells is a man of *crotchets*; vividly admiring a good thing at one time; and coolly ignoring a thing equally as *good* or *better* at another time (as the temporary mood dictates)." By the end of the decade, Hayne was so exasperated by Howells that he determined never to contribute to the magazine again.

There were, however, other reasons for Hayne's failure to remain a regular contributor. For one thing, he began to publish rather extensively at this time (1876–1880) in *Scribner's*, *Lippincott's*, and weeklies like the *Christian Union* and the *Independent*; in the second place, he may have worn out his welcome at the *Atlantic* by occasionally flooding the editorial offices with verse (from January 3 to January 5, 1874, for example, he sent four poems to Howells, all

6. *A Collection of Hayne Letters*, ed. Daniel Morley McKeithan (Austin, Texas, 1944), pp. 193–194.

of which were declined); finally, he may have incurred the editor's displeasure by mailing a poem to him and to another editor at the same time and withdrawing it from one when it had been accepted by another, though this was apparently an oversight on Hayne's part. Whatever the reason, Hayne did not publish again in the *Atlantic* until 1884, well after Howells was out of his old chair and more than three years after Thomas Bailey Aldrich had replaced him.

Aldrich's succession to the editorship in 1881 led Hayne to hope for better days with the *Atlantic*, for he had admired the editor as "a true poet and consummate artist (in his own special line)" and had corresponded with him intermittently since 1860. On March 14, 1881, he congratulated Aldrich on assuming the new post but also offered "condolences" on the unpleasant duties accompanying it, especially those which involved "disappointed contributors." A month later, however, he was sure that Aldrich "*must fail in the end*," and by the following January Hayne had resolved anew not to contribute to the *Atlantic* again—a resolution broken only on several occasions when he published brief quatrains in the issues of September and November, 1884.

Thus Hayne's relations with the *Atlantic* concluded on much the same note they had ended on with the other great Northern monthlies. A proud man, Hayne could not understand why a poet of his experience and stature should not be a regular contributor to magazines of national reputation and circulation. The editors, on the other hand, had to consider many things and, for various reasons not always related to their merits, frequently could not accept his contributions or give him the attention he desired. Thus he turned more and more in the 1880's to weeklies like the *Independent* and the *Christian Union* and to Southern journals like *Home and Farm* and the *Southern Bivouac*. It was galling for one who had been an honored contributor to the great monthlies to conclude his career with them on such terms, but he acknowledged the situation and commented on it forthrightly in the spring of 1885 in a letter to A. A. Lipscomb: "These Yankee periodicals are crowded with contributions from England & the No & No-western States of America; & invariably they give the preference to Englishmen & their own writers. The poor Southerner stands at the foot of the authorial class, unless he chances to be a *clever* & unscrupulous *Renegade*; then he will not find it 'a long cry to Loch Ame!' as the Highlandmen used to say!" By the following autumn things had not improved, and he confided to Charles Gayarré that the chief monthlies were "closed practically" to him; and before he could counteract the trend, his health began to deteriorate rapidly. On July 6, 1886, Hayne closed his account with the magazines and the world and put to the final test the faith and vision so serenely expressed two months earlier in *Harper's* in "Face to Face," his last poem published by one of the important monthlies:

Sad Mortal! couldst thou but know
  What truly it means to die,
The wings of thy soul would glow,
  And the hopes of thy heart beat high;
Thou wouldst turn from the Pyrrhonist schools,
  And laugh their jargon to scorn,
As the babble of midnight fools
  Ere the morning of Truth be born:
But I, earth's madness above,
  In a kingdom of stormless breath —
I gaze on the glory of Love
  In the unveiled face of Death.

Harriet R. Holman

Magazine Editors and the Stories of Thomas Nelson Page's Late Flowering

Like his enemies, the stories a writer has trouble selling are one measure of the man; they also tell the reader of a later generation something of his time and place, and they make a useful gauge of his editors. The stories of Thomas Nelson Page's late flowering are a case in point. They consist of eleven atypical stories employing characters, settings, techniques, and themes significantly different from Page's earlier stories of planation life in antebellum piedmont Virginia. Consideration of these stories and the correspondence relating to them suggests that Page was more than a writer of local-color stories and that after his initial success his editors too often proved prescriptive rather than perceptive, wholly concerned with the preference of their readers, inhospitable to innovation, and consequently more aware of the day's marketplace than of either literary values or the future. A writer more greatly gifted than Page, or arrogant, or more aggressive in marketing what he wrote might have evaded their limitations without damage to himself, but that is speculation unrelated to consideration of these eleven non-Southern stories Page wrote to please himself.[1]

The stories have been so generally ignored by critics and literary historians that some word on them is prerequisite for understanding what Page's editors found objectionable. All are social commentary verging upon protest, all attack man's inhumanity to man, and all imply criticism of whole castes, if not classes, in the American social structure. Though at first glance they appear mannered, dated, a little remote and genteel, they are close to the spirit of protesters like

1. Published in *Under the Crust* (New York, 1908), included also in the collected Plantation Edition, and *The Land of the Spirit* (New York, 1913).

Veblen, young Garland, young Robert Herrick, and occasionally Frank Norris. They fall into three groups—five stories with New England settings, three strong stories which differ from each other and all his other fiction, and three stories with religious themes.

The New England stories are "Miss Godwin's Inheritance," published in *Scribner's Magazine*, 1904; "The New Lebanon Agent," originally called "The New Agent at Lebanon Station," *Ladies' Home Journal*, 1905; "Leander's Light," first called "Naboth's Vineyard," *Century*, 1907; "My Friend the Doctor," *Scribner's Magazine*, 1907; and "The Bigot," *Scribner's Magazine*, 1910. Page knew New England. Though Maine was his summer home for thirty years and local citizens counted him one of their own,[2] he made no pretense to write from the inner consciousness of the villagers, as the local-color writers had done. By thus admitting the limitations of his own perceptions and experience, he avoided the condescension of summer-visitor writers like Edith Wharton, who had irritated Mary Wilkins Freeman and other native New Englanders. As usual, he was too honest an observer to risk faking what he did not know. The intent of the early Southern stories was to evoke time, place, and mood through the particulars of local color; in these New England stories the intent was quiet revelation of character, with setting only incidental. They appear in a volume significantly titled *Under the Crust*. For Page the shift involved innovations in technique as well as subject-matter and, less obviously, in center of interest. "The New Lebanon Agent," for example, is essentially objective. "Miss Godwin's Inheritance," which Charles Scribner considered "perfectly charming, and as a piece of art almost perfect,"[3] differs from Page's earlier stories in having as both narrator and center of interest the *simpatico* summer visitor. In these New England stories Page makes his criticism explicit through the words of characters like Lishy Dow's widow in "My Friend the Doctor" when righteous indignation moved her to tell the self-gratifying Mrs. Durer exactly what she was.

By use of a different technique in three strong stories—"A Brother to Diogenes," *Scribner's Magazine*, 1906; "The Goth," *Scribner's Magazine*, 1907; and "The Outcast," in this country unpublished except in Page's *The Land of the Spirit* (1913)—Page leaves to the

2. Neighbors selected Page to make the address celebrating the 250th anniversary of the establishment of York Harbor.

3. Scribner to Page, April 25, 1904, the Thomas Nelson Page Collection, the Manuscript Department, William R. Perkins Library, Duke University.

reader the responsibility for providing his own commentary. "A Brother to Diogenes" is essentially objective, that is, dramatic, with its central figure an unhappily materialistic man insensitive to the human values which Page believed sweeten life. The taut ending shows the story well made from the beginning. Page called it his California story because it evolved from a winter spent in Santa Barbara. "It contains some of my philosophy," he wrote his mother from Naples within sight of smoking volcano and unbelievably blue sea.[4] That philosophy—the healing power of nature in mountain, field, and plain, coupled with the conviction that wealth limited to material things is ultimately poverty of spirit—is part of an agrarian revolt against the anonymity and increasing complexity of life that came with industrialization, thereby showing Page surprisingly akin to the Jack London of *Martin Eden*, the Booth Tarkington of the Growth trilogy, the Willa Cather of *O, Pioneers!*, the Ellen Glasgow of *The Voice of the People*, the Vanderbilt Fugitives, and the Maxwell Anderson of *High Tor*. By contrast, "The Goth" has its setting in Monte Carlo. This slice-of-life story of an international gambler given the cut direct by an acquaintance reads rather like a Richard Harding Davis story of fashionable society illustrated by Charles Dana Gibson; it happens to be a direct result of Page's reading a book on the psychology of compulsive gamblers at about the time he made two visits to Monte Carlo as an interested spectator in the winter of 1905–1906. Both this story and "The Outcast" demand that the reader produce his own commentary. "The Outcast" centers on a judge hearing the case of a prostitute accused of murder. In its dramatic presentation Page attempts to assess the basic responsibility for her situation, which by implication he attributes to her fatherless home.[5] The situation clearly shows injustice, but Page did not demand what Brand Whitlock called instant reform. He was too good a lawyer, too knowledgeable in the ways of the world to expect that to work.

The final group of three stories is built around religious themes. "The Stranger's Pew," published in *Scribner's Magazine* in 1910, an effective retelling of the familiar story of a coldly formal church

4. Page to Elizabeth Burwell (Nelson) Page, March 4, 1906, the Thomas Nelson Page Collection in the Clifton Waller Barrett Library of the University of Virginia (published in Thomas Nelson Page, *Mediterranean Winter 1906: Journal and Letters*, ed. H. R. Holman, Miami, 1971, p. 95).

5. Page noted with ironic satisfaction that it was his story most widely known in Italy during his ambassadorship.

whose members could not recognize Christ in the flesh, reflects Page's continuing disavowal of worldliness within the church.[6] "The Shepherd Who Watched by Night," Page's tribute to a brother who served as Episcopal rector in Virginia, Texas, and New York, is, he said, "real enough to be a transcription of fact."[7] Page never offered it to magazine editors, giving first rights instead to the Episcopal Church to use in raising funds for superannuated ministers. "The Stable of the Inn," which appeared in *Scribner's Magazine* in 1912, is another affirmation of his religious commitment; derived from the Biblical account of the first Christmas, it is "to some extent based on the Golden Legend."[8] These religious stories are workmanlike examples of a kind rarely commanding the attention of scholars and critics. In subject-matter they bear some relation to the stories with which Henry Van Dyke had been instructing the multitudes, but they differ from his in being more restrained and comparatively sparse stylistically. Page claimed no literary excellence for them, but they had a certain appeal, as readers often reminded him.

However diversified the settings of these eleven stories, they have in common the subject of responsibility, which Page designated duty to God and man. As any reader who knows Page's earlier stories will recall, it was duty that sent Marse Chan to war, and duty that put iron into the soul of the old colonel who spiked his guns and sank them in the river before surrendering. The difference in emphasis, however, combined with new settings and experiments in technique, makes the later stories seem the work of another writer. The change, which was the basic cause of the editors' disaffection, challenges the reader to reassess for himself both the earlier stories and the later. After all the intervening years, of course, it is not likely that Page would find a wide audience of admirers again, but the reader who judges these stories of his late flowering by any objective standards will recognize in them evidence of a control of material, a knowledge of men and the world, and a more encompassing compassion than could have been predicted from the local-color stories on which Page's reputation still rests.

His apprenticeship to editors made him properly hesitant about going counter to their recommendations. Moreover, never a man to

6. See newspaper reports of his speech at New Hampshire's Old Home Week and a *New York Times* editorial August 26, 1900, p. 18.

7. "Preface," *The Land of the Spirit* (New York, 1913), p. vii.

8. Ibid., p. vi.

ignore an obligation, Page did not forget that without the active encouragement of the editors who came to Richmond to talk with him after publication of "Marse Chan" he would never have developed into a writer. William Dean Howells and Richard Watson Gilder made recommendations for cutting the long manuscript that fifteen years later became *Red Rock* (1898). Gilder urged him to record for the nation the recollections of a child growing up within sound of the battlefields; that account became *Two Little Confederates,* first published in 1888 and never out of print since. Robert Underwood Johnson suggested the theme of "Meh Lady." Editors taught him to shape and control his stories and to see all about him materials with fresh appeal to readers.

But those lessons had been learned in 1884–1886. Ten years later, the lyric impulse stilled by his wife's early death, Page was a different man with something else to say. By choice and conviction always a Virginian, he had in the intervening years lost the limitations of provincial horizons. Legal work for business interests he served had taken him into Colorado mining country and some even more inaccessible areas of the Appalachians. He carried letters of introduction from editors when he went to London to confer with financial backers. There his good breeding and charm continued to provide opportunities for intellectual and social life which included lunch with Edmund Gosse and W. M. Rossetti, Gosse's literary At-Homes, an afternoon with Kipling in his Embankment rooms, a Sunday with Thomas Hardy at the salon of Mrs. Francis Jeune, diplomatic receptions, days in the galleries of Parliament to study the oratory of Parnell, the theater with redoubtable old Countess Burdett-Coutts, friendship with Ada Rehan[9] and the violinist Johannes Wolfe, beefsteak suppers in the Green Room of the Lyceum Theatre with Sir Henry Irving and the Beerbohm Trees, and a walking tour through Norway with the Irish editor of the London *Sun.* As a Southerner only a generation away from war and reconstruction, he found British attitudes toward life more congenial than those prevailing among Americans in the industrial and urban North, but when the financial panic of 1891 ended his English negotiations, he returned immediately home to Richmond. He was a cosmopolitan who kept his native roots.

9. See H. R. Holman, "Attempt and Failure: Thomas Nelson Page as Playwright," *Southern Literary Journal*, III (Fall, 1970), 72–82.

The crucial year for Page, however, was 1892, when he "lectured"—that is, he read his own stories—from Boston to Denver and Palm Beach. Everywhere except in the impoverished South he saw the kind of wealth that, properly used, could found great libraries or free gifted individuals for work in the service of humanity and art,[10] and what he saw aroused him to a sense of urgency: men of vision must take into the new industrial era the old aristocratic ideals of responsible leadership and service for the common good. A year later in Chicago his marriage to Mrs. Henry Field introduced him to the world of her Bryan and Lathrop relatives, unmistakably a moneyed aristocracy meeting its responsibilities in a mushrooming metropolis; her uncle was credited with bringing the Columbian Exposition to Chicago, her cousin served as secretary to liberal governor John Peter Altgeld, her brother gave sacrificially to support cultural activities, and Mrs. Page herself gave the nucleus of paintings for the Chicago Art Institute. Because her family was actively involved in the business of the city, they could give Page a depth of awareness that he might not have achieved without them. It has generally escaped the attention of critics that a full decade before the Muckrakers began spectacular disclosures about the new robber barons, Page was working into his stories satirical portraits of individuals who assumed money to be the one final measure of value. More significantly, he was writing stories of little people engulfed by urban blight and ill-planned industrialization, victims of what Kimball King called "an affluent society which has lost the traditional virtues of an aristocracy."[11] So long as these portraits were embedded in stories of plantation society, nobody seemed to pay much attention.

But increasingly when this new Page turned from accounts of a vanished past, the magazine editors did not like the change. They based their objections sometimes upon the story, sometimes upon Page's reputation, sometimes upon his "strong" language, and sometimes upon the expectation of their readers. Of the eleven short stories which I have been able to identify as part of this late burgeoning, Page managed to peddle nine essentially unchanged for magazine publication and gave to his church first-publication rights to a

10. With no resources except faith and vision Page had established in memory of his wife the first public library in Richmond. He was profoundly moved by the great collections of books and manuscripts at the University of Wisconsin.

11. "Satrical Portraits by Thomas Nelson Page," *Mississippi Quarterly: A Journal of Southern Culture*, XVIII (Spring, 1965), 74–81.

tenth one;[12] of an additional group of manuscripts written in a new, sparse style from about 1897 to 1911 on subjects too powerful or controversial for editors to touch, however, Page seems to have saved intact only "The Outcast."

By this time Page had small need to turn out pot-boilers, because he was receiving a steady stream of book royalties from Scribner's. Though his wife's wealth paid most of their household bills, he remained scrupulously self-supporting. His chief expense was subsidies for an astonishingly long list of unfortunates, many with no claim upon him except that they had nowhere else to turn. If financial pressures eventually caused Page to alter what he had written (as I can only surmise that in some cases they did) and if the pressures certainly caused him to publish poor material previously witheld, like "The Old Planters," it was essentially because he would not allow his wife or anyone else to meet responsibilities he had assumed for cousins in reduced circumstances, sick lawyers, a succession of widows and orphans, and former slaves who had never belonged to his family.

Letters to and from editors constitute the best evidence about the reaction to new developments in Page's writing. Page wrote Gilder in 1897 to suggest that he was experimenting deliberately with a way of writing which differed from his customary method. Ordinarily, except when he was writing an anecdote of the kind which gave him the reputation of *raconteur par excellence*,[13] he began with a sketch-like impression of character or scene, in subsequent drafts revising form and action into it, often over a period of years. He seems to have suggested to Gilder in this letter that he was trying a direct story line to fit subject matter different from his plantation stories: "It's all right about the story," he wrote after Gilder had rejected an unspecified manuscript.

> I am sorry it does not appeal to you; but that's the test in a way. . . . It is not homogeneous—not complete up close enough—and the episodes are episodes rather than segments of a well rounded and compact story. All this I know and shall remedy. But the *succinct, colorless, direct narrative is what I am after here, and the style was deliberately adopted. I want to try it, and it must go so or not at all.*[14]

12. "The Shepherd Who Watched by Night" was given multiple separate publications, apparently by individual dioceses, the proceeds going to ministerial relief. Presbyterian churches subsequently made similar use of it.

13. For example, those he contributed to "The Editor's Drawer" of *Harper's Monthly*, collected afterwards as *Pastime Stories*.

14. Page to Gilder, December 23, 1897, Duke. Italics mine.

This was probably the "novelette or Long Story" which Edward Bok had wanted to see but returned because the *Ladies' Home Journal* required "the predominance of the feminine."[15]

Careful attention to background was "the color" that editors not only expected, but demanded from Page. When he did not give it to them, they rejected his work. A case in point is the urban novel, *The Untried Way*, on which he had been working for several years in the directly simple style appropriate to the subject. In rejecting it, E. L. Burlingame of *Scribner's Magazine* explained:

> I really do not think that the story would be successful, judged by your own standards and the standards of your previous work; and I cannot help thinking it likely that a re-reading after an interval may make you agree with me, at least with regard to the present form. It seems to me, frankly, bald and held down very close to the actions of the plot, without the color which you usually give (except perhaps in the first sketch of the hero in the opening chapter) and it affects me rather like the *scenario* of a story than like the story itself in your usual sense. If I did not know to the contrary, I should imagine it had been sketched out long ago with the intention of founding something upon it later; but I know that it is sometimes the effect when a warm colorist, in some sudden mood of reaction, keeps himself pretty rigidly in line. The experiment is always a hard one to try; and in this case I think the reader will not read as much into the result as you yourself had in mind in making the sketch.[16]

It is significant that Burlingame, acting here in dual editorial roles, with this same letter both rejected the manuscript for *Scribner's Magazine* and accepted it for book publication by Charles Scribner's Sons if Page insisted. But in this instance Page's literary judgement must have yielded to his quick pride. I found no manuscript of *The Untried Way* in the vast Thomas Nelson Page collections, in the Clifton Waller Barrett Library at the University of Virginia and in the William R. Perkins Library at Duke University. Apparently Page uncharacteristically destroyed it, or possibly he made subsequent use of it as foundation for *John Marvel* (1909) or, more probably, *Gordon Keith* (1903).

Magazine editors also gave Page trouble about all his other long manuscripts except *Red Rock* (1898). In these manuscripts he was writing of prostitution, mercenary marriages, the urban poor and conspicuous consumers of wealth, the staggering impact of alien

15. Bok to Page, January 28, 1898, Virginia.
16. Burlingame to Page, July 29, 1898, Virginia.

migrations into the Anglo-Saxon culture of middle America, and of Southerners as corrupt politicians, money-grabbers, and the self-serving rievers and destroyers of a mountain mining town. No one, editors or reviewers, seems to have been bothered by his failure to grapple with the basics of economics and human relations, or by his offering as solution for all problems the domestic virtues of duty and compassionate brotherly love. What did bother the reviewers was exactly what his editors had objected to. "It is when the action of his stories changes to the North that we miss something of the charm of Mr. Page's earlier work," Herman Knickerbocker Vielé wrote in *The Bookman*,[17] as if Virginia possessed inherent powers to cast charm upon unscrupulous business dealings and violent death. "There are many who can paint the railroad strikes of *John Marvel* or the speculation of *Gordon Keith*," Arthur Hobson Quinn later wrote regretfully; "no one but a Southern gentleman could have written *Red Rock* or *Meh Lady*."[18]

Moreover, *John Marvel*, innocuous as that work now seems, was kept out of sight in English circulating libraries except when a patron specifically requested it. "God bless the smug souls of the English Circulating Libraries!" Page exploded to Charles Scribner.

> Are not they a choice lot? Think of [Elinor Glyn's] *Three Weeks* and George Moore and *Man and Superman* [Page after all belonged to the audiences that Shaw enjoyed shocking] and a few other choice morsels of pruriency and the way in which they turned them over their tongues, and smacked their greasy lips at their salacious taste, and then consider John Marvel *doubtful*!
>
> I should not mind anything but doubtful, but if it does not go head on against their whole position of smuggy bourgeois hypocrisy, it is nothing. . . .[19]

In effect, then, what his magazine editors and individual readers were demanding of Page was more Southern material of the kind he had been writing twenty years before. The notable exception was *Scribner's Magazine*, whose editors, though sometimes unenthusiastic about his finished product, made no effort to dictate what he wrote.

17. XVII (July, 1903), 513.

18. "Mr. Page in Fiction and Poetry," *The Book News Monthly*, XXVIII (November, 1909), 144. But the public bought the novels, 97,000 copies of *Gordon Keith* in the first seven months and enough of *John Marvel* to keep it on the best seller list for two years.

19. Page to Scribner, March 12, 1910, Virginia.

Charles and Arthur Scribner had assembled an editorial staff including W. C. Brownell, E. L. Burlingame, and Robert Bridges, whose perceptive awareness of many kinds of excellence established the liberal milieu which Maxwell Perkins later inherited. Unlike some others, they did not reject good work in favor of inferior. Perhaps it was because they were also editors for the publishing house, with an obligation to keep a successful novelist happy. More probably, simply because they were editors for Charles Scribner's Sons they had a less restricted vision of what literature and the world are in reality, and thus a clearer understanding of the editor's relationship to the writer.[20]

Among other editors, S. S. McClure asked for a series of articles on race relations in the South, subsequently collected as *The Negro: The Southerner's Problem.* He also asked Page for stories, but turned down two of the New England group as "what you might call a Northern story, a field in which we get plenty of stories,"[21] and Page vowed to send him no more. Nor could Page place with his usual editors an article on the education of poor country girls in the South —of vital concern to Page and his father before him—and so he sold "A Neglected Class" to *Good Housekeeping* at about half his usual rates. Yet at the same time a Southern plantation story, like "Mam Lyddy's Recognition," bought by Charles Belmont Davis at *Collier's*, commanded top prices.

The editor who most frequently transgressed against Page's sense of values was Robert Underwood Johnson, who combined with an infinite capacity for detail a remarkable insenitivity to persons, managing to create one uproar after another without any awareness of storms about the break upon his head. Because Johnson was one of the editors cordial to him in the early years, Page swallowed without comment such judgments as "though it is not a 'Marse Chan,' and depends upon its interest rather than on its charm (a quality we hope to find in the Xmas story) we shall be glad to publish 'The New Lebanon Agent.' . . ."[22] But the condescending cajolery of another

20. Because much of Page's dealings with the men at Scribner's was face to face, letters are often too elliptical to be useful in identifying what the editors accepted without enthusiasm. It should be noted, however, that Page's documented experience with these editors contradicts what Thomas Wolfe and other admirers of Maxwell Perkins said about them.

21. McClure to Page, February 27, 1904, Duke, in rejecting "Leander's Light." McClure had earlier rejected "The New Lebanon Agent."

22. Johnson to Page, May 13, 1904, Duke.

letter proved too much for Page. "At the earliest moment practicable," Johnson wrote,

we have read "My Friend Naboth," and Mr. Gilder desires me to say how we feel about it.

We find it not a story, in the sense of dramatic movement and interplay, but a sketch—to be sure, complete and rounded out with your wonted geniality—a typical though not very vivid sketch of our time. Now, what we are always hoping you will do for your old friends of *The Century* is to send them a first-rate breathless story which we can say is among your very best. As we have said, this is a sketch rather than a story. We want to have you in *The Century's* pages but we do not quite feel up to paying story prices for it. We do not like any more than you the bargaining side of literature, but unfortunately it is one that has to be fronted. . . .

We hope that you will put it within our reach.[23]

Page fired off a reply by return mail:

As . . . you do not think it a story at all, but only a sketch, and not a very vivid sketch at that, I am going to get you to send it back to me, and see if I can't write "horse" plainly enough on it to have someone recognize the genus. . . .

This is the second piece of writing on paper that I have sent to *The Century* under the impression that it was a story, but which has been stamped sketch and returned to me. I do not in the least question the sincerity of your views about it, for I am conceited enough to believe that you would be reasonably glad to publish a "story" by me; and, of course, I know that what you call an acceptable story must be of more immediate value to you than what you call a sketch, and what I call a story, but I do not know just what constitutes the difference.

I would call "Rab and His Friends" [by Dr. John Brown] and "Posson Jone" [by George W. Cable] stories, as I did call "A Brother to Diogenes" a story, though none of these has in it what I understand by "dramatic movement and interplay," each of them being, in fact, but a story of one dog, or one man, in which is grouped or is attempting[?] to be grouped, a picture of a segment of life amid which the scene is placed.

Referring to some of the "authorities," I find that one Joseph Addison, himself a writer of sketches, defines a story as "the relation of an incident or minor event, a short narrative, a tale," while in a recently published authority of great weight[24] I find that a story in the sense in which the term is used in literature is defined as "a narrative; a tale written in more or less imaginative style, especially a fictitious tale, shorter and less elaborate than a novel," while I find a sketch appears to have as an essential a brief, slight, or hasty delineation or composition. Now, I am afraid you read *The Century Dictionary* too much and Addison too little. I know

23. Johnson to Page, December 21, 1906, Duke.
24. That is, *The Century Dictionary*.

that often a man is not a good judge of his own work, so I let pass the fact that I think "My Friend Naboth," a name for which I shall substitute "Leander's Light," a pretty good relation, I mean for me, of minor events in the life of an old Maine countryman and his sister. It was written with a view to showing that under their hard and repellant exterior there lies a deep vein of sentiment that makes them close kin to the rest of Anglo-Saxondom, to whom the love of home and family is the most vital and lasting of all principles.[25]

Though neither Page nor his editors knew it then, Page had the future on his side, for the short story as written by Sherwood Anderson and all his literary descendants resembles more nearly Page's picture of a "segment of life" than Johnson's plotted "dramatic movement and interplay." In this matter, by insight or accident, the writer evidenced better judgment than his editors.

Johnson rejected "The Stranger's Pew" because it lacked "the novelty which the public would expect from you. . . admirable as it is in feeling and direction of purpose."[26] Of course he and other editors meant novelty acceptable to them, not a shocker like "A Modern Brutus," later renamed "The Outcast." "Your story, 'A Modern Brutus,' is terribly impressive," wrote H. M. Alden from *Harper's Magazine*.

It does not read like a piece of fiction but like a strong narrative of fact. I do not think a story of this kind presented in this way will be kindly received by our readers. The sheer strength of the presentment seems to make it impossible. I am sorry that I must return it. . . .[27]

Similarly, Charles Belmont Davis returned it because

notwithstanding the power with which you have told this big story, we cannot believe it is the best *kind* of story for *Collier's*. . . . Certainly no charge of pruriency could be brought against this tale. . . . I can only hope you will send us something else that will come more within the scope of what we believe our readers want.[28]

25. Page to Johnson, December 22, 1906 (carbon copy), Duke. *Century* wanted "Leander's Light," but not at Page's usual rates of $1,000; *McClure's* turned it down; *Metropolitan* turned it down; Franklin B. Wiley of *Ladies' Home Journal* negotiated back and forth over length and other stipulations that Page considered necessary because of that magazine's reputation for "editing" without permission of the author; *Scribner's* wanted it for $800; Page finally—and generously—placed it with *Century* at their original low price. (Correspondence at Duke.)

26. Johnson to Page, April 21, 1910, Virginia.

27. Alden to Page, January 12, 1910, Virginia.

28. Davis to Page, February 4, 1910, Virginia.

No other magazine editor would publish it. In 1913, while clearing his desk before he went to serve as Ambassador to Rome, Page included it in *The Land of the Spirit*, a volume of short stories which was not republished as part of his collected edition. Three years later, to Page's distress, "The Outcast" was made into a movie with Mae Marsh in the lead; special preshowings to local clergymen to attest that it was a proper movie for a decent community were emphasized by screaming advertisements.[29]

From about 1895 when he was writing *The Untried Way*, unpublished and now lost, editors again and again asked Page for stories, and what they bought again and again was material related in some fashion to the plantation stories that had brought him fame. Again and again, with such grace as was given to them, editors returned other materials to him with a variety of explanations: too stark, too bald, too lacking in warmth and color, too powerful, a sketch rather than a plotted story, or simply not what they wanted from him. Comparing what any one editor bought with what he rejected makes clear the fact that what they wanted of Page was Southern materials, Southern plantation material only. Johnson, who longed for another "Marse Chan" at bargain prices, bought "The Old Planters," a derivative and rambling piece that Page had pulled from his files and rewritten, but he returned "The New Lebanon Agent," which by any objective standards is better work, and S. S. McClure commissioned controversial articles on race relations in the South but turned down two quiet New England stories. The fact that few of these later stories of Page's have great appeal for the general reader of a later day is quite beside the point: The combined influence of the magazine editors was against change, experimentation, or innovation in form, content, or style.

This record of Page and his editors offers support for a theory by which Fred Lewis Pattee explained the plight of distinguished local colorists, like Mary Noailles Murfree, who in their later writing years were reduced to peddling stories from editor to editor. When Garland wrote Pattee that "the writer can't go on doing it over and over," Pattee philosophised, "And yet the reading public, or perhaps it is the publishers, brand their new writers with a herd mark and do not let

29. See H. R. Holman, "Attempt and Failure: Thomas Nelson Page as Playwright," p. 72.

them escape the ranch where they made their first appearance."[30] For Page, the record clearly shows, magazine editors with the notable exception of those at *Scribner's* did what they could to restrict him to plantation Virginia and the kind of stories he had been writing when first he came to their attention.

30. *Penn State Yankee* (State College, Penn., 1953), pp. 274–275.

Elizabeth C. Saler and Edwin H. Cady

The St. Nicholas *and the Serious Artist*

Roswell Smith and J. C. Holland founded *St. Nicholas: Scribner's Illustrated Magazine for Girls and Boys* in 1873 to create a children's magazine equal in standards of format and content to *Scribner's Monthly*. Edited by Mary Mapes Dodge, already a famous children's writer, *St. Nicholas* also enjoyed the services of *Scribner's* illustrators. Despite the depression of 1873, it quickly established itself as the most highly regarded children's magazine in the country.[1] Inevitably the tone of *St. Nicholas*, following the dictum "train up a child in the way he should go, and when he is old he will not depart from it," was consciously didactic. But it was also a deliberately literary magazine, firmly intended to introduce children to good reading—classic and contemporary—and provide them gentle, sagacious instruction in how to read and respond to literature. With such ambitions, *St. Nicholas* became an important factor in establishing the reading habits and literary values of thousands of Americans during the late nineteenth and early twentieth centuries. Because it occupies an important place in the development of American literary tastes, it deserves fuller study than has yet been given it.

I

The drive behind much of *St. Nicholas*'s impact derived from Mrs. Dodge, whose availability had been essential to Smith and Holland's plan. She named the magazine and laid down its policies. Famous for *Hans Brinker and the Silver Skates* (1865), she brought solid prestige, wide experience, excellent contacts, and a dominant per-

1. Frank Luther Mott, *A History of American Magazines, 1865–1885* (Cambridge, Mass., 1938), pp. 500–505. Summary of the form and publishing history of *St. Nicholas*.

sonality to her job. She held firm opinions about the ideal children's magazine:

> Sometimes I feel like rushing through the world with two placards—one held aloft in my right hand, BEWARE OF CHILDREN'S MAGAZINES! the other flourished in my left, CHILD'S MAGAZINE WANTED! A good magazine for little ones was never so much needed, and much harm is done by nearly all that are published.

She insisted that a children's magazine had to be "stronger, truer, bolder, more uncompromising," than an adult magazine, full of cheer, freshness and heartiness, never filled with condescending "editorial babble."[2]

Seeing that busy school children would not tolerate sermons in a magazine presented as entertainment, Mrs. Dodge called for lively contents suited to children's actual interests. Though she valued moral and other instruction, she held that "it must be by hints dropped incidentally here and there." "In all except skillful handling of methods," she warned, "we must be as little children if we would enter this kingdom."[3] Thence she listed editorial aims for *St. Nicholas*: to help children have real fun; to help them grow morally and physically; to prepare them for life as it is; to teach them appreciation of art; and, finally, "to give them reading matter which every parent may pass to his children unhesitatingly."[4]

Though in literary content *St. Nicholas* was rigidly "suitable," Mrs. Dodge applauded Sir Philip Sidney's coupling of instruction with delight, and her literary offerings were positively chosen with juvenile preferences and limitations in mind. And she was prepared to make definite statements about the reading she thought appropriate. Most such statements appeared in the popular "Jack-in-the-pulpit" department, presented as vignettes openly addressed to her child readership: do not read books you are ashamed of; find enlightening books but do not overwhelm yourselves with difficulty. Mrs. Dodge opposed the overburdening of children with adult reading. Writing as "Joel Stacy," she condemned a reading list compiled by Lindley Murray, "the father of English grammar." Murray prescribed that

2. Mary Mapes Dodge, "Children's Magazines," *Scribner's Monthly*, VI (July, 1873), 352.
3. Ibid.
4. Alice B. Howard, *Mary Mapes Dodge of St. Nicholas* (New York, 1943), p. 157.

teenage girls read (with "girlish alacrity") *Guthrie's Geography*, *Paradise Lost* and *Paradise Regained*, *Gisborn on the Duties of the Female Sex*, *Beattie's Evidence of the Christian Religion*, *Newton on the Prophecies*, and Boswell's *Life of Johnson*. "There is the list," said Mrs. Dodge, "with many a good book in it, but rather appalling to poor Miss Alice, I should say."[5]

To cultivate a taste for good reading, *St. Nicholas* sought to guide readers to their own sense of what a good book is. Children were taught to abandon the intent of reading for moral or mental improvement. For instance, in the September 1876 issue "Olive Thorne" (Mrs. Harriet Mann Miller) suggests self-directed learning which follows the line of live interests and takes advantage of new interests as they arise. One's approach to reading, Mrs. Miller says, not the number or categories of titles read, counts.[6] Mrs. Dodge stood confident that children would learn a great deal from independent reading. Though articles in the magazine constantly warned that not all books are equally worthwhile, in sum the gospel according to *St. Nicholas* was that all pleasurable reading is important because reading skill can help foster a clearer yet more imaginative vision of the world.

St. Nicholas aimed to make the best possible literature available so that children would enjoy and value it. Beginning in December, 1880, this emphasis was reflected in a department called "The *St. Nicholas* Treasure-Box of Literature."[7] The idea was to reprint, from month to month but not every month, selections of such "standard" poems, sketches, and stories as would be thought important parts of a child's reading but might not be available to children without libraries. Works were published whole or in part, according to the demands of space and the suitability of certain lines or stanzas to young readers. Little information was supplied about the authors in the hope (the implied assurance) that readers would undertake to find out about the authors on their own initiative. Mrs. Dodge hoped the "treasure boxes" might stimulate children even to memorize good things, and she foresaw that in reading literature valued by adults, children might acquire a better understanding of their parents' feelings and attitudes.

5. *St. Nicholas*, X (July, 1883), 715.
6. *St. Nicholas*, III (Sept., 1876), 702–704.
7. *St. Nicholas*, VIII (Sept., 1880), 139.

The first treasure box held Hawthorne's "David Swan: A Fantasy," and "King Canute" by Thackeray. Later selections, with varying amounts of accompanying commentary, presented Irving, Kingsley, Barry Cornwall, Lowell, Wordsworth, Herrick, Scott, Bryant, Longfellow, and the Brownings. Though the department was discontinued in 1882, it served the editor's intention to supplement school reading and encourage children to discover the classics for themselves—or to suppose that they had done so. As *St. Nicholas* stood for uplift, it stood for entertainment. But it also stood for a functional literacy the seriousness of which was meant to be limited only by considerations of appropriateness to children. It undertook to serve, though for broader and infinitely more sophisticated audiences, functions like those of television's famous "Sesame Street."

From like intentions eventually sprang the influential *St. Nicholas* League for Young Contributors. There Robert Benchley, Stephen and William Benét, Faulkner, Fitzgerald, Ring Lardner, Welty, and E. B. White won, as juveniles, first recognition. They and their many thousands of contemporaries less gifted, precocious, or lucky, fared richly. Through generations *St. Nicholas* won, perhaps in certain cases it created, extraordinary contributors. After Mrs. Dodge herself, writers as various as John Kendrick Bangs, Oliver Herford, Edith M. Thomas, J. T. Trowbridge, and Carolyn Wells seem almost to have made careers in *St. Nicholas*. The general list of contributors is an army with banners: Louisa May Alcott, Boyesen, John Burroughs, Bryant, Cable, Charles E. and Guy Wetmore Carryl, Rebecca and Richard Harding Davis, Eggleston, Frederic, Harte, Joel Chandler Harris, G. A. Henty, Howells, Jewett, Joaquin Miller, Harriet Monroe, Thomas Nelson Page, Mayne Reid, Riley, Theodore Roosevelt, Stevenson, Tennyson, Celia Thaxter, Whittier, Kate Douglas Wiggin, Mary Wilkins Freeman—during Mrs. Dodge's editorship.

Though there were other great years, the *annus mirabilis* came in 1894. Its meteors were Cable, with *New Orleans*; Clemens, with *Tom Sawyer Abroad*, "by Huck Finn. Edited by Mark Twain"; Palmer Cox, with "Brownies" (again); and Kipling, with "Rikki-Tikki-Tavi," "Toomai of the Elephants," and the root inventions of both *The Jungle Book* and *Just-So Stories*. In brief, *St. Nicholas*, for all it was "nice," served as a major resource for the children who would become the serious artists of "modern" literature.

II

Since it paid enough in cash and prestige to command many of the best writers, *St. Nicholas* naturally became embroiled, after its fashion, in their wars. And from the time of its founding until well after Mrs. Dodge died in 1905, the major literary conflicts swirled around "realism." The battles of the Realism War were fought among three partisan groups: the romantics, idealists, and conservators of romance; the realists, disillusioned humanists, and enemies to romance; the neo-romantics, "idealizers," lovers of romantic effects but believers in neither humane nor romantic ideas.

Amid the turmoil of skirmish and foray, much of the best of the magazine's serious literature was compatible with the judgments expressed in the following *St. Nicholas* poem (November, 1891) by W. D. Howells's daughter Mildred:

ROMANCE

Down from the sunken door-step to the road,
 Through a worn garden full of old-time flowers,
Stretches a pathway, where the wrinkled toad
 Sits lost in sunlight through the long summer hours.

Ah, little dream the passers in the street,
 That there, a few yards from the old house door,
Just where the apple and the pear trees meet,
 The noble deeds of old are done once more!

That there, within the gold-lit wavering shade,
 To Joan of Arc angelic voices sing,
And once again the brave inspired maid
 Gives up her life for France and for her king.

Or now no more the fields of France are seen, —
 They change to England's rougher, colder shore,
Where rules Elizabeth, the Virgin Queen,
 Or where King Arthur holds his court once more.

The stupid village folk they cannot see;
 Their eyes are old, and as they pass their way,
It only seems to them beneath the tree
 They see a little dark-eyed girl at play.

So far as the poem took them, Mildred Howells, Howells himself, and Mrs. Dodge went hand in hand. Fable, fantasy, the circus with its monsters and spangles, and all flighting unreality is right for children—and for men and women on moral holiday. But *St. Nicholas* was not finally to decide before the late 1890's, and then in the Rooseveltian (Romantic) way Howells thought wrong, which party to join in the Realism War. As Stephen Crane thought, it had sinned unpardonably against boyhood by stunning the world with *Little Lord Fauntleroy* (November, 1885–October, 1886). Perhaps it next only sought to balance the forces a little. At any rate, though one finds it with a certain shock, it is not surprising to discover that in the February, 1887, issue there appeared a lightly veiled act of literary warfare, "Little Effie's Realistic Novel." Its author, Alice Marland Wellington Rollins (1847–1897) was a Bostonian transplanted to New York who wrote verse good enough to be represented in Stedman's *American Anthology*, and travel books and magazine pieces enough to win recognition as "an efficient and favorite member of the N.Y. literary circles."[8] Her "Little Effie" had been invented to serve as a vehicular heroine of Mrs. Rollins's most ambitious effort, a slum-reform novel, *Uncle Tom's Tenement* (1888); and "Little Effie's Realistic Novel" must have been a by-product of that project.

Just as her novel allied itself to the socialism of concern which Howells monthly preached from his "Editor's Study" in *Harper's*, Mrs. Rollins's sketch harmonized with his militant realism. It opens upon a dialog between Effie and her Mama which is almost explicitly Howellsian:

> "Mama, I don't see why I couldn't write a novel, now that it is the fashion to put into novels just the plain things that everybody sees every day. You know we have been studying recent literature in Miss Owen's class at school, and it seems as if it would be ever so easy to write a story like those Mr. Howells writes."
>
> "But why do you try to make a novel out of it, Effie? Perhaps you would not find it quite so easy after all. Why not take just a simple story?"
>
> "Why, Mama, a realistic novel *is* just a simple story. That's why I like it, and why I think I can do it. It's just an account of what real people do every day of their lives, and you don't have to invent anything at all. It's very absurd, Mr. Howells says, to put troubadours and knights and all sorts of unnatural adventures into a story nowadays. People are tired of such things."
>
> "Well, but what will it be, Effie? A love story?"
>
> "No; I think not a love story."
>
> "How are you going to write a novel without a love story in it."

8. *An American Anthology, 1787–1900*, ed. Edmund Clarence Stedman (Boston, 1900), pp. 499–500, 819.

"Why, Mama, that's just it again! A realistic novel doesn't have to have lovers. Indeed, it mustn't have lovers. All that sort of thing is very old-fashioned in a novel."

"But, Effie," objected Lillian, Effie's older sister, "I'm quite sure Mr. Howells has lovers in his. Why, don't you remember, one of his stories was called 'Their Wedding Journey,' and I think somebody is always married in all of them."

"Well," said Effie, thoughtfully, "I'll tell you how I think it is: You can have people engaged and married, if you can't think of anything better for them to do, only you mustn't make a great fuss about it. There mustn't be all sorts of objections from the parents, and they mustn't turn pale with passion, and rave at each other in sonnets, and all that sort of thing. They must just get engaged sensibly and then go and get married, the way people really do."

"But what will you have your heroine do, if she doesn't fall in love or get married?"

"I don't know yet; I haven't made up my mind; but I think I shall have her go into a convent."

"Oh, Effie! Mr. Howells wouldn't do that. He wouldn't use a convent at all!"

"Why not? There *are* convents. It is perfectly realistic to take things that really do exist."

"But then there are so few convents; and comparatively few girls go into them nowadays. I think, if you are going to be realistic, you will have to tell just what the average girl, and not the exceptional girl, does."

"Oh, well; of course there are lots of other things she can do," said Effie. "I only happened to think of a convent just then."

Actually writing a "novel" is of course harder than Effie supposes, and it gets her teased by Papa, whom Mrs. Rollins invented to provide comic relief and the exposition of perspectives beyond Effie's ken. In Effie's hands realism becomes tepid romance, weak-kneed mediocrity. But Papa explains:

"It's all right about using our imaginations for common things; only you make a mistake in thinking that imagination is inventing things. Imagination is not *inventing* things; it is *seeing* things; but it is seeing things that are out of sight—it is seeing intellectual and spiritual things, just as the eye sees really visible things. . . .

"I think you will find out, as you go on, that it requires a great deal more imagination to write a realistic novel than to write a fairy-tale; because the object of a realistic story is not to repeat common things, but to interest people in common things; not to create uncommon things, but to show people that common things are not by any means so uninteresting as they seem at first sight. The realistic writer must see, not new things, but new qualities in things; and to do that, he must have plenty of imagination.

. . . This is the difference, Effie; those whom you call the 'old-fashioned writers' imagined that they must describe the thoughts and looks and clothes and actions of a princess, or some creature out of the range of every-day life; but the realistic writers have discovered that the thoughts and clothes and looks and actions of a little beggar-girl can be made just as interesting to people, if only you can *see what is unseen* about them with your mind's eye. Now, which would you say had really the nobler imagination —a man who went into his library and wrote a remarkable poem about the golden apples of the Hesperides, that were pure creations of his fancy, or Sir Isaac Newton when he went and sat down under a common apple-tree, and set his imagination to work to find out what made the apple fall to the ground? The realistic writer is satisfied with the every-day apple-tree—that is quite certain; but here is your mistake about him, Effie: *He isn't* satisfied with telling you that the apples fell; he shows you how they fell, and what a great, beautiful, wonderful law of the universe caused them to fall; and he makes you feel that the law was all the more beautiful and wonderful for not applying merely to one particular apple, or even to the whole class of apple-trees, but to everything."

In the upshot, revelation comes to Effie, and she tells her friends at school recess:

"I've given up my novel, and I'm just going to try fairy-tales." And she added, with a little sigh, "Papa says that I may write very good fairy-tales, but that I haven't imagination enough to be a realistic writer."

Mrs. Rollins had seen into certain essentials of realistic doctrine further than many of the nation's best-known critics and found a means of stating them for which Howells himself might have been grateful. In the end, however, the interest of her sketch lies with its placement in *St. Nicholas*. If, as seems probable enough, Howells read "Little Effie's Realistic Novel," he did not permit gratitude to warp his review of *Uncle Tom's Tenement* about fourteen months after the appearance of Mrs. Rollins's sketch.[9]

In his conversational way, Howells came in his "Study" to Mrs. Rollins by way of Cable's *Bonaventure*. It is, he says, "the work of a master," and Cable is not to be put down by "any provincial censure." But it is "no such book as the *Grandissimes*," which is "one of the great novels of our time . . . ." Conscience gives "final value" to everything Cable does and *that* will not suffer us ". . . to forget that art is the clearest medium of truth."

9. Since Howells submitted his "Editor's Study" manuscript about three months before publication, he probably wrote his review in June, 1888; it appeared in the October, 1888, *Harper's Monthly*.

It is a very delicate medium, however, and it breaks unless the ethical intention it is meant to carry is very carefully adjusted. One feels that something of this sort is the trouble with Mrs. Alice Wellington Rollins' book, which she calls *Uncle Tom's Tenement.* It is the work of an intellectual woman, and it is written with noble purpose from abundant knowledge; it interests, it touches, it stirs; but it is wanting in aesthetic solidarity, and one is sensible at last that, with all the fervor of its episodes, it must be judged on its economic side, if it is to be judged for what mainly occupied the writer. She has found that the tenement-house curse of New York has its origin primarily in the rapacity of the landlords, and secondarily in the savagery of the tenants; the former have accustomed the latter to squalor, till now they prefer it. The reform must begin in the consciences of the landlords, who ought to give their tenants improved tenements, and then the tenants ought to be educated up to their opportunities by surveillance and discipline. The abuses alleged are all undeniable and sickening enough; the extortions practiced are atrocious; the abominations and indecencies unspeakable. If ever prosperity visits these miserable homes in the shape of better wages, it is seized and confiscated to the landlord's behoof in an increased rent. The disease is well studied, and the symptoms all clearly ascertained; the remedy proposed is more conscience in the landlords. But is there any hope of permanent cure while the conditions invite one human creature to exploit another's necessity for his profit, or a bad man, under the same laws, may at any moment undo the work of a good one?

In short, the critic feels Mrs. Rollins insufficient in her powers of aesthetic realization and social perception. *Uncle Tom's Tenement* he finds wanting in both realism and socialism. In all charity, judged by major standards Effie's inventor stands under the same condemnation as Effie: she doesn't have imagination enough. But that is only to say that Mrs. Rollins failed in the major vein. "Little Effie's Realistic Novel" and its place in *St. Nicholas* remain interesting evidence of her cultural alertness and her power to succeed in a minor vein.

For it seems clear enough that any of the realists—Boyesen, Clemens, Crane, Garland, Howells, James—would cheerfully have admitted that romance and romanticism were right for *St. Nicholas* because they were right for children. There stood exactly the realistic point: the milk of romance for babes; the meat of realism for adults; the poison of neo-romanticism for oblivion. Mrs. Rollins planted a clear declaration, and in language the editors thought communicable to their readership, in one of the least predictable places. What the fact illustrates is that we have still much to learn from alert study of the American magazines.

James Woodress

The Pre-eminent Magazine Genius: S. S. McClure

In every account of American journalism between 1890 and the First World War *McClure's Magazine* stands out like Gulliver among the Lilliputians. Its founder, the ebullient, irrepressible Sam McClure, intended that it should be the best magazine published, and he quite literally carried out his resolve. When the first issue appeared on the newsstands in June, 1893, Dr. Albert Shaw in the *Review of Reviews* commented editorially that it "throbs with actuality from beginning to end,"[1] and the Philadelphia *Public Ledger* gave it "front rank at once."[2] Ray Stannard Baker, who became one of *McClure's* star reporters in 1898, recalls in his autobiography that he bought every issue and read every line while he was a newspaperman in Chicago: "*McClure's* was something fresh and strong and living in a stodgy world."[3] Mark Sullivan in his memoirs remembers the magazine as "the most alive and energetic periodical of its time."[4] Ellery Sedgwick at the end of a long editorial career looked back on the magazine as having had "the most brilliant staff ever gathered by a New York periodical,"[5] and Will Irwin believed that "*McClure's* virtually founded national journalism."[6]

More of these superlatives are easily obtainable. A large number of the most talented journalists of the era, which surely was the golden age of the American magazine, have left memoirs that corroborate the above testimony. But the best witness to put on the stand is the magazine itself, for even today one can read through the files of *Mc-*

1. VIII (July 1893), 99.
2. 13 June 1893.
3. *American Chronicle* (New York, 1945), p. 78.
4. *The Education of an American* (New York, 1938), p. 177.
5. *The Happy Profession* (London, 1948), p. 136.
6. *The Making of a Reporter* (New York, 1942), p. 148.

Clure's with a mounting sense of excitement and wonder at the intrinsic interest the dusty volumes still have. *McClure's* biographer, Peter Lyon, summarizes the accomplishment and impact of the magazine:

McClure's was the most exciting, the liveliest, the best illustrated, the most handsomely dressed, the most interesting, and the most profitable of an abundance of superior magazines. Indeed, for the fifteen years from 1895 to 1910 *McClure's* was probably the best general magazine ever to be published anywhere. Judged from the standpoint of impact on its times, of the daring and vision of its editorial formula, of the sustained excellence of its editorial matter, *McClure's* has never had a peer.[7]

The purpose of this paper is to inquire into the nature of this journalistic phenomenon, to isolate the factors that made the magazine an astonishing success, and to probe the reasons for its demise. *McClure's* was a supernova in the journalistic heavens. While *Harper's* and the *Atlantic* still wheel through the periodical skies, *McClure's* burned out half a century ago, and its founder's own brilliancy in subsequent years dimmed to near invisibility. What happened? Why? How did the magazine achieve its pre-eminence? Where did it get the remarkable vigor and fecundity that lifted it quickly to national stature? Who and what were responsible for the rise and fall? These are provocative questions for anyone interested in American culture. The answers lie in the abundant memoirs of the age, the bound volumes of the magazine, and the large collection of McClure and Phillips Papers at Indiana University's Lilly Library.[8]

One discovers upon investigating the history of *McClure's Magazine* that the journal and its founder are synonymous, and to get at the secrets of the periodical, one must fathom the nature of the man. Emerson's idea that an institution is the lengthened shadow of one man applies accurately to McClure and his enterprise. McClure conceived of the magazine, named it for himself, hired the staff, struggled at first to keep it solvent, then plowed his profits back into the project. All the while he supplied inexhaustible energy and enthusiasm. Mark

7. *Success Story: The Life and Times of S. S. McClure* (New York, 1963), p. 113. Lyon, who is McClure's grandson, may exaggerate a bit here, but his book is an excellent though unfootnoted study based on the extensive McClure papers.

8. A new book, Harold Wilson, *McClure's Magazine and the Muckrakers* (Princeton, N. J., 1970), is a well-written, carefully documented study based on a wide use of the manuscript sources at Indiana University and elsewhere.

Sullivan wrote: "Samuel S. McClure, I thought at the time and still think as I look back, was the pre-eminent magazine genius, easily first, in a period in which magazines flowered as never before."[9] William Allen White in his autobiography ranked McClure "among the ten first men who were important in the American scene."[10] Dr. Shaw, editor of the *Review of Reviews*, believed that McClure had gone through "a sort of training which gives him altogether exceptional qualifications for the conduct of a magazine." He added: "McClure's name is familiar wherever daily newspapers are read, for he stands at the head of the literary 'syndicate' business. He has within the past ten years made the acquaintance of more authors of standing in different countries than any other man knows or ever knew."[11]

McClure in real life was the American dream come true, an actual Horatio Alger, who came from his native Irish bog at the age of nine with his widowed mother. He struggled through dire poverty to get an education and in 1882 graduated from Knox College. His early successes included marrying the daughter of a prominent professor over strenuous parental objections and talking himself into the editorship of a bicycle magazine. He wasted no time in journalistic apprenticeship, and two years after college, he began a newspaper syndicate. He does not get actual credit for inventing the syndicate ("the thing was in the air," as he puts it in his *Autobiography*), but his enterprise was the first important venture of this kind, and he was a pioneer among syndicators. Then he launched the magazine, unfortunately in the midst of the Panic of 1893; but he survived by grim persistence, and within three years the magazine had reached a circulation of more than 300,000. The December, 1896, number, as McClure modestly wrote, had "more pages of paid advertising than any other magazine at any time in the history of the world."[12]

Genius he seems to have been, but what were the traits that made his magazine go off like a skyrocket? He himself could not write, and though he occasionally produced editorial notes for the magazine, he did not contribute articles to it. When he came to write his autobiography, he had to get Willa Cather to do it for him. The source of his genius lay in his lively, inquiring mind, his tireless energy, and

9. *Education*, p. 193.
10. *The Autobiography of William Allen White* (New York, 1946), p. 386.
11. *Review of Reviews*, VIII (July, 1893), 99.
12. *McClure's*, VI (Feb., 1896), 304.

his engaging personality. His restless curiosity kept him travelling incessantly across continents and oceans looking for writers and material, and it kept him devouring shelves of books, tons of magazines, and armloads of daily newspapers. The result was a geyser of ideas that erupted regularly and abundantly. His irresistible charm could persuade almost anyone he wanted to write or work for him, and he had a remarkable ability to spot talent, both journalistic and belletristic.

Coupled with his ability to recognize talent was a shrewdness in knowing what the growing middle-class public wanted. His taste was largely intuitive, but it was nonetheless reliable. He had what one writer called "a very highly developed 'sense of the interesting.'"[13] He did not cater to the lowest common denominator but aimed rather at his public's aspirations. McClure was essentially a romantic and believed passionately in the American dream. Though he led the muckraking movement, he was no stern reformer. He merely wanted the dream to come true. He had a rather simple faith that truth and justice could triumph and a rather naive trust in people and institutions. When his downfall came, it resulted from an excess of his virtues. As a natural phenomenon, perhaps like a nuclear reaction, he had to be carefully controlled, and when the controls went out, disaster occurred.

McClure's ability as talent scout and his genius for winning friends and influencing people are nowhere better illustrated than in his relationship with Ida Tarbell. She was perhaps his greatest discovery and for the first thirteen years of the magazine his greatest asset. She not only wrote brilliantly, but she also was a close friend and editorial advisor. She could put a cork on McClure's volatility, and her balance and sanity were vitally needed in keeping the magazine running smoothly. In her autobiography she describes her first meeting with him, in Paris, the summer before he began the magazine. She had gone to France on savings from a former editorial job in order to write a biography of Mme Roland, but she needed additional means of support and in 1892 was free lancing. She sent McClure's syndicate a two-thousand word article "cribbed from a French newspaper"[14] on Jean Alphand and his services to the city of Paris in paving its

13. *Outlook*, XLVIII (15 July 1893), p. 133.
14. *All in the Day's Work* (New York, 1939), p. 100.

streets. McClure's partner John Phillips bought it for ten dollars and McClure happened to read it in proof. He said to Phillips: "This girl can write. I want to get her to do some work for the magazine."[15]

Sometime later McClure passed through Paris on one of his innumerable trips to Europe and hunted up Ida Tarbell. He ran up the eighty steps to her apartment and breathlessly announced: "I've just ten minutes . . . must leave for Switzerland tonight. . . ." He was, writes Tarbell, "close to my own age [35], a vibrant, eager, indomitable personality that electrified even the experienced and the cynical. His utter simplicity, outrightness, his enthusiasm and confidence captivated me."[16] She was so charmed that she forgot to ask him how much he would pay for the articles he wanted her to write. At the end of the visit, which lasted two hours instead of ten minutes, McClure realized that he did not have time to go to the bank and still catch his train for Geneva.

"Could you lend me forty dollars?" he asked her. It was a large sum at that point in her career, and she only happened to have it because she was leaving for a vacation the next day. She handed it over to him unquestioningly, however; then after he had dashed down the stairs she wondered if he ever would remember borrowing it. He did. McClure wired his London office that night to send her a check, and thus began a vital personal relationship which survived after the business connection was severed in 1906. During the Depression when McClure was a defeated old man living in genteel poverty in a New York hotel, Ida Tarbell organized an anonymous pension fund from among his old and more affluent friends.

Booth Tarkington was another of McClure's discoveries, and the publisher's effect on him in 1899 was similar. When McClure accepted *The Gentleman from Indiana* for publication in book form (he had hired F. N. Doubleday and gone into the book business in 1897), he invited Tarkington to come to New York to cut his manuscript for serialization in the magazine. Tarkington, after years of collecting rejection slips, was exhilarated finally to have his first novel accepted, and he dashed off to New York. When he arrived at the office, he was treated as though McClure's only aim in life was to welcome fledgling authors. McClure took him around the office to meet Hamlin Gar-

15. S. S. McClure, *My Autobiography* (New York, 1963), p. 218.
16. Tarbell, *Day's Work*, p. 118.

land, Doubleday, and others, and when they came to Ida Tarbell, he said: "This is to be the most famous young man in America."[17] A few days later McClure installed Tarkington in his Long Island home and put him to work cutting his manuscript. A week after they had met, he was inviting Tarkington to go to Europe with him the next summer and was offering him an editorial job (not accepted) on the magazine.

Willa Cather was another writer who got her first important recognition from McClure. This was in 1903 when she was a high school English teacher in Pittsburgh. H. H. McClure, cousin of S. S. McClure and head of the newspaper syndicate, passed through Lincoln, Nebraska, on a talent-scouting trip, and while there he heard about Willa Cather. He relayed the tip to cousin Sam, who invited her to submit some work. She mailed him a few stories but did not expect anything to happen. A week later, however, she received a telegram from McClure summoning her to New York immediately. As soon as she could get away from her school, she took the train east and presented herself. Life was never the same after that interview. Willa Cather walked into the office at ten o'clock one morning, not worrying much about streetcar accidents and such; at one o'clock she left stepping carefully. She had suddenly become a valuable property. McClure had offered her the world. He would publish her stories in book form but first use them in the magazine. Those that he could not fit into the magazine he would place for her in other magazines. He wanted to publish everything she wrote from then on, and when she told him that previously she had submitted stories to *McClure's* but that they had been rejected, McClure called in his manuscript readers and asked them in her presence to give an accounting of themselves.

That wasn't the end. McClure took her home to meet his wife, children, and Mrs. Robert Louis Stevenson, who was visiting. He wanted to know all about her, who she was, where she came from, what she had done up to that time. He began planning her future for her, and she wrote later that if he had been a religious leader, he would have had people going to the stake for him. He had a genius for proselyting, she thought, and took a hold of one in such a personal way that business was forgotten. McClure did publish two of her stories in the magazine and then brought out in book form her first

17. James Woodress, *Booth Tarkington: Gentleman from Indiana* (Philadelphia, 1955), p. 77.

fiction, *The Troll Garden* (1905). Later when he needed some new editorial hands after the celebrated exodus of his all-star staff in 1906, he remembered Willa Cather. He swooped down on Pittsburgh and carried her off to a new career in New York.[18]

That McClure was a fascinating character is clearly evident from the literary use his contemporaries made of him. Howells, whom McClure admired vastly, put him into *A Hazard of New Fortunes* as the newspaper syndicate operator Fulkerson. There he is the engaging, self-made westerner who persuades Basil March (Howells's alter ego) to join him in starting a magazine. McClure actually tried to make the fiction come true by offering to make Howells editor of a new magazine, but Howells was not yet ready to leave *Harper's*.[19] Harold Frederic, whom McClure met in London during his Syndicate days, borrowed his experiences and personality in creating the character of Reuben Tracy, the self-made man, in *The Lawton Girl*. Frederic was working up material for his novel when McClure arrived for an evening and day of total talk. His youthful struggles went into the book in somewhat the same language that Willa Cather recorded in his *Autobiography* a quarter of a century later.[20] Robert Louis Stevenson, another of McClure's literary passions, also put him into a novel, *The Wrecker*, where he is Jim Pinkerton, an insensitive journalist-promoter. The sculptor-narrator of the novel complains that his friend has dished him up "with a sauce of penny-a-lining gossip" and butchered his person and his works of art "to make a holiday for readers of a Sunday paper."[21]

This was rather shabby treatment on Stevenson's part, but McClure's reaction to it throws light on an important aspect of his character: McClure never could believe anything bad about a friend. His genius for taking an interest in people often produced great results, but in the struggle for survival in the magazine world a modest belief in natural human depravity might have been useful. McClure early developed a warm admiration for Stevenson, who called it in the novel a "doglike service of admiration" (p. 97), and went to great

18. James Woodress, *Willa Cather: Her Life and Art* (New York, 1970), pp. 108–110.

19. Edwin H. Cady, *The Realist at War: The Mature Years, 1885–1920, of William Dean Howells* (Syracuse, N. Y., 1958), pp. 163–164; Lyon, *Success Story*, pp. 100–101.

20. Robert H. Woodward, "Reuben Tracy and S. S. McClure: Self-Made Men," *The Frederic Herald*, II (Sept., 1968), 5.

21. *The Works of Robert Louis Stevenson: Vailima Edition* (London, 1922), XVII, 87.

lengths to secure his work for the syndicate. He paid him handsomely for his fiction and advanced him $10,000 for a series of travel letters from the South Seas. When these letters turned out to be a bore, McClure never complained, and later after *The Wrecker* appeared, he claimed never to have read Stevenson's satiric portrait.[22] McClure's *Autobiography* is filled with admiring reminiscences of Stevenson. He named his son after the novelist and in a letter written to Stevenson soliciting a story in 1890, McClure said he was building a new house with a suite especially furnished in case Stevenson ever came to visit him. He was, he wrote, "full of longing to see you again."[23]

Kipling was another author on whom McClure made an indelible impression. He let McClure syndicate his fiction and later published a great deal of his work in the magazine. When McClure was looking for material to put into the first issue of the magazine, he went to Vermont where Kipling then was living. Kipling remembers in his autobiography that McClure was on fire with enthusiasm for the new project and talked for "some twelve—or it may have been seventeen—hours, before the notion was fully hatched out." Kipling "liked and admired McClure more than a little" and prized his "genius and simplicity."[24] He also thought that Stevenson's fictional portrait was far less original than McClure actually was. He used to say: "McClure, your business is dealing in brain futures."[25] They remained friends, and McClure often visited Kipling in England on his frequent talent-scouting and idea-searching trips.

McClure's trip to Vermont to see Kipling, his numerous visits to Europe, his excursion to Pittsburgh to snatch Willa Cather from her classroom—all these were characteristic acts. He was always on the move and believed a magazine could not be conducted properly by a sedentary editor. In his syndicate days he travelled from coast to coast selling fiction, and he roamed incessantly in his search for talent. During his career he crossed the Atlantic 149 times. "I sometimes spent as many as seventeen consecutive nights on sleeping-cars," he writes in his autobiography; "I never got ideas sitting still. I never saw so many possibilities for my business or had so many editorial ideas as when I was hurrying about from city to city, talking with editors

22. Lyon, *Success Story*, p. 108.
23. S. S. McClure to R. L. Stevenson, 12 Sept. 1890 (McClure papers).
24. *Something of Myself: For My Friends Known and Unknown* (London, 1937), pp. 124–125.
25. McClure, *Autobiography*, p. 230.

and newspapermen."[26] On one occasion in 1903 when he visited London, he spent the night in Sussex with Kipling, lunched the next day with Conan Doyle, talked in the afternoon to Anthony Hope Hawkins and William Heinemann. Then he lunched the day after with Conrad and Ford Maddox Hueffer before keeping a date with Mrs. Humphry Ward and catching a train for France.[27] When he hired Lincoln Steffens to be one of his editors, he told him he couldn't learn the job in the New York office. Steffens asked:

> "Where then can I learn? Where shall I go to learn to be an editor?" He sprang up and waved his hand around a wide circle. "Anywhere," he said. "Anywhere else. Get out of here, travel, go—somewhere. Go out in the advertising department. Ask them where they have transportation credit. Buy a railroad ticket, get on a train, and there, where it lands you, there you will learn to edit a magazine."[28]

Steffens did just that. The advertising department gave him an order for a ticket to Chicago, and there he began the investigations that resulted in *The Shame of the Cities*.

Of course, Steffens never learned to be a desk editor, but he produced brilliant articles, and the ideas came to him while he was moving around. McClure also was never an editor in the usual sense of the term. He could not sit still long enough to put out the magazine, and if it had not been for his associates John Phillips and Albert Brady, both Knox College classmates, who handled the editorial minutiae and the business affairs, the magazine never would have appeared at all. But McClure had a genius for picking his staff, and the quiet, scholarly, efficient Phillips was content to stay in New York managing things while McClure raced about the world. While McClure was on his travels, he would send back from Europe or elsewhere fat packets of newspaper articles "usually not cut out but torn out, jagged, scored and underlined, as suggestions for 'stupendous new series of articles.' "[29] Or after his trips he would descend on the office bursting with ideas.

Ida Tarbell remembered that McClure's returns from his foraging expeditions were "the most creative moments of our magazine life. He was an extraordinary reporter; his sense of the meaning, the meat of a man or event, his vivid imagination, his necessity of discharging

26. Ibid., p. 182.
27. N. W. Gillespie to Mrs. S. S. McClure, 17 Nov. 1903 (McClure papers).
28. Lincoln Steffens, *Autobiography* (New York, 1931, 1958), p. 364.
29. Baker, *American Chronicle*, p. 96.

on the group at once, before they were cold, his observations, intuitions, ideas, experiences, made the gatherings on his return amazingly stimulating to me."[30] Baker recalled that on those occasions McClure's ideas "literally erupted, like a live volcano,"[31] and William Allen White used to say that "Sam had three hundred ideas a minute."[32] Edith Lewis, Willa Cather's lifelong friend and companion, then a proof-reader on the magazine, wrote that "ideas flew from him like showers of sparks" and he wanted them all acted on immediately. "Some of his ideas were journalistic inspirations, some, of course, were very impractical; he did not bother to sort them out, he expected his staff to do that."[33] Mark Sullivan called him an "ideas-man" only: "His gift was idea-origination and, in occasional moments of calm, idea-valuation, a valuation usually achieved, like most of his functioning, by instinct."[34]

The editing of the magazine consisted largely of screening the one most practical idea out of the hundred that McClure suggested and then seeing that this idea was thoroughly researched and ably presented. McClure could trust John Phillips to see that this was done. The difference between *McClure's* and the more staid periodicals like *Harper's* or the *Atlantic* was that the latter kept their staffs at home and waited for manuscripts to come in. Then they selected the best of the weekly quota of arrivals and paid the usual honorarium of perhaps two hundred dollars. McClure sent out his staff, able people like Steffens, Tarbell, Baker, Will Irwin, George Kibbe Turner, George Kennan, Burton Hendrick, Cather, and many more, to get the stories. Sometimes it took more than one reporter, and McClure did not begrudge spending several thousand dollars for a single article. He put his profits back into the magazine.

Capping the geyser of ideas was a perennial task. McClure told Sullivan: "I get an idea . . . It comes to me in the night. I lie awake until morning. I rush to the office with it—and they throw cold water on it."[35] Whenever McClure was in town, Phillips and Tarbell had to keep the boss from disrupting the office with his ideas. He would, if not prevented, snatch from the magazine an article already in type in order to replace it with an unwritten piece that he thought more

30. Tarbell, *Day's Work*, p. 199.
31. Baker, *American Chronicle*, p. 96.
32. White, *Autobiography*, p. 386.
33. *Willa Cather Living* (New York, 1953), p. 60.
34. Sullivan, *Education*, p. 198.
35. Ibid., p. 194.

interesting. "The staff worked under some natural law of desperation," remembered Sedgwick; "the chief was forever interrupting." There were attempts at self-preservation and schemes constantly were made to circumvent McClure. Since there were no quiet offices, the staff would rent a secret room in a nearby hotel in an effort to finish articles to meet deadlines. Phillips and Tarbell had to get the magazine out according to some reasonable time schedule. Sedgwick concluded: ". . . a week in the McClure office was the precise reversal of the six busy days described in the first chapter of Genesis. It seemed to end in a world without form and void. From order came chaos."[36] Edith Lewis compared working on *McClure's* with "working in a high wind, sometimes of cyclone magnitude."[37]

After leaving the magazine, Willa Cather wrote a story called "Ardessa" about the restless Marcus O'Mally, editor of a "red-hot magazine of protest, which he called 'The Outcry.'" It was a restful time in the office when the editor went to look after his mining interests in Goldfield, Nevada, and everyone could relax and do his thing. Then, Cather writes, "the great men of the staff . . . as contemplative as Buddhas [sat] in their private offices, each meditating upon the particular trust or form of vice confided to his care."[38] So it was when McClure departed for London or San Francisco and left the staff to get out the magazine without his help.

There may have been less difficulty in getting out the magazine on time when McClure was in Europe, but the staff could not have functioned without his irrepressible enthusiasm. Sedgwick, again an articulate witness, rated McClure's enthusiasm as his most important trait. It was a burning force. "He never liked the word 'crusade' but when he went crusading, he might have given points to Peter the Hermit. Everyone about him caught fire and he would inflame the intelligence of his staff into molten excitement. The mood would be too hot to last but would bring results." If anyone complained that some other magazine had already treated the same subject, McClure would only reply: "A story is never told until McClure tells it."[39] Edith Lewis recalled that McClure's "electric energy keyed the whole office to a high tension which never relaxed so long as he was in the place."[40]

36. Sedgwick, *Happy Profession*, p. 142.
37. Lewis, *Willa Cather Living*, p. 60.
38. *Century*, XCVI (May 1918), 105, 107.
39. Sedgwick, *Happy Profession*, p. 139.
40. Lewis, *Willa Cather Living*, p. 60.

That McClure had an intuitive sense of public taste is documented by all of the witnesses. As we already have noted, Sullivan reports that when McClure could sit still long enough, he could evaluate his ideas intuitively. He evaluated fiction and nonfiction the same way. When he told in his autobiography about buying Conan Doyle's Sherlock Holmes stories, he reported: "I had but one test for a story . . . simply how much the story interested me. I always felt that I judged a story with my solar plexis rather than my brain; my only measure of it was the pull it exerted on something inside of me."[41] Though Conan Doyle was unknown at this time, McClure's instincts were sound. He was equally canny in buying Stevenson, Kipling, Rider Haggard, Anthony Hope Hawkins, Conrad, Jack London, Crane, Tarkington, Cather, and others. His method was to read a story three times within seven days to see if his interest kept up. Willa Cather comments in her story "Ardessa" that "he knew what the West wanted, and it proved to be what everybody secretly wanted."[42] Baker remembers that "McClure's instinct for that which was really alive, timely, interesting, . . . enabled him to pick out many stories and articles by unknown writers which proved unusually successful."[43]

McClure's sound intuition, his buoyant enthusiasm, and his inexhaustible imagination were perhaps enough to make an exciting magazine, but another trait—his insistence on careful, painstaking workmanship—made the periodical an organ of real significance. All of his star reporters recognized and paid tribute to this characteristic. When Baker joined *McClure's*, he found everything different from the haste and superficiality of the newspaper world. He was commissioned on one occasion to write an article on General Leonard Wood, who had distinguished himself in the Spanish-American War. He visited Cuba, Massachusetts, and Washington to gather material and returned to New York full of his subject after five or six weeks of research. All the while he was on salary and expense account, and the cost of the article to McClure was many times the amount magazines usually paid. "What a boon to the writer!" writes Baker. "To be able really to take his time, saturate himself with his subject, assure accuracy . . . and then, above all, to be able to write and rewrite."[44] Ida Tarbell is equally explicit in her memoirs:

41. McClure, *Autobiography*, p. 204.
42. Cather, *Century*, XCVI (May, 1918), p. 105.
43. Baker, *American Chronicle*, p. 94.
44. Ibid.

"He [McClure] did not ask that you produce a great serial in six months. He gave you years if it was necessary. I spent the greater part of five years on 'The History of the Standard Oil Company.' . . . I know of no other editor and no other publisher who has so fully recognized the necessity of generous pay and ample time."[45] Of course, Tarbell wrote other articles while at work on the Standard Oil series, but her time was her own, and the result, in the opinion of Peter Lyon, was "the best-grounded, most careful, most substantial, and most devastating contribution made by the muckrakers to the general enlightenment" of the public.[46] When Willa Cather became a contributing editor to the magazine, McClure sent her to New England for more than a year to rewrite and check the facts in Georgine Milmine's interesting but poorly written life of Mary Baker Eddy. It was McClure's passion for accuracy and careful research that made the magazine what Will Irwin believed to be the first exemplar of a truly national journalism.

McClure in explaining his practices wrote: ". . . no staff writer can produce more than three or four good articles a year. A man spends as much time on an article for *McClure's* as would produce a book."[47] On another occasion, when the Nashville *Banner* implied that an article on hook worm in the South was "yellow" journalism, McClure fired off an indignant letter to the editor. "There never appears a single article or statement in *McClure's* that is not based on the very best authority. This article . . . represented the results of several months of investigation on the part of a member of the staff and several years of investigation on the part of the national government, and of certain Southern boards of health." Further, the article had been reviewed by several outside experts before being printed. He concluded: "The magazine values its reputation for absolute accuracy and authority above all things." Then he offered to send a representative to Nashville to go over all the material with the *Banner's* editor.[48] This letter is fairly typical of McClure's attitude towards his magazine and the quality of its contents.

45. Tarbell, *Day's Work*, p. 258. McClure in *My Autobiography* (p. 245) recalls that the fifteen articles that made up the Standard Oil series "were produced at the rate of about three a year, and cost the magazine about four thousand dollars each." This is somewhat exaggerated, for Tarbell's salary (according to an unpublished manuscript in the McClure papers) was $10,400 a year at that time.

46. Lyon, *Success Story*, p. 210.

47. Undated autobiographical manuscript written about 1910 (McClure papers).

48. S. S. McClure to the editor of the *Banner*, 8 Oct. 1909 (McClure papers).

The variety of its contents also was noteworthy. Besides the liberal quantities of good fiction, already noted, *McClure's* was the sort of magazine that people read from cover to cover. It contained a great deal of Civil War material during the decade of the nineties when the country had an insatiable desire to read about that conflict. Tarbell's Lincoln series was followed by Hamlin Garland on Grant, and later the magazine scored a real coup in getting Carl Schurz to write his memoirs for serialization. Hardly an issue went by that did not carry well-written articles about animals, exploring, mountaineering, and especially railroading, the latter a topic of perennial appeal at the turn of the century. McClure also filled his magazine with illustrations and spent large sums supporting the lavish tastes of his able art editor, August Jaccaci. He exploited brilliantly the popular interest in personalities, publishing all kinds of interviews, profiles, and sketches of interesting people. One series that was especially successful was called "Human Documents," a series of photographs mostly, with modest amounts of accompanying text. McClure led off his first issue with a series called "Real Conversations," in which the novelist H. H. Boyesen interviewed Howells. Later Edward Everett Hale talked to Oliver Wendell Holmes, Robert Barr discussed matters with Conan Doyle, and Garland interviewed James Whitcomb Riley.

McClure's interest in science also produced many absorbing articles and frequent "scoops." The first issue carried Henry Drummond's popular article on "Where Man Got His Ears," and the early volumes contained interviews with Edison and Alexander Graham Bell, which were part of a series that McClure called "The Edge of the Future." McClure was perpetually peering over the edge of the future, and *McClure's* carried the first magazine accounts of both the Wright Brothers' flight and Marconi's wireless transmissions. On another occasion when McClure read in the paper a brief report on Roentgen rays, he dispatched H. J. W. Dam to Würzburg to get a story on this new marvel, and he had an article on this subject in print within three months. Some of Tarbell's first assignments before she returned from Paris were to write about the Mont Blanc observatory and the latest methods of criminal detection developed by the French police.

Although McClure discovered in 1903 that he was leading the muckraking movement, his interest in political and social reform began in the early years of the magazine. Volume IV (December, 1894–May, 1895) carried two articles by Elisha Edwards on Tammany Hall, and these were followed by similar articles in subsequent issues. William Allen White's profile of Senator Thomas Platt, boss of New York State, in 1901 brought threats of a libel suit against the magazine. As early as the first issue of the magazine McClure had published a strong letter from James Parton championing civil service reform. This letter elicited a message of commendation from Theodore Roosevelt: "I wish to congratulate you on behalf of all civil service reformers . . . You have rendered a real service to the cause of good government."[49]

Yet the mix of articles and fiction of *McClure's* first decade was general—interesting stories of a romantic cast, popular science, adventure, human interest—all blended with material on public affairs. The magazine really was a great deal like the best general magazines of the day, *Harper's* and the *Century*—in no way inferior to them in contents but much cheaper. In 1894–1895 while the *Century* was serializing a novel by F. Marion Crawford, *McClure's* was running one by Anthony Hope Hawkins. The former published short fiction by Kipling, Sarah Orne Jewett, Richard Harding Davis, and Kate Chopin, while the latter printed Kipling, Stevenson, Bret Harte, Conan Doyle, and Octave Thanet. The *Century* ran pieces on innoculation for diptheria, women's colleges, flying machines, and published some of Hawthorne's letters and Mrs. Fields's memoirs of Oliver Wendell Holmes. At the same time *McClure's* carried articles on evolution, flying, snake poison and serum, and printed Tarbell's account of French criminal detection, and excellent photographs of the moon's surface from the Lick Observatory. Both magazines were running series on Lincoln and Napoleon.

McClure had the bad luck to begin his magazine at almost the precise moment when the Panic of 1893 struck the United States. The first number appeared in June as banks were closing and businesses were going bankrupt. There were thousands of periodical failures in this sharp financial crisis,[50] but *McClure's* survived its traumatic birth. The pertinacity and singleness of purpose that McClure had displayed earlier in launching the newspaper syndicate again saved him. What he said afterwards about the syndicate was equally true of the

49. Theodore Roosevelt to S. S. McClure, 29 May 1893 (McClure papers); printed in Wilson, *McClure's Magazine*, p. 128.

50. Frank Luther Mott, *A History of American Magazines, 1885–1905* (Cambridge, Mass., 1957), p. 15.

magazine: "It became an obsession with me. Again I was a man of one idea, as I had been when I was determined to get an education, as I had been when I was determined to get my wife."[51] Considering that McClure and John Phillips began the magazine with $7,300, it is a miracle that the venture did not founder during its first few months. Twelve thousand copies of the first issue of 20,000 were returned unsold, and most of the initial capital was gone before the second issue ever appeared. McClure had to pour on the charm and persuasion to raise additional funds that first year, but he managed: $3,000 from Professor Drummond, the popular lecturer on anthropology who had contributed to the first number; $1,000 from Col. Albert Pope, McClure's first employer and bicycle manufacturer as an advance on advertising; $5,000 from the mortgaging of John Phillips's father's house in Galesburg. During the second year Sir Arthur Conan Doyle invested $5,000 in the enterprise at a critical moment, and so it went. By November, 1894, after eighteen months of hand-to-mouth existence, circulation reached 60,000.[52] Then as business was picking up, McClure scored a bulls-eye with the public in Ida Tarbell's "Life of Napoleon" series, which boosted circulation from 40,000 to 100,000. From that time on the magazine kept climbing in circulation and advertising. Tarbell's "Life of Lincoln" the next year sent circulation soaring to 250,000 by December, 1895.

While McClure's initial timing was bad, his general timing was perfect. The age of the cheap magazine was just beginning. The great success of Edward Bok's *Ladies Home Journal* had proved that a ten-cent magazine could build a circulation of over half a million and return handsome profits. McClure priced his magazine at fifteen cents, and once the economy recovered from the Panic, he began tapping a large new potential audience. The older established magazines like *Harper's* or the *Century* cost thirty-five cents and their potential market was limited. When McClure began his magazine, those two periodicals, plus *Scribner's*, *Munsey's*, and the *Cosmopolitan* at twenty-five cents, dominated the field. Their combined circulation, however, was not over 500,000. McClure knew that there was a potential mass market, for he had been reaching a market several times this large with his newspaper syndicate. As soon as McClure

51. McClure, *Autobiography*, p. 166.

52. Circulation figures come from the McClure papers, but there is a great deal of information on this topic in both Lyon and Wilson.

began publishing, both the *Cosmopolitan* and *Munsey's* cut their prices to meet the competition, and all of them prospered.

The success of the cheap magazines owed a great deal to the advances in printing technology that were taking place in the early nineties. The invention of the photoengraving technique known as the halftone introduced a cheap process for illustrations, and it became feasible to publish a copiously illustrated magazine at a fraction of the former cost. Where the *Century* had spent as much as $5,000 per issue on woodcuts alone in the previous decade, McClure could in the nineties publish an entire issue for less.

Without advertising, however, the cheap magazine could not have existed, and the development of the modern advertising industry dates from this period. Magazines like *McClure's* provided the possibility of national advertising and national markets, and the advertising agency was a natural growth. By December, 1895, *McClure's* was setting records for the number of pages of advertising it carried, and a decade later it was averaging 165 pages of advertising per month at $400 per page. *Printer's Ink* declared that in the years 1895–1899 *McClure's* carried the greatest quantity of advertising of any magazine in the world,[53] and in April, 1905, the magazine's advertising income was larger than it ever had been before.[54] Several other magazines did almost as well.

H. L. Mencken with his characteristic wit, vigor, and wrongheadedness later accused McClure of displacing such splendid general magazines as the *Century* with yellow magazine journalism: "What McClure—a shrewd literary bagman—did was to apply the sensational methods of the cheap newspaper to a new and cheap magazine. Yellow journalism was rising and he went in on the tide."[55] Although these remarks were made many years later in 1919, from the beginning there were viewers with alarm. When *McClure's* and the *Cosmopolitan* reduced their price to ten cents in July, 1895, the New York *Independent* commented editorially that the effect on magazines like the *Century* and *Harper's* was hard to foresee but that they probably would "wish to maintain that higher, purer, literary standard which succeeds in securing the best but not the most numerous readers."[56] McClure answered this comment with a lively editorial

53. Mott, *History of American Magazines*, p. 597.
54. J. S. Phillips to S. S. McClure, 22 Mar. 1905 (McClure papers).
55. *Prejudices: First Series* (New York, 1919), p. 175.
56. Reprinted in *McClure's*, V (Aug., 1895), 287.

the following month. The editor of the *Independent,* he thought, must be pulling someone's leg, and then he went on to list more than three dozen of the most prominent contemporary writers whose work had appeared in *McClure's* since it began twenty-six issues before. These included Stevenson, Kipling, Howells, Sara Orne Jewett, Herbert Spencer, Conan Doyle, William Gladstone, Anthony Hope Hawkins, Joel Chandler Harris, Hamlin Garland, Henry M. Stanley, Sir Walter Besant, J. M. Barrie, and Charles A. Dana.[57]

As we have noted, the magazine reached a circulation of 300,000 early in 1896, and its subscription list continued to grow. In the same year *McClure's* acquired its own printing plant, which cut costs and improved considerably the technical excellence of the magazine. For the rest of the century its progress was an uninterrupted success story. Then in 1902 McClure discovered that he was leading the muckraking movement, and in the often-reprinted editorial appearing in the January, 1903, issue he noted that there were appearing simultaneously an article by Lincoln Steffens on "The Shame of Minneapolis," a chapter from Ida Tarbell's series on the Standard Oil Company, and a piece by Ray Stannard Baker, "The Right to Work," on racketeering in the labor movement. "We did not plan it so," wrote McClure; "it is a coincidence that the January *McClure's* is such an arraignment of American character as should make every one of us stop and think." And he added that all of the above-named articles could have been called "The American Contempt for Law": "Capitalists, workingmen, politicians, citizens—all breaking the law or letting it be broken. Who is left to uphold it? . . . There is no one left: none but all of us. . . . We have to pay in the end, every one of us. And in the end the sum total of the debt will be our liberty." Thus the muckraking movement was under way in earnest, and the part *McClure's* played in the exposures of graft and corruption in the decade before World War I is a well-known story.[58]

While the muckraking movement was going full blast, a revolution overtook the magazine. John Phillips, Ida Tarbell, Lincoln Steffens, and Ray Stannard Baker all left McClure in 1906 and started

57. Ibid.

58. See C. C. Regier, *The Era of the Muckrakers* (Gloucester, Mass., 1957; originally published in 1932); Louis Filler, *Crusaders for American Liberalism* (Yellow Springs, Ohio, 1950; originally published in 1939); Wilson, *McClure's Magazine.* Filler reproduces (p. 84) the famous editorial from the January, 1903, issue of *McClure's.*

their own periodical. There isn't space here to recount the story of this celebrated shake-up, but it is fully told in Lyon's biography of McClure and Wilson's study of the magazine. Also it is dealt with in some detail in Tarbell's autobiography and of course in the McClure and Phillips Papers. Sometime before the split, McClure decided to launch a new magazine, and neither Phillips nor Tarbell could talk him out of it. As he went ahead planning a grandiose new project, it seemed to his associates that he was designing a sure plan for bankruptcy. As the scheme grew, it came to include a People's University and a textbook publishing business, a People's Life Insurance Company, and a People's Bank. McClure apparently believed that his career had been based on surmounting impossible obstacles, and nothing could convince him that he ought not to proceed with these new enterprises. Finally Phillips and Tarbell presented McClure with an ultimatum: either he buy them out or they would buy him out. They could not go on working for the magazine unless they could control their lives. The outcome was that McClure bought them out and they departed.

The break between McClure and his old associates was full of drama and pathos. Phillips and McClure had been together since they edited the *Knox* [College] *Student* a quarter of a century before. Then as later Phillips had been the ballast and anchor for the fast-moving McClure. Ida Tarbell too had been his indispensable co-worker for thirteen years. Both Phillips and Tarbell tried energetically to stop their friend's folly but without success. Phillips attributed McClure's abberations to ill health, and indeed McClure had been away from the office a great deal in previous years on doctors' orders. Phillips wrote him affectionately in January, several months before the break, that McClure simply must obey his doctor and slow down. Tarbell kept a journal during this period in which she recorded her agonized reactions to the inevitable rupture. When it was all over and he realized what had happened, the break was traumatic for McClure too. Writing to Robert Mather in April about Phillips and Tarbell, McClure said: "I am certain that it is not in my power to reward them for their services, which were such as no money could pay for. They leave me retaining my deepest love and affection and esteem and confidence. I think I may say it is the greatest tragedy thus far of my life to lose them."[59]

59. S. S. McClure to Robert Mather, 14 April 1906 (McClure papers).

McClure bounded back after this great split, however, and even before the exodus, began putting together another staff. It was then that he hired Willa Cather. He also hired in rapid succession Perceval Gibbon, George Kibbe Turner, Henry Kitchell Webster, Will Irwin, Ellery Sedgwick, George Kennan, and Cameron Mackenzie. Witter Bynner, then the office boy, stayed on with McClure and so did Viola Roseboro', his accomplished chief manuscript reader, who started off the new era by discovering Damon Runyon. Most of the new people McClure hired did not stay very long, as they found McClure too volatile a genius to work for. Will Irwin later recalled his short tenure on the magazine: "As a curb on genius I was not a success."[60] Willa Cather lasted longer than anyone, until 1911, and did not leave until about the time McClure himself was forced out of the control of his magazine. From 1908 on she served as managing editor and got along with McClure perfectly. It was a frustrating existence for her, however, as she was cut out to be a creative writer and not a magazine executive. McClure had a sort of hypnotic influence on her and very nearly succeeded in making another Ida Tarbell out of her. She was worn to a nub when she finally made the break, and in sum her experience on the magazine cost her six years' delay in getting on with her literary career.

McClure's continued to sell briskly during the era from 1906 to 1912, but viewed in retrospect one can see that the magazine was running on earlier momentum. Yet the circulation continued to climb modestly, and the issue of June, 1910, was the largest in the magazine's history.[61] Two years later the circulation was 450,000, but the end for McClure was only a matter of time. Without the talents of John Phillips, McClure could not survive indefinitely. He could generate the ideas for articles, he could buy good fiction, but he could not fend off the predators from the capitalistic jungles. Editorial brilliancy and innovation ultimately succumbed to the exigencies of the counting house.

In the first place, buying out Phillips and Tarbell started the new

60. Irwin, *Making of a Reporter*, p. 137.

61. Woodress, *Willa Cather*, p. 136. The figure, while not stated, was certainly under 500,000. N. W. Ayer and Son's *American Newspaper Annual and Directory* gives the circulation for 1910 as 425,000 and for 1912 as 450,000. The magazine customarily printed many more copies than were sold so that the print orders probably averaged 100,000 more than Ayer's *Directory* was willing to accept. When *McClure's* had a circulation of 425,000, *Munsey's* had 500,000. The *American Magazine*, under Phillips and Tarbell, did not reach 275,000 until 1912.

era with a large debt, and within two years McClure found himself saddled with an unscrupulous partner whom he had naively allowed to buy into the business. In order to oust this partner, McClure had to reorganize and borrow money at a ruinous interest rate of sixteen percent, and by 1911 still another financial reorganization was needed despite the flourishing circulation of the magazine. To get new capital McClure finally signed a contract for the lease of his magazine with an option to buy. The contract provided that he was to be retained as editor-in-chief, but as Curtis Brady, the business manager, said later: "What was going to happen . . . was so clear a blind man could have felt it with his cane."[62]

At that point both Brady and Willa Cather, his managing editor, retired from their positions, and the following year McClure was ousted completely. Even when he was being thrown out after twenty years of brilliant editorship, McClure could not believe it was happening or could happen. He was always the incurable optimist. In the financial crisis of 1908, for example, when Mary Bisland, head of his London office, was writing that she had only twelve pounds in the bank and owed authors some 1,500 pounds, McClure was writing an old friend that things were coming along well except for "gross blunders in the diversion and squandering of money." The magazine was never so popular or profitable, he added.[63] Yet it is a fact that the last year that *McClure's* made a profit was 1905, the year before the departure of Phillips, Tarbell, Steffens, and Baker.[64]

McClure was only fifty-five at the time he lost his magazine, but the rest of his career is all anti-climax. First he promoted the work of Maria Montessori in the United States; then during World War I he got involved in editing the New York *Evening Mail*, which was owned by a pro-German capitalist. For several years in the early twenties he once again became editor of *McClure's*, but his financial backers were penny-pinchers, he was a has-been, and the magazine eventually was sold to Hearst in 1926. It then became *McClure's: the Magazine of Romance*, "a sordid and vulgar thing, filled with leering fiction fit to be read only by adolescents behind the barn."[65] It ended in 1929 as "the greatest mess of shrieking type and bad illustration"

62. Lyon, *Success Story*, p. 335.
63. Mary Bisland to S. S. McClure, 26 Mar. 1908; S. S. McClure to M. M. Bennett, 13 Mar. 1908 (McClure papers).
64. Wilson, *McClure's Magazine*, p. 191.
65. Lyon, *Success Story*, p. 399f.

on the newsstands[66] after a brief ownership by the publisher of *Photoplay*, who rechristened it *The New McClure's—A Man's Magazine.* In the late twenties McClure went to Italy where he developed a rather notorious enthusiasm for Mussolini and fascism, but after his wife died in 1929 he lapsed into obscurity. He ended his career a lonely old man living in a room in the old Murray Hill Hotel. He spent his days surrounded by piles of clippings and letters in a corner of the Union League Club's library where he worked endlessly over a never-finished manuscript, "The Science of Human Self-Organization." When he died in 1949 at the age of ninety-two, he already was a ghost out of the American past and already a character in the published political and social histories of the United States.

66. Mott, *History of American Magazines*, p. 607.

Donald Pizer

A Summer at Maumee: Theodore Dreiser Writes Four Stories

As part of his campaign against the forces of American puritanism, H. L. Mencken undertook in early 1916 to write a long essay in defense of Theodore Dreiser. Mencken had known Dreiser since 1908, but he was uncertain about the facts of Dreiser's early career and therefore wrote him in May, 1916, requesting pertinent background information for use in his essay. Dreiser's reply is an important autobiographical document. Although he was later to publish two lengthy autobiographies—*A Book About Myself* (1922) and *Dawn* (1931)—these accounts close with the winter of 1894–95, when Dreiser gave up newspaper work. He never wrote the two projected volumes which were to cover the remainder of his career—*Literary Apprenticeship* and *Literary Experiences*—and thus the period between early 1895 and 1907 (when he became editor of the prominent *Delineator*) is especially misty.

In his letter of May 13, 1916, to Mencken, Dreiser briefly sketched his years as a newspaperman and free-lance magazine writer during the 1890's. He then went on to describe his beginnings as a writer of fiction:

> It was he [Arthur Henry] who persuaded me to write my first short story. This is literally true. He nagged until I did, saying he saw short stories in me. I wrote one finally, sitting in the same room with him in a house on the Maumee River, at Maumee, Ohio, outside Toledo. This was in the summer of 1898 [1899]. And after every paragraph I blushed for my folly—it seemed so asinine. He insisted on my going on—that it was good—and I thought he was kidding me, that it was rotten, but that he wanted to let me down easy. Finally, HE took [it], had it typewritten and sent it to *Ainslee's*. They sent me a check for $75. Thus I began.
>
> The above is exact and sacredly true.
>
> Later he began to ding-dong about a novel. I must write a novel, I must

write a novel. By then I had written four short stories or five, and sold them all:

1. "Of the Shining Slave Makers"
2. "The Door of the Butcher Rogaum"
3. "The World and the Bubble"
4. "Nigger Jeff"
5. "When the Old Century Was New"[1]

It is necessary, first of all, to say something about Arthur Henry, the now obscure writer who played such an important role at this turning point in Dreiser's life. The two men had met and had taken an instant liking to each other in March, 1894, when Henry was city editor of the *Toledo Blade* and Dreiser worked briefly for that newspaper. They saw each other occasionally in New York between 1895 and 1899 while Dreiser edited the magazine *Ev'ry Month* and then established himself as a magazine writer, but they began the most intimate phase of their friendship in mid-1899. Henry and his wife Maude owned a large house on the Maumee River. In the summer of 1899, Henry invited Dreiser and his wife Sallie to spend the summer at Maumee. Henry and Dreiser would write and rusticate, and the two women would do the housekeeping.

Despite his avowal of exactness to Mencken, Dreiser's memory played him false in his recollection that the visit to Maumee occurred in the summer of 1898 (there is no doubt that it was 1899) and that his work of the summer represented his first efforts at fiction. He had written, though not published, several stories during the winter of 1894–95,[2] and he had published at least one fictional sketch in *Ev'ry Month*.[3] Moreover, he had sold none, not all, of his Maumee stories by the time he began to write *Sister Carrie* in October, 1899. Dreiser's correspondence at the University of Pennsylvania Library reveals that both *Harper's Monthly* and the *Century* declined "The Shining Slave Makers," for example,[4] and that "Nigger Jeff" was not accepted by *Ainslee's* until the summer of 1900.[5] Indeed, because of

1. *Letters of Theodore Dreiser*, ed. Robert H. Elias (Philadelphia, 1959), I, 212–213. As Elias notes, "The World and the Bubble" has never been identified. It is perhaps an unpublished story which is no longer extant. Mencken's essay is in his *A Book of Prefaces* (1917).

2. See Donald Pizer, "Theodore Dreiser's 'Nigger Jeff': The Development of an Aesthetic," *American Literature*, XLI (Nov., 1969), 332, n. 4.

3. Theodore Dreiser, "Forgotten," *Ev'ry Month*, II (Aug., 1896), 16–17.

4. W. A. Swanberg, *Dreiser* (New York, 1965), p. 84.

5. Arthur Henry to Theodore Dreiser, [August, 1900], in the University of Pennsylvania Library.

these and other rejections and because of the usual delay between acceptance and publication, the four stories were not published until 1901, from one-and-a-half to two-and-a-half years after their composition. Their original titles and the journals in which they appeared are: "When the Old Century Was New," *Pearson's*, XI (January, 1901), 131–40; "The Shining Slave Makers," *Ainslee's*, VII (June, 1901), 445–50; "Nigger Jeff," *Ainslee's*, VIII (November, 1901), 366–75; "Butcher Rogaum's Door," *Reedy's Mirror*, XI (December 12, 1901), 15–17.

The relationship between each story and the magazine in which it appeared is of some interest and importance. *Pearson's* and *Ainslee's* were among the many new ten-cent monthlies which had sprung up in the mid and late 1890's after the great success of *McClure's* and *Munsey's*.[6] During his years as a free-lancer, from 1897 to 1899, Dreiser had contributed the bulk of his articles to journals of this kind, articles about famous people, well-known places, and current events which were simply written, fully illustrated, and brief. *Pearson's* and *Ainslee's* were magazines which depended on mass circulation for their appeal to advertizers and were therefore equally dependent on mass taste in their choice of material for publication. It is not surprising to find "When the Old Century Was New" in *Pearson's*, since the story is in the manner of the light historical romance then much in vogue. It *is* surprising, however, to find "The Shining Slave Makers" and "Nigger Jeff" in *Ainslee's*. The raw violence of both stories, as well as the subject matter of rape in the second, was not the typical fare of *Ainslee's*. The stories were published in the magazine despite their anomalous contents because of Dreiser's special relationship with the journal. He was a close friend of Richard Duffy, one of its editors, and had published regularly in it since its initial issue in March, 1898. Indeed, he occasionally designated himself a "consulting editor" of the magazine.[7] *Reedy's Mirror*, in which "Butcher Rogaum's Door" appeared, represents another phenomenon of turn-of-the-century magazine publishing—the radical journal, often dominated by a single personality, with a small but permanent audience. William Marion Reedy, who was later to discover Edgar Lee Masters, published what he liked, and he particularly liked writing which

6. See Frank L. Mott, *A History of American Magazines, 1885–1905* (Cambridge, Mass., 1957).

7. Swanberg, p. 76.

challenged conventional taboos and ideas.[8] The theme of "Butcher Rogaum's Door" is hardly radical, but one of its scenes is in a whorehouse and a principal character is a prostitute. This was strong stuff for the magazine world of 1900, and it is no wonder that Dreiser was reduced to publishing the story in a relatively obscure and poorly paying weekly.

Dreiser's experience in placing his four stories is a paradigm of his career as a magazine writer. He could always publish popular material in popular journals, and was to do so without hesitation for over forty years in order to keep the pot boiling.[9] But in order to publish work which represented his essential interests and beliefs, he required either a close relationship with an editor (as with H. L. Mencken during the years he edited *Smart Set*) or a radical journal of limited circulation (as with the Socialist *New York Call* from 1913 to 1921 and with many left-wing magazines and newspapers during the 1930's).

Dreiser's Maumee stories are uneven in quality, ranging from the almost worthless "When the Old Century Was New" to the powerful "Nigger Jeff.' But they are important as a group because they reveal a no longer youthful Dreiser (he was 28 on August 27, 1899) working with subject matter, themes, and techniques which were to reappear as major characteristics of his best work for the remainder of his career. It is this aspect of the four stories—their usefulness in clarifying and isolating significant elements in Dreiser's novels—that I would like to explore at some length.

I should note, however, that I am going to discuss the four stories which Dreiser published in 1901 and not the revised versions which appear in *Free and Other Stories* (1918). He revised "When the Old Century Was New" only slightly, but he made major changes—almost all additions—in the other three stories. Some of these additions merely make more explicit themes already present in the original version of the story, but others—particularly in "The Shining Slave Makers" and "Nigger Jeff"—move the stories in the direction of Dreiser's philosophical speculations in *Hey Rub-a-Dub-Dub* (1920). Dreiser's 1918 revisions are of course of great interest, but since my concern at this time is with the Dreiser of 1899, I will disregard them in this essay.

8. See Max Putzel, *The Man in the Mirror: William Marion Reedy and His Magazine* (Cambridge, Mass., 1963).

9. See my "The Publications of Theodore Dreiser: A Checklist," *Proof: The Yearbook of American Bibliographical and Textual Studies*, I (1971), 247–292.

"When the Old Century Was New" is set in the Manhattan of 1801. We follow William Walton, a prosperous young merchant, as he engages in the activities of a day, a day which closes with his successful proposal of marriage to a young belle of the town. The story is basically a version of historical romance. Dreiser gives much attention to specific historical figures, places, and events of early nineteenth-century New York, and the whole is knit together by a light love plot. "The Shining Slave Makers" is in the form of a dream vision. McEwen has taken refuge from the heat and turmoil of the city in a park. He discovers a group of ants at his feet, and as he studies their activities he finds himself transformed into a member of the Shining Slave Makers, one of the warring tribes he has been watching. He joins in their quest for food and in their battles, and is at last mortally wounded. As he is about to die, he is again in the park, gazing at armies of warring ants. "Nigger Jeff" is primarily an initiation story. A lighthearted young St. Louis newspaperman is sent to a rural village to investigate reports that a Negro who has attacked a white girl may be lynched. In pursuit of his story, he follows a mob and observes the capture and hanging of the terrified Negro. The next day he visits the home of the Negro and encounters his grief-stricken mother. The reporter now senses the tragic nature of the events he has been observing and determines that he will try to embody this quality in his story. "Butcher Rogaum's Door" is in part a New York City local color story. Rogaum, a German-American Bleecker Street butcher, attempts to rule his family with an iron hand. His young daughter, Theresa, rebels by staying out late with her beau, and Rogaum locks her out for the night. Both Theresa and Rogaum soon regret their actions. She is frightened of her boy friend's intentions and Rogaum begins to worry. He is particularly terrified when he discovers a dying young prostitute on his doorstep and momentarily mistakes her for his daughter. But Theresa is found by the police before any harm comes to her, and she and her family are reunited.

Despite the fact that each of the four stories can be placed in a distinctive genre of short fiction, all rely on one of two kinds of subject matter. "When the Old Century Was New" and "The Shining Slave Makers" depend heavily on research. The Dreiser of 1899 who had written articles on "Japanese Home Life"[10] and "Electricity in the

10. *Demorest's*, XXXV (April, 1899), 123–125.

Household"[11] could also turn to historical accounts of New York and to scientific treatises on ant life for his new ventures in fiction. Indeed, Dreiser was incensed when an editorial assistant of the *Century* questioned the accuracy of his material in "The Shining Slave Makers" and cited Sir John Lubbock's *Ants, Bees and Wasps* as his source.[12] "Nigger Jeff" and "Butcher Rogaum's Door" derive primarily from personal experience. Dreiser himself had reported a rural lynching in 1893 while a St. Louis newspaperman,[13] and he was familiar with lower Manhattan street life as a resident of the area since late 1894. But both stories are also autobiographical in a more significant sense. It was Dreiser himself who had begun to realize the tragic nature of life when, as a reporter, he had constantly encountered the consequences of human inadequacy. And it was Dreiser who had observed in his own family the clash between thick-skulled parental authoritarianism and rebellious youth eager for life.

These two kinds of material—research and personal experience—were to be Dreiser's principal resources as a novelist. Sometimes the research element is paramount, as in the Cowperwood trilogy, with its detailed and thinly veiled accounts of Philadelphia and Chicago business and political history. In other works autobiography is the major source, as in Dreiser's close use of his family in *Jennie Gerhardt* and of his own marriage in *The "Genius."* His best novels are a skillful blend of the two. In *Sister Carrie* and *An American Tragedy* a solid base of historical detail is lent emotional power by Dreiser's projection of his own experiences and longings into his major figures.

"The Shining Slave Makers" contains a theme frequently associated with Dreiser—that life is a struggle for existence. McEwen's initial responses to ant life, after he discovers that he has become a Shining Slave Maker, are still human. He expects other ants to share food with him and has a sympathetic awareness of the victims of war. But he quickly adapts to a life of continuous combat and becomes a merciless and prodigious warrior. When he awakens at the end of the story, he views the struggling ants at his feet with "sorrow" and "a vague, sad something out of far-off things"[14]—that is, with a sense of loss rather than of relief at his escape from life as an ant. McEwen

11. *Demorest's*, XXXV (Jan., 1899) 38–39.
12. Dreiser to Robert Underwood Johnson, January 9, 1900; *Letters*, I, 45–46.
13. See Pizer, "Theodore Dreiser's 'Nigger Jeff'," p. 331, n. 2.
14. *Ainslee's*, VII, 450.

has thus discovered not only the Darwinian truth that man retains powerful vestiges of his animal past and that these vestiges surface readily when needed but also that a life of animal combat can be pleasurable despite its dangers and destructiveness. McEwen had quickly accepted the ethic of tribal loyalty which controls ant life and had focused his loyalty on a particular warrior ant, Ermi, from whom he is soon inseparable. Moreover, he had "reveled" in the sport of pillaging and killing and had developed a "lust" for warfare.[15] The truth of human experience which Dreiser is attempting to capture in these "positive" characteristics of McEwen's dream vision is that struggle lends life its color and excitement and drama and that human relationships can be emotionally satisfying and therefore covertly and obliquely "moral" despite the cosmic amorality in which they exist.

Dreiser was always enthralled by the extreme consequences of the struggle for existence in human affairs—a titanic Cowperwood at one end, a fallen Hurstwood at the other—and only toward the close of his career did he stress that such consequences were the product of remediable social injustice. In the major portion of his career, as in the Cowperwood trilogy, the theme of "The Shining Slave Makers" is expressed with little reservation. For Frank Cowperwood, life is a battle for power and beauty, and he is ruthless in his efforts to gain these goals. As in his portrait of McEwen the Slave Maker, Dreiser neither condemns Cowperwood nor is he sympathetic toward his victims. A similar ethic pervades both the story and the trilogy: life is a struggle, but the excitement of battle and the rewards of victory are well worth the hazards of combat.

Within the struggle for survival in "The Shining Slave Makers," the relationship between McEwen and Ermi is in one sense merely an illustration of the mechanistic power of tribal loyalty to bind members of the tribe into an effective destructive force. But the relationship is also one of sympathy and unselfishness and thus has the emotional coloration of a "good" which is good for reasons other than tribal. Like many writers of his time, Dreiser found that the image of social life as a struggle for existence was apt and convincing. But he also acknowledged that his mother's all-embracing love had been a powerful force in the midst of the poverty and hardship that was his youth, and he had recently discovered within the cut-throat competitive world of New York journalism a fully satisfying friendship with

15. Ibid., p. 449.

Arthur Henry. From his earliest *Ev'ry Month* editorials of 1895 to his death in 1945, Dreiser argued that experience was chaotic, directionless, and valueless. At the same time, though in varying ways and degrees of emphasis, he dramatized that it had both meaning and value.

Dreiser was also absorbed throughout his career by the themes of the power of sex and the pull of family loyalty. In "Nigger Jeff" it is the first flush of spring and Jeff, a poor, ignorant Negro, attacks a white girl—a girl who knows him and whom he meets in a lane. " 'Before God, boss, I didn't mean to . . . . I didn't go to do it,' " Jeff cries to the mob.[16] Although sexual desire may not lead to the destruction of a Cowperwood, it is nevertheless a dominant, uncontrollable force in almost all of Dreiser's principal male characters. Hurstwood, Lester Kane, Eugene Witla, and Clyde Griffiths are at its mercy. A force of equal strength in "Nigger Jeff" is that of family love and loyalty. Jeff returning to say good-bye to his mother despite the certainty of capture by the sheriff; the mother mourning over the body of her dead son; the attacked girl's father intent on vengeance—moments such as these reappear as major motifs in Dreiser's later novels. For it is the strength of family love which binds the Gerhardts together, which is the final refuge of Clyde Griffiths, and which creates the tragic tension of Solon Barnes's loss of his children.

Dreiser often combined the theme of sexual attraction and that of the lure of the city. The budding Theresa, in "Butcher Rogaum's Door," "loved to walk up and down the . . . street, where there were voices and laughter, and occasionally moonlight streaming down."[17] Her street is of course a commonplace working class thoroughfare, but to Theresa—because of her powerful desire to experience "life"—it is a place of romance and beauty. In Theresa, Dreiser begins to sketch one of his great themes—the power of the youthful, questing imagination to create the beautiful and desirable out of the tawdry and cheap. So Carrie and Clyde find in Chicago and Kansas City an Arabian Nights wonderland, a world of excitement and beauty which is primarily the product of their need for the exciting and beautiful. Dreiser's success in rendering this theme arises from his ability to dramatize both the objective and subjective reality of the city—the superficial glamour of a Green-Davidson Hotel and Clyde's wide-eyed responsiveness to its superficiality. Dreiser's tone at such mo-

16. *Ainslee's*, VIII, 372.

17. *Reedy's Mirror*, p. 15.

ments is one of sympathetic wonder at the strength of the human quest for beauty and of compassionate recognition that the flawed understanding of the seeker and the limitations of his world will cause him to mistake the tinsel for the beautiful and desirable.

In Dreiser's best novels, the themes of the power of sex and the lure of the beautiful move toward tragic statement. Hurstwood and Carrie are tragic figures, the first reaching out for life in the form of Carrie but unable to hold what he has won, the second desiring and gaining the beautiful but discovering that once gained it is no longer desirable or beautiful. These two major kinds of human desire, the sexual and the aesthetic, appear in a single character in the only work of fiction which Dreiser explicitly called a tragedy. The tragedy of Clyde Griffiths is that of the seeker of sex and beauty who is destroyed by weaknesses within himself and his society as he attempts to fulfill his quest. To Dreiser, tragedy arises out of the reality of human desire. This reality does not lend nobility to his characters. Like Clyde or Jeff, they are often weak and contemptible. But their capacity to feel combined with their incapacity to act wisely or well is to Dreiser the very stuff of man's tragic nature and thus gives meaning and poignancy to their fate whatever their class or condition.

Despite the superficiality of "When the Old Century Was New," it too anticipates one of Dreiser's major themes. The story dramatizes the thesis that life is both permanent and impermanent, both solid and dream-like. The New York of 1801 is the capital of the country, Wall Street is only semi-urban, and the Bowery is completely rural. Moreover, by setting the story exactly 100 years before its publication date Dreiser enforces the moral that the New York of 1901, with its seemingly indestructible solidity, will also someday disappear or be changed. To Dreiser, who was later to write an essay on "Change" as the great principle of life,[18] the theme of impermanence had a twofold implication. For a character of great strength, such as Cowperwood, the theme is worked out on the cosmic scale of the transience of wealth and power. More often, however, the theme takes the complementary form of the reality of dreams in relation to the transience of the material. For Dreiser's questing characters—Carrie, Jennie, Eugene, and Clyde—the material world has great importance but the permanent in their lives is nevertheless their unending quest for beauty or love, a quest which is both intangible and changeless.

18. *Pagan*, I (Sept., 1916), 27–28; republished in *Hey Rub-a-Dub-Dub* (1920).

Thus, Dreiser's early stories, despite their frequent thinness—the fluff of "When the Old Century Was New," the melodrama of "Butcher Rogaum's Door," the hackneyed dream-vision frame of "The Shining Slave Makers"—begin to sound the notes that appear in more full-bodied form in his novels. In Dreiser's major novels, however, no one theme dominates a single work, as in his early stories. Rather, there is a mingling of themes, for in the greater length of the novel Dreiser found a more satisfactory form for the expression of his belief that the principal realities of life are found in interwoven patterns rather than single strands. *An American Tragedy* offers a good example—the struggle for power and survival, the strength of sex and family loyalty, the lure of the city, the unending cycle of a boy seeking pleasure—all are present in varying degrees and constitute in their totality Dreiser's complex yet coherent vision of life.

Dreiser's Maumee stories also reveal characteristics of form and technique which reappear in various guises in his novels. Dreiser's basic tendency as a novelist was to establish a clear central structure (Hurstwood's fall and Carrie's rise; Cowperwood's alternating business and love affairs; Clyde's parallel life in Kansas City and Lycurgus; Solon's double life as a businessman and Quaker), to pursue this structure to its seeming conclusion (death or emotional equilibrium), yet to suggest by means of symbols developed within the narrative (a rocking chair, deep sea fishes, a street scene, a brook) that life is essentially circular, that it moves in endless repetitive patterns. His early stories anticipate this tendency without achieving it fully in any one instance, with "The Shining Slave Makers" and "When the Old Century Was New" offering the best examples. "The Shining Slave Makers" has a single important character relationship, that of McEwen and Ermi; its "inner" time scheme is complete in that it comprises McEwen's life as an ant; and it has a circular form imposed upon it by its dream allegory structure of awake-dream-awake. "When the Old Century Was New" is in form the Cowperwood trilogy in miniature. We follow Walton during a day's activities of love and business, with the circularity motif introduced by the implied similarity between 1801 and 1901.

Another pervasive structure in Dreiser's novels is best illustrated by "Butcher Rogaum's Door." The three principal figures in the story—Rogaum, Theresa, and Almerting—can be characterized as a well-meaning but ignorant and authoritarian parent; a girl seeking the wonder and excitement of life; and a seducer who takes advantage of the conflict between parent and child. Rogaum, blind to the needs of youth, drives Theresa to rebellion, and she is almost seduced by Almerting. This "triangle" and the narrative which derives from it constitute an "archetypal" structure within the world of Dreiser's novels, though it is a structure which appears in increasingly complex and "displaced" forms. It is present in Carrie's departure from the Hansons' and her seduction by Drouet and Hurstwood, in Clyde's rebellion against his parents and his seduction by the pleasures associated with the Green-Davidson, in Roberta's parallel experience with her parents and Clyde, and in Solon's unworldly authoritarianism, which drives his children into various kinds of worldliness while he himself comes to realize that he too has been seduced by a form of worldliness.

A third significant characteristic of the form of Dreiser's early stories is their tendency toward the parody of sentimental or hackneyed narrative patterns. In "The Shining Slave Makers," the relationship between McEwen and Ermi is an unconscious caricature of the "comrades in arms" motif in the historical romance, complete with a battlefield farewell and death scene. In "Butcher Rogaum's Door," Theresa's adventures are parallel to those of the poor but honest working girl who faces the dangers of the city in sentimental popular fiction. And in "When the Old Century Was New," Walton's experiences among the elite of New York are in the mode of high society romance popularized by Anthony Hope and Richard Harding Davis. Throughout his career as a novelist Dreiser was to rely on similar formulas, particularly those of the "seduced country girl" in *Sister Carrie* and *Jennie Gerhardt*, and the Horatio Alger myth in the Cowperwood trilogy, *The "Genius,"* and *An American Tragedy*. In most instances he both used the myth and reversed some of its principal assumptions. Carrie "rises" not only despite her seduction but because of it, and Clyde finds that he has neither luck nor pluck in his attempt to succeed. Like many major American novelists, Dreiser used the mythic center of American life as a base from which to remold myth into patterns more closely resembling experience as he knew it.

There is at least one important characteristic of Dreiser's technique as a novelist which is scarcely present in his short stories—his reliance on the aesthetic effect of massed, repetitive detail. Hurstwood's decline, Jennie's relationship with Lester Kane, the triangle of Clyde, Roberta, and Sondra—these and many more of Dreiser's most effective fictional situations achieve much of their power from his ability to associate a character's desires, fears, and hopes with the details of concrete social reality and thus, through repetition and accumulation of detail, to raise the level of fictional intensity. The short story, of course, does not lend itself to this technique, though Dreiser anticipates the later prominence of the technique in his work by his reliance upon a local color background in "Nigger Jeff" and "Butcher Rogaum's Door."

I have been discussing Dreiser's novels as though they comprised a single static moment in his creative life, while obviously there is much difference between the Dreiser of *Sister Carrie* and the Dreiser of *The Bulwark*. Moreover, I have perhaps overreached for some of my analogies between his early stories and his novels, as is perhaps inevitable in a comparative study. Yet despite these limitations, I hope that I have demonstrated that Dreiser's early stories reveal in simplified form many of the themes and techniques of his novels. The summer at Maumee was not only of value to Dreiser but also is still of value to the critic interested in the configuration of his literary imagination.

C. Hugh Holman

Thomas Wolfe, Scribner's Magazine, *and "The Blest* Nouvelle"

Thomas Wolfe's four novels and two volumes of short stories, short novels, and sketches all form the incomplete effort to reproduce one man's experience in America and the world, a twentieth-century equivalent of Whitman's desire "to put *a Person*, a human being (myself, in the latter half of the Nineteenth Century, in America,) freely, fully and truly on record."[1] That Wolfe made this effort, and that he failed, at least in terms of form and structure, are critical truisms. *Look Homeward, Angel* had been cast in the form of a *Bildungsroman*, and it had the natural although loose shape of the novel of development.[2] In the nine years that remained in his career after its publication, he never found an adequate structure for imprisoning and ordering his experience, although he grappled mightily with the problem, projecting vast schemes, borrowing organizational principles from mythology, and attempting to substitute theme or leitmotif for plot and causal development.[3] For him event was seldom as important as the impact of event on his protagonist; the emotion aroused in Eugene Gant or George Webber was as important as the action producing the emotion; hence his willingness to describe, to explain, and also to rhapsodize. The failure to find a satisfactory form for the representation of his protagonist's experiences is, then, a major and overwhelming failure, and one that cannot be explained away

1. "A Backward Glance o'er Travel'd Roads," *Leaves of Grass*, Comprehensive Reader's Edition, ed. H. W. Blodgett and Sculley Bradley (New York, 1965), pp. 573–574.

2. This idea has been discussed by many critics; perhaps its best and most succinct statement is in Richard S. Kennedy, "Wolfe's *Look Homeward, Angel* as a Novel of Development." *South Atlantic Quarterly*, LXIII (Spring, 1964), 218–226.

3. The most detailed examination of these efforts is in Richard S. Kennedy, *The Window of Memory: The Literary Career of Thomas Wolfe* (Chapel Hill, 1962), particularly Parts IV and VII. It is worthy of note, however, that Joseph Warren Beach recognized and described Wolfe's efforts at non-novelistic organization as early as 1940, in *American Fiction, 1920–1940* (New York, 1941), pp. 173–215.

either by his verbal success or the effectiveness of many of his individual scenes.

Even his severest critics have recognized his ability to realize fully and intensely a dramatic scene or situation. Bernard De Voto, perhaps Wolfe's harshest attacker, praised his "ability to realize all three [intuition, understanding, and ecstasy] in character and scene, whose equal it would have been hard to point out anywhere in the fiction of the time. . . . [Such scenes] seemed to exist on both a higher and a deeper level of realization than any of Mr. Wolfe's contemporaries had attained."[4] John Peale Bishop, in an early and brilliant analysis of Wolfe's failure to give objective structure to his work, asserted that "the most striking passages in Wolfe's novels always represent these moments of comprehension. For a moment, but a moment only, there is a sudden release of compassion, when some aspect of suffering and bewildered humanity is seized, when the other's emotion is in a timeless completion known. Then the moment passes, and compassion fails."[5] At the time that this essay was first published, Bishop had no way of being acquainted with the evidence that the manuscripts and the publishing history of Wolfe's work now give us that at least a portion of the responsibility for the fleeting quality of these moments of awareness of others resulted not from how Wolfe originally wrote but how he later fragmented and assembled scenes in making the larger works.

Clearly it was how Wolfe wrote that is one key to the success of his scenes and the weakness of his larger structures. Much has been written about Wolfe's methods, and most of it has been romanticized or has so centered on quantity and frenzy rather than artistry that a seemingly permanent picture of Wolfe as the eternal *naïf* has emerged. In fact, his method seems to have been to deal with individual scenes, characters, actions, or emotions in depth and at length and then later to fit them into the larger composition. One example, which is typical of his method, will illustrate this aspect of his work. The first thing published by Wolfe after *Look Homeward, Angel* was a short novel *A Portrait of Bascom Hawke*, which appeared in *Scribner's Magazine* in April, 1932. It was consciously written as a

4. "Genius is Not Enough," *Forays and Rebuttals* (Boston, 1936), p. 324; originally published in the *Saturday Review of Literature*, April 25, 1936, pp. 3–4, 14–15.

5. "The Sorrows of Thomas Wolfe," *Collected Essays of John Peale Bishop*, ed. Edmund Wilson (New York, 1948), p., 135; originally published in the *Kenyon Review*, I (Winter, 1939), 7–17.

unit,[6] and as late as March, 1934, he thought of it as independent of the "work in progress," *Of Time and the River.*[7] Yet when the novel appeared in 1935, Wolfe had found a place for the episodes of *A Portrait* among the adventures of Eugene Gant. But it is fragmented into eight parts and distributed among Eugene's varied experiences.[8] Before his death thirty-eight stories or sketches by Wolfe had been published in magazines.[9] Of these, twenty reappear as parts of the novels, with portions of a number being in more than one book. The 12,000-word story "The Train and the City," which was published in *Scribner's Magazine* in May, 1933, is distributed among *Of Time and the River, The Web and the Rock,* and *You Can't Go Home Again.*[10] Those not utilized in the novels are reprinted in *From Death to Morning*[11] and *The Hills Beyond.*[12] While it is true that in many cases editors like Maxwell Perkins or agents like Elizabeth Nowell selected from the larger manuscripts episodes sufficiently self-contained to be given separate life, this fact does not invalidate the claim that Wolfe's natural method of writing was in reasonably brief and self-contained units.

Here a case can be made (and I believe should be made) that Maxwell Perkins's insistence that *Look Homeward, Angel* should be followed by a "big book" was injurious to Wolfe's career. He wanted to follow it with a brief novel, *K 19,* which was actually put in production by Scribner's and a salesman's "dummy" containing boards, jacket, and the first signature was prepared before Perkins decided against going ahead with publication.[13] Wolfe wanted them to publish *No Door* as a separate volume and at one time thought that it would appear in the early autumn of 1933.[14] To speculate on the effect such publications might have had on the shape of Wolfe's

6. *The Letters of Thomas Wolfe,* ed. Elizabeth Nowell (New York, 1956), p. 330.

7. *The Letters of Thomas Wolfe to His Mother,* ed. C. Hugh Holman and Sue F. Ross (Chapel Hill, 1968), p. 225.

8. *Of Time and the River* (New York, 1935), pp. 104–111, 116–130, 132, 136–141, 141–150, 177–184, 185–186, and 192.

9. A convenient listing in chronological order of these publications is given in *Letters of Wolfe to His Mother,* pp. xxv–xxviii. Many other magazine publications have appeared since his death.

10. *Of Time and the River,* pp. 407–419; *The Web and the Rock* (New York, 1939), pp. 441–449; *You Can't Go Home Again* (New York, 1940), pp. 3–4.

11. New York, 1935.

12. New York, 1941.

13. A copy of this salesman's dummy is in the Thomas Wolfe Collection in the Pack Memorial Library, Asheville, N. C.

14. *Letters of Wolfe to His Mother,* p. 207.

career, although interesting, is futile. Kennedy is probably correct in his judgment that *K 19* was simply a bad book.[15] However, it is difficult to read *The Story of a Novel* without believing that the agony of struggling over the years to make the "big book" in the face of growing critical skepticism which he describes there was fundamentally injurious to his work.[16] Certainly the effect of this urging by his editor was to center Wolfe's attention on a large work for which he had no clearly defined organizational principle.[17]

Many of the incidents that were the bases of Wolfe's short, separate compositions were incidents that he had witnessed rather than participated in or involved characters other than himself who had fascinated him. In producing them both his natural inclination for the dramatic scene and his considerable experience in writing for the theater helped in the creation of an objective world of great specificity and integrity. When he incorporated these incidents into his novels, they tended to lose their separate integrity and to become a part of the protagonist's experience; hence their value underwent a shift from objective reality to subjective interpretation, and the apparent self-centeredness of the protagonist cast over them an often unpleasant autobiographical light.[18]

The length that seemed most congenial to Wolfe's talents and methods was that of the short novel, if the fairly common definition of 15,000 to 40,000 words is accepted for that form.[19] Eight of Wolfe's magazine publications fall within the short novel limits: *A Portrait*

15. *Window of Memory*, pp. 247–248. He does not put it this bluntly but clearly implies this judgment.

16. *The Story of a Novel* (New York, 1936), pp. 13–17.

17. Perkins probably underestimated Wolfe's lack of self-confidence. See his account of the relationship in his Introduction to *Look Homeward, Angel*, Scribner Library Edition.

18. I have discussed this aspect of Wolfe's work at some length in my introduction to *The Short Novels of Thomas Wolfe*, ed. C. Hugh Holman (New York, 1961), pp. xviii–xx. This volume reprints the magazine versions of *A Portrait of Bascom Hawke, The Web of Earth, No Door, "I Have a Thing to Tell You,"* and *The Party at Jack's.* The introduction and headnotes give the histories of these short novels. It is worthy of note that in *You Can't Go Home Again*, a work with a formal shape with which Wolfe had little to do, the separately published works undergo much less fragmentation, and George Webber is a more shadowy figure than the protagonists in the other novels.

19. Leo Hamalian and Edmond L. Volpe use this length in their collection, *Ten Modern Short Novels* (New York, 1958), p. x. Richard M. Ludwig and Marvin B. Perry, Jr., use the limits of 15,000 to 50,000 in their collection, *Nine Short Novels* (Boston, 1952), p. vii. Edward Weeks uses the limits of 20,00 to 60,000 in his collection, *Great Short Novels* (New York, 1941).

of Bascom Hawke, 32,000 words; *The Web of Earth,* 39,000 words; *Death the Proud Brother,* 22,000 words; *No Door,* 31,000 words; *Boom Town,* 20,000 words; *"I Have a Thing to Tell You",* 21,000 words; *The Party at Jack's,* 20,000 words; and (a borderline case) *The Lost Boy,* 15,000 words. In addition, three of Wolfe's most successful shorter works, "The Train and the City," "The Child by Tiger," and "Chickamauga" are each approximately 12,000 words. Although "Only the Dead Know Brooklyn," "In the Park," and "The Face of the War" are probably Wolfe's only outstanding examples of short stories of the traditional length, Kennedy's statement that "it was almost impossible for him to write a short story" is extreme.[20] If to the works separately published as short novels we add the materials of short novel length which he probably composed as units for the first two novels—the Laura James episode in *Look Homeward, Angel,* and the death of Gant, the picture of Professor Hatcher's drama class, and the portrait of Abraham Jones in *Of Time and the River*—the extent to which materials fell between 15,000 and 40,000 words for him becomes apparent.[21]

The short novel form was remarkably well suited to Wolfe's method of writing. It seems, indeed, to have built into it some of the safeguards that Wolfe's approach to writing made desirable, while at the same time it allowed him some of that expansiveness of attitude which his special concerns made imperative. And just what special qualities or virtues exist for the writer in the short novel that do not exist for him in the short story or the full-length novel? A definitive answer would, of course, chop up the protean form of the short novel and force it to fit the Procrustean bed of the particular critic's special attitudes. Yet it is possible to suggest some of the distinctive qualities of the form.

The short novel, declares Howard Nemerov in the most courageous and persuasive attempt that I know of to get at its essence, is "neither a lengthily written short story nor the refurbished attempt at a novel sent out into the world with its hat clapped on at the eightieth page."[22]

20. *Window of Memory,* p. 243.

21. The materials I am listing here from *Of Time and the River* have also been fragmented, except for the death of Gant. I have reassembled them in the sequences in which they were probably originally written, if they were produced by Wolfe's customary method, in *The Thomas Wolfe Reader,* ed. C. Hugh Holman (New York, 1962).

22. "Like Warp and Woof: Composition and Fate in the Short Novel," *Graduate Journal,* V (Winter, 1963), 375.

Yet it can best be discussed with reference to these two things which it is not.

The strength of the short story lies in its power of concentration. Like a lyric poem it places a premium on preciseness and control, and it demands some sharply realized principle around which its materials are organized. That principle may be quite varied, ranging from the neatness of a well-made plot to the presentation of a single character or the explication of a theme or a symbol to Poe's famed "effect." But in all cases the focusing principle is there, and through its operation the short story shares with the lyric poem the quality of exclusion, of shutting out in order to arrange, concentrate, and unify. But this quality of exclusion and concentration in the short story is bought for a price, that of the showing of a scene in a continuum of action, of the development as opposed to the revelation of character, of the adjudication among conflicting themes or the exploration of complexities of symbol. The short story reveals, discloses, shows a person, an action, a situation as it is at the moment of the story. This revelatory quality in the short story probably was in James Joyce's mind when he called his short stories "epiphanies." An epiphany gives us immediate—and unexpected—access to the heart of a mystery, but it does not show the development of that mystery. It is beautifully suited to showing an event or a person at a special time; but it is poorly equipped to show an event or a person *in* time. It is, perhaps, this inability of the short story to deal with "time in process" that yielded it a generally unfruitful form for Wolfe, whose obsession with time was deep and pervasive.

The novel, on the other hand, is primarily characterized by the quality of expansiveness, of inclusion. As Howard Nemerov suggests, readers "tend to live in novels, and sometimes they live there very comfortably indeed: thus you have descriptions which are nothing but description, thus you have philosophical excursions, set pieces, summaries, double-plot and full orchestration, not to mention that all the chairs are heavily upholstered and even the walls padded."[23] Mr. Nemerov is clearly exaggerating, but the thrust of his remarks is true. The special forte of the novel is not revelation but development, not comment or demonstration but presentation in the fullest possible sense. For this reason we accept and believe in characters and actions in a novel which would be incredible to us if presented in the

23. Ibid., pp. 379–380.

same way in a short story. The novel is remarkably well adapted to the demonstration of the effects of time on character, to seeing the meaning of an incident in terms of the continuum of events within which it exists. Perhaps no other literary medium is as immediately suited to showing the corrosive effects of the passage of time as the novel. The events of a novel picture a growth and they demand—and when they succeed, receive—a concurrent growth in the reader's mind. This evolving process gives a novel a sense of depth in experience and a quality of richness in interpretation that even the finest short story at best can merely suggest, although a few masters of the short story craft have made their suggestions remarkably powerful.

The short novel at its best unites the concentrated focus of the short story with the expansiveness and the scope of the novel. It tends toward the concentration and the unity of the short story, working within more obvious limits more consciously imposed that those of the full-length novel. One of the reasons that Wolfe's short novels took on extra wordage and diffuseness and often were fragmented when they became part of his long novels was that in the longer form they lost some of their artistic and inherent right to the unifying exclusiveness of the short form. Yet within the short novel form, the author has—always within fairly strict limits—the privilege of developing and creating rather than revealing and demonstrating his materials. Henry James had this quality in mind when, in the preface to *The Author of Beltraffio* volume in the New York edition, he characterized the short story as "the concise anecdote" and found it suitable for material where it was possible "to follow it as much as possible from the outer edge in." The short novel, which he called the *nouvelle*, resulted, he thought, from the opposite method of pursuing its subject "from the centre outward." He set the short story against the short novel, of which, he declared, "the subject treated would perhaps seem one demanding 'developments,'" and added, "There is of course neither close nor fixed measure of the reach of a development which in some connexions [the short story] seems almost superfluous and then in others [the short novel] to represent the whole sense of the matter."[24]

Howard Nemerov defined the short novel as well as that impossible

24. *The Art of the Novel: Critical Prefaces by Henry James*, ed. R. P. Blackmur (New York, 1934), pp. 232–233.

task has ever been done: "What are short novels? For the writer who is by habit of mind a novelist, they must represent not simply a compression but a corresponding rhythmic intensification, a more refined criterion of relevance than the one he usually enjoys, an austerity and economy perhaps somewhat compulsive in the intention itself. For the writer who habitually thinks in short stories—a bad habit, by the way—the challenge is probably greater: he will have to learn as never before about the interstices of his action, he will have to think about a fairly large space which must be filled, not with everything (his complaint against the novelist), but with something definite which must be made to yield in a quite explicit way its most reserved and recondite ranges of feeling; he will have to think, for once of design and not merely of plot."[25]

Such terms as "the effect of time on character," "rhythmic intensification," "the interstices of his action," "recondite ranges of feeling," and "design and not merely . . . plot" point to those intrinsic qualities of the short novel that are well adapted to Wolfe's special kinds of creative problems. Although he was skilled at the revelatory vignette —a fact demonstrated repeatedly in his novels and a few times in stories such as "Only the Dead Know Brooklyn"—those characters and actions that were central to his interpretation of experience he saw in relation to the expanding pattern of life. One of the distinctive aspects of his imagination is the tendency to see life as a thing of "becoming." He saw time—"dark time"—as being at the center of the mystery of existence, and its representation on three complex levels as a major philosophical and technical concern. The individual scene or person had little permanent value to him; it had to be put back in time—the complex time which he described as tripartite in *The Story of a Novel*: present chronological time, past time impinging upon, making, and modifying the present, and "time immutable, the time of rivers, mountains, oceans, and the earth; a kind of eternal and unchanging universe of time against which would be projected the transience of man's life, the bitter briefness of his day."[26] Hence the ultimate use he made of the apparently self-contained materials of his

25. "Like Warp and Woof," p. 375.

26. *Story of a Novel*, pp. 51–52. There have been several excellent studies of Wolfe's concept of time: Karin Pfister, *Zeit und Wirklichkeit bei Thomas Wolfe* (Heidelberg, 1954); Louis D. Rubin, Jr., *Thomas Wolfe: The Weather of His Youth* (Baton Rouge, 1955), pp. 28–54; Margaret Church, "Thomas Wolfe: Dark Time," *Time and Reality* (Chapel Hill, 1963), pp. 207–226.

art was to make them portions of the continuum of experience of his protagonist, and thus to strip them of the unity and independence which they enjoyed in their first forms.

Yet the fact remains that one of Wolfe's most effective mediums was the short novel. Such a fact made him by no means unusual among the world's writers of fiction. On the Continent fiction in the intermediate length—what Henry James called "the beautiful and blest *nouvelle*"—enjoyed critical acclaim and reader acceptance. "It was," James asserted, "under the star of the *nouvelle* that, in other languages, a hundred interesting and charming results, such studies on the minor scale as the best of Turgenieff's, of Balzac's, of Maupassant's, of Bourget's, and just lately, in our own tongue, of Kipling's, had been, all economically arrived at . . . ."[27] A host of other distinguished names rush to mind to join James's examples: Goethe, Voltaire, Thomas Mann, Anatole France, Anton Chekhov, André Gide, François Mauriac, Albert Camus, and Franz Kafka. In England and America, on the other hand, as James lamented, "Shades and differences, varieties and styles, the value above all of the idea happily developed, languished, to extinction, under the hard-and-fast rule of the 'from six to eight thousand words.' "[28]

Yet English masters of the form are not hard to find. Perhaps the earliest decisive example is Laurence Sterne's *A Sentimental Journey,* and few school boys will forget such differing short novels as Stevenson's *Dr. Jekyll and Mr. Hyde* and George Eliot's *Silas Marner.* The distinguished work of Joseph Conrad cannot be overlooked—indeed, the *nouvelle* has frequently been called his most agreeable medium, with such works as *The Shadow Line, Typhoon, Youth, Heart of Darkness, The End of the Tether,* and *The Nigger of the Narcissus* cited in proof. Virginia Woolf wrote short novels, as did John Galsworthy, notably in *The Apple Tree* and even in *The Forsyte Saga,* where his use of the *nouvelle* for *Indian Summer of a Forsyte* represents the use of the short novel as an element in a vast work somewhat like Wolfe's use of it in *A Portrait of Bascom Hawke* and *The Party at Jack's.*

Despite the indifference of the public and the purblindness of many critics, the short novel can almost be said to be a natural mode for the American writer. A casual roll-call of American short novels shows its significant place in our literary history. Melville's finest accom-

27. *The Art of the Novel,* p. 220. 28. Ibid.

plishments after *Moby-Dick* are short novels, *Benito Cereno* and *Billy Budd*. Stephen Crane was at his best in this length, as witness *Maggie, A Girl of the Streets* and *The Red Badge of Courage*. Simms, Cooper, and Howells used the short novel, as did Mark Twain in *The Mysterious Stranger* and *The Man That Corrupted Hadleyburg*. Edith Wharton, in such works as *Ethan Frome*, *False Dawn*, and *The Old Maid*, and Willa Cather, in *A Lost Lady* and *My Mortal Enemy*, found the form congenial. John Steinbeck in *Of Mice and Men*, *The Pearl*, and *The Red Pony*, Thornton Wilder, in *The Bridge of San Louis Rey*, Eudora Welty in *The Robber Bridegroom* and *The Ponder Heart*, James Gould Cozzens, in *S.S. "San Pedro"* and *Castaway*, Katherine Anne Porter, in *Pale Horse, Pale Rider* and *Noon Wine*, William Faulkner, in *The Bear* and *Knight's Gambit*, DuBose Heyward, in *Porgy*, and Ernest Hemingway, in *The Old Man and the Sea*, have all employed the short novel effectively and successfully. And such distinguished—and different—craftsmen as Gertrude Stein, Truman Capote, Robert Nathan, and Nathanael West have used it as their characteristic mode of expression.

The American novelist Henry James was also the major American practitioner of the short novel. As Charles G. Hoffman has shown, "The short novel, as a distinct art form, can be said to begin in America with Henry James," for he brought to it "an awareness of its technical possibilities, a consciousness of its ideal balance between development of idea and economy of execution, and the full measure of his craftsmanship."[29] Yet James, whose short novels include such distinguished work as *Madame de Mauves*, *The Aspern Papers*, *The Turn of the Screw*, *Daisy Miller*, *The Lesson of the Master*, and *The Beast in the Jungle*, complained bitterly of "the blank misery of our Anglo-Saxon sense . . . [that] a 'short story' was a 'short story,' and that was the end of it," and sadly pictured the American writer forced to compress a *nouvelle* to a standard length as "the anxious effort of some warden of the insane engaged at a critical moment in making fast a victim's straight-jacket."[30] James found escape from what he called "the rude prescription of brevity at any cost"[31] in the pages of Henry Harland's *Yellow Book*, which gave him freedom as to length

29. *The Short Novels of Henry James* (New York, 1957), p. 123.
30. *The Art of the Novel*, p. 220.
31. Ibid., p. 219.

and thus made it possible for him happily to produce short novels for its pages—a type of writing which he declared to be "foredoomed . . . in more cases than not, to editorial disfavour."[32]

Wolfe, somewhat like Henry James and *The Yellow Book*, was fortunate in having available to him the pages of a magazine interested in the short novel and anxious to give it an audience. That magazine was *Scribner's*, under the editorship of Alfred Dashiell from 1930 to 1936. When he became editor of the magazine, Dashiell began a series of efforts at variety and new forms of reader interest. These included two $5,000 Short Novel Contests, a Life in the United States Narrative Contest, and a series of Scribner's Biographies. The Short Novel Contests and the short novels that grew from it constitute a significant, though minor, chapter in American literary history and a major one in the career of Thomas Wolfe.

In 1930 *Scribner's Magazine* began its first Short Novel Contest, in order, the magazine said, "to provide a market for and to stimulate the writing of the long story (a neglected and highly important literary form)."[33] *Scribner's* was most inconsistent in the name it applied to the genre, using "short novel," "novelette," "long story," and even "long short story" at various times. "[T]here has not been an appropriate name given to the principal piece of fiction appearing in *Scribner's* each month," the editors declared, adding that Wolfe's *A Portrait of Bascom Hawke* "can't be labelled."[34] But they were quite explicit about the purpose of the Short Novel Contests, which were three in number: "to give an opportunity for established writers to function in the field of the long short story, which has been dormant by reason of technical barriers (too long for a short story, too short for a serial, or a novel, etc.)";[35] "to uncover promising new talent";[36] and "to open the field permanently to novels of this length."[37] At another time, they said, "The chief purpose of the contest is to free writing from another commercial limitation."[38]

In their attempts to define the short novel as a genre, the editors were most specific about length—"between 15,000 and 30,000

32. Ibid., pp. 217–220, 268.
33. *Scribner's Magazine*, LXXXVIII (Sept., 1930), 33 of front matter.
34. Ibid., XCI (March, 1932), 1 of front matter.
35. Ibid., LXXXVIII (Dec., 1930), 86 of back matter.
36. Ibid.
37. Ibid., LXXXIX (Feb., 1931), 233.
38. Ibid., XC (Aug., 1931), 19 of front matter.

words."[39] They reported that of the 1,672 manuscripts submitted in the first contest the average length was 25,000 words.[40] When they moved from measurable specifics to attempts to define the form in aesthetic terms, they encountered the common problems of its critics. They spoke of "the excellence of this literary form which seems to us to have so many possibilities."[41] They declared of a short novel by Grace Flandrau, *The Way of Love*: "It is impossible to conceive of this tale in any form but the one in which it now appears. It is not a short story; it is not a novel; it is the long story brought to the heights."[42] They listed as the characteristics of the short novel "adequate space for development of character and situation, combined with precision and solidity of structure" and argued that these qualities made it "intrinsically ideal for magazine publication. Since a signal virtue of this type of writing is its unity, the complete story appears in a single issue."[43] And they were finally reduced to definition by example, citing as distinguished examples of what they meant Edith Wharton's *Ethan Frome,* Conrad's *Youth,* Willa Cather's *A Lost Lady,* de Maupassant's *Boule de Suif,* and Katherine Mansfield's *Prelude.*[44]

Twelve short novels were published in the first contest: *S.S. "San Pedro",* by James Gould Cozzens inaugurated the first contest in the August, 1930, issue. (The judges were to select among short novels published the best at the end of the contest.) *Many Thousands Gone,* by John Peale Bishop followed in September. It was followed by *The Way of Love,* by Grace Flandrau (October, 1930); *Hard Wood,* by W. R. Burnett (November, 1930); *Lesby,* by Elizabeth Willis (December, 1930); *Mortal Man,* by James B. Wharton (January, 1931); *The Fighter,* by Carroll E. Robb (February, 1931). In March, 1931, the decision of the judges was announced; Gilbert Seldes, Malcolm Cowley, and John Hall Wheelock had adjudged John Peale Bishop's *Many Thousands Gone* the winner of the contest.[45] And a noncontest short novel, *The Weigher of Souls,* by André Maurois, in that issue could be viewed by the editors as proof that the contest was "open-

39. Ibid., LXXXVIII (July, 1930), 26 of front matter; XC (Aug., 1931), 18 of front matter.
40. Ibid., LXXXIX (Jan., 1931), 26 of back matter.
41. Ibid., LXXXVIII (Aug., 1930), 25 of back matter.
42. Ibid., LXXXVIII (Oct., 1930), 345.
43. Ibid., XC (Aug., 1931), 18 of front matter.
44. Ibid.
45. Ibid., LXXXIX (March, 1931), 29 of front matter.

[ing] the field permanently to novels of this length."[46] Short novels that merited publication from the first contest continued to be published. *Jacob's Ladder*, by Marjorie Kinnan Rawlings, was in the April, 1931, issue, and was followed by *Behind the Swamp There was a Village*, by Nahum Sabsay (May, 1931); *Guardian Angel*, by Margery Latimer (June, 1931); *Ohio in Her Bones*, by D. V. Carlaw (July, 1931); and *Call It a Day*, written and illustrated by Edward Shenton (August, 1931). With the publication of *Call It a Day* the first contest was completed and a "New $5,000 Prize Contest for Best Short Novel" was announced, to close February 1, 1932, the editors reiterating their concern with establishing not only a market for the short novel but also with helping to lessen the "severe handicap to many writers who functioned best in works of this length."[47]

The new contest got underway with *A New Break*, by Josephine Herbst (September, 1931), followed by *An Affair of the Senses*, by Grace Flandrau (October, 1931); *The Cloud of Witnesses*, by Cornelia Evans Goodhue (November, 1931); and *Mill Girls*, by Sherwood Anderson (January, 1932).

When Thomas Wolfe turned over to Maxwell Perkins the manuscript of *A Portrait of Bascom Hawke* in January, 1932, he had had only one magazine publication, "An Angel on the Porch," in the August, 1929, *Scribner's Magazine*, and this work had been drawn directly out of *Look Homeward, Angel.* Apparently he was oblivious of the Short Novel Contests. Perkins purchased the short novel for $500 and entered it in the contest without Wolfe's knowledge,[48] and it was published in the April, 1932, issue.

Other novels in the second contest were *Her Son*, by Edith Wharton (February, 1932); *Love's a Grown-Up God*, by Arthur Tuckerman (March, 1932); *The Cracked Looking-Glass*, by Katherine Anne Porter (May, 1932); and *The Big Short Trip*, by John Herrman (August, 1932). In August the editors announced that the judges—Burton Rascoe, William Soskin, and Edmund Wilson—had selected *A Portrait of Bascom Hawke* and *The Big Short Trip* as co-winners of the second contest from the nine short novels published in the magazine and drawn from the more than 1,500 entries in the competition.[49]

46. Ibid., LXXXIX (Feb., 1931), 233.
47. Ibid., XC (Aug., 1931), 18 of front matter.
48. *Short Novels of Thomas Wolfe*, p. 3.
49. *Scribner's*, XCII (Aug., 1932), 10 of back matter.

The magazine continued to reap the benefits of its short novel competition. In June, 1932, it had published a *nouvelle* by Grace Flandrau, *The Happiest Time.* In July, 1932, it had published Thomas Wolfe's *The Web of Earth,* which, learning of the contest, he had written frantically for entry. Although he missed the closing date—February 1—*The Web of Earth* was an important bonus both for him and for *Scribner's,* for it is one of his finest pieces of work.[50] When in 1934 Alfred Dashiell, the *Scribner's* editor, collected his favorite stories in *Editor's Choice, The Web of Earth* led the volume and Dashiell commented, "The virtue of the long story is amply demonstrated in 'The Web of Earth.' Reduced to five thousand words... the story would have lost much of its effectiveness. Liberated from the space formula, it becomes the rich story of a life...."[51]

In December, 1932, *Scribner's* published another short novel, *Hill Idyll,* by Emmett Gowen, but with the January, 1933, issue it began publishing its series of *Scribner's* biographies. It returned in the June, 1933, issue to the short novel with *Death the Proud Brother,* by Wolfe, and followed in the next issue with *No Door,* by Wolfe. This version of *No Door* was a 19,000 word section of the short novel, with 12,000 words—later published in August, 1934, as "The House of the Far and the Lost"—removed from it.[52] *No Door* was the last of Wolfe's works of more than 15,000 words which Dashiell published before his editorship of the magazine ended with the issue of September, 1936. Between August, 1930, and July, 1933, Dashiell published twenty-six short novels, twelve in the first contest, nine in the second, and four independent of the contests. However, between April, 1932, and July, 1933, he published eight *nouvelle* of which four were by Wolfe. After *Scribner's* turned to other things to bolster its sagging subscription lists—serials, "Life in the United States" narratives, biographies—Wolfe felt the lack of a market for a form that was natural to his talents and interests. Writing to Hamilton Basso, while he was working on *The Party at Jack's,* Wolfe said: "It is all very well to talk of classic brevity etc. but this story cannot be written that way: if it is it becomes something else. And if I do it right it is certainly worth doing. But to get it published? I don't know. All this talk about there being a market or a publisher nowadays for any good

50. *Short Novels,* pp. 75–76.
51. *Editor's Choice* (New York, 1934), p. 111.
52. The details of these publications are given in *Short Novels,* pp. 157–158.

piece of writing is nonsense. A writer's market, unless he chooses to live and work and publish like James Joyce or to be one of the little magazine precious boys, is still cabin'd and confined to certain more or less conventional and restricted forms and mediums."[53]

Perhaps it was his experience with *Boom Town* which he had in mind. This satiric picture of Lybia Hill was originally a short novel of about 20,000 words, written in its first form in 1932. His agent, Elizabeth Nowell, sold it in its third revision to *The American Mercury* in 1934, and it was published in the May, 1934, issue, but only after it had undergone extensive editing and cutting by one of the *Mercury* editors.[54] Wolfe did not return to the short novel form until the fall of 1936, when he imprisoned his impressions of Nazi Germany in a *nouvelle* which was serialized in three parts in the *New Republic* (March 10, 17, 24, 1937).[55]

The Lost Boy, a work of almost 15,000 words, may be considered a short novel. It was written in 1935 and published, in an abridged form, in *Redbook Magazine* in November, 1937.[56] Then in 1937 he turned again to the short novel form for *The Party at Jack's.*[57]

From this spotty and inconclusive history, some speculations may be drawn. One is that Wolfe found the short novel form attractive and liked to work in it; another is that he felt the constriction of the usual length limits of magazines. A third is that his short novels were generally conceived as independent units. He was explicit about this fact in regard to *A Portrait of Bascom Hawke*; *The Web of Earth* and *Death the Proud Brother*, neither of which he ever incorporated into longer works but republished as short novels in *From Death to Morning*; "*I Have a Thing to Tell You*," which he wrote as a short serial; and *The Party at Jack's*. Whether *No Door* represents a rearrangement of material already written for *Of Time and the River*, as Richard S. Kennedy claims,[58] or whether *No Door* was the means through which Wolfe discovered a structure for the novel, as I believe,[59] will probably never be fully resolved. The *Notebooks*, which

53. *Letters*, p. 631.
54. Ibid., pp. 333, 401, 406, 409. The editor, Charles Angoff, in "Thomas Wolfe and the Opulent Manner," *Southwest Review*, XLVIII (Winter, 1963), 81–84, describes the editing, which he now views as excessive and unfortunate.
55. *Short Novels*, pp. 235–236.
56. *Letters*, p. 488.
57. *Short Novels*, pp. 281–282.
58. *Window of Memory*, p. 261.
59. *Short Novels*, pp. xii–xiv, 157–158.

would normally be expected to help toward a solution, in fact complicate the issue.[60]

Another tenable speculation is that the interest of *Scribner's Magazine* in the short novel was an inspiriting and strong influence on Wolfe's career, for it provided him with a market for a form of writing which he liked. It is appropriate that the final issue of *Scribner's Magazine*, that of May, 1939, should have published posthumously as a part of a new—and never completed—Short Novel Contest Wolfe's last short novel, *The Party at Jack's*. Thus five of the eight *nouvelle* which he published in magazines appeared in *Scribner's*. The hope of encouraging the form which Alfred Dashiell announced in 1930 was thus realized in the work of one of the most important writers whom the magazine published. *Scribner's* served for Wolfe as *The Yellow Book* did for James the vital role of giving him a welcome market for the "blest *nouvelle*."

60. *The Notebooks of Thomas Wolfe*, ed. Richard S. Kennedy and Paschal Reeves (Chapel Hill, 1970).

Clarence Louis Frank Gohdes

(1901–   )

Chronology

Born San Antonio, July 2, 1901.

A.B. Capital University, 1921; A.M. Ohio State University, 1922; A.M. Harvard University, 1928; Ph.D. Columbia University, 1931.

Assistant professor of English, Southern Methodist University, 1926–1927.

Instructor in English, New York University, 1929–1930.

Assistant professor of English, Duke University, 1930; associate professor, 1934–1938; professor, 1938–1971; James B. Duke Professor, 1961–1971.

Visiting professor at Columbia University, Harvard University, the universities of Pennsylvania, Utah, and California.

Managing editor of *American Literature*, 1932–1954; editor, 1954–1969.

Guggenheim Fellow, 1962.

Member of the Modern Language Association, American Historical Association, Phi Beta Kappa.

Bibliography

Books

The Periodicals of American Transcendentalism. Durham, N.C.: Duke University Press, 1931; reprinted New York: AMS Press, 1970.

Uncollected Lectures by Ralph Waldo Emerson. New York: W. E. Rudge, 1932.

Letters of William Michael Rossetti Concerning Whitman, Blake, and Shelley to Anne Gilchrist and Her Son Herbert Gilchrist. (Edited with

P. F. Baum.) Durham, N.C.: Duke University Press, 1934; reprinted New York: AMS Press, 1968.

American Literature in Nineteenth-Century England. New York: Columbia University Press, 1944; reprinted Carbondale, Ill.: Southern Illinois University Press, 1963.

Sidney Lanier, *The English Novel and Essays on Literature.* (Edited with Kemp Malone.) *Centennial Edition of the Works of Sidney Lanier,* Vol. IV. Baltimore: The Johns Hopkins Press, 1945.

Walt Whitman, *Faint Clews and Indirections: Manuscripts of Walt Whitman and His Family.* (Edited with Rollo G. Silver.) Durham, N.C.: Duke University Press, 1949; reprinted New York: AMS Press, 1964.

The Later Nineteenth Century, Part III of *The Literature of the American People,* edited by A. H. Quinn. New York: Appleton-Century-Crofts, Inc., 1951, pp. 569–809.

America's Literature. (Edited with James D. Hart.) New York: Dryden Press, 1955, reprinted New York: Holt, Rinehart and Winston, 1960, 1963, 1965.

Bibliographical Guide to the Study of the Literature of the U.S.A. Durham, N.C.: Duke University Press, 1959; 1960. Second edition, revised and enlarged, 1963; third edition, 1970.

Literature and Theater of the States and Regions of the U.S.A.: An Historical Bibliography. Durham, N.C.: Duke University Press, 1967.

Hunting in the Old South: Original Narratives of the Hunters. Baton Rouge, La.: Louisiana State University Press, 1967.

Essays on American Literature in Honor of Jay B. Hubbell. Durham, N.C.: Duke University Press, 1967.

Russian Studies of American Literature: A Bibliography. Compiled by Valentina A. Libman; translated by Robert V. Allen; edited by Clarence Gohdes. Chapel Hill, N.C.: University of North Carolina Press, 1969.

Articles

"Henry Thoreau, Bachelor of Arts." *The Classical Journal,* XXIII (Feb., 1928), 323–336.

"A Note on the Bibliography of Keats." *Modern Language Notes,* XVIII (June, 1928), 393.

"Whitman and Emerson." *Sewanee Review,* XXXVII (Jan., 1929), 79–93.

"*The Western Messenger* and *The Dial.*" *Studies in Philology,* XXVI (Jan., 1929), 67–84.

"Ethan Allen and His Magnum Opus." *The Open Court,* XLIII (March, 1929), 129–151.

"Some Remarks on Emerson's Divinity School Address." *American Literature,* I (March, 1929), 27–31.

"A Brook Farm Labor Record." *American Literature,* I (Nov., 1929), 297–303.

"Aspects of Idealism in Early New England." *Philosophical Review,* XXXIX, (Nov., 1930), 537–555.

"Alcott's 'Conversation' on the Transcendental Club and *The Dial.*" *American Literature*, III (March, 1931), 14–27.

"A Gossip on Emerson's Treatment of Beauty." *The Open Court*, XLV (May, 1931), 315–320.

"Getting Ready for Brook Farm." *Modern Language Notes*, XLIX (Jan., 1934), 36–39.

"The 1876 English Subscription for Whitman." *Modern Language Notes*, L (April, 1935), 257–258.

"The Theme Song of American Criticism." *The University of Toronto Quarterly*, VI (Oct., 1936), 49–65.

"On the Study of Southern Literature." *William and Mary College Quarterly Historical Magazine*, XVI (Jan., 1936), 81–87.

"Gossip about Melville in the South Seas." *The New England Quarterly*, X (Sept., 1937), 526–531.

"A Utopian Doctoral Thesis in English: An Outline." *The English Journal* (College Ed.), XXVII (March, 1938), 262–265.

"The Study of American Literature in the United States." *English Studies* (Amsterdam), XX (April, 1938), 61–66.

"Three Letters by James Kay Dealing with Brook Farm." *Philological Quarterly*, XVII (Oct., 1938), 377–388.

"Some Letters by O. Henry." *The South Atlantic Quarterly*, XXXVIII (Jan., 1939), 31–39.

"Some Notes on the Unitarian Church in the Ante-Bellum South." Chapter in *American Studies in Honor of W. K. Boyd*. Durham, N.C.: Duke University Press, 1940, pp. 327–366.

"Longfellow and His Authorized British Publishers," *PMLA*, LV (Dec., 1940), 1165–1179.

"A Check-List of Volumes by Longfellow Published in the British Isles during the Nineteenth Century." *Bulletin of Bibliography*, XVII (Sept.-Dec., 1940), 46; XVII (Jan.-April, 1941), 67–69; XVII (May-Aug., 1941), 93–96.

"A Note on Whitman's Use of the Bible as a Model." *Modern Language Quarterly*, II (March, 1941), 105–108.

"British Interest in American Literature during the Latter Part of the Nineteenth Century as Reflected by Mudie's Select Library." *American Literature*, XIII (Jan., 1942), 356–362.

"Some Letters of Joaquin Miller to Lord Houghton." *Modern Language Quarterly*, III (June, 1942), 297–306.

"Check List of Bret Harte's Works in Book Form Published in the British Isles." *Bulletin of Bibliography*, XVIII (May-Aug. and Sept.-Dec., 1943), 19, 36–39.

"Melville's Friend 'Toby.'" *Modern Language Notes*, LIX (Jan., 1944), 52–55.

"A Department of American and Comparative Literature." *Modern Language Journal*, XXXIII (Feb., 1949), 135–137. (Written in collaboration with W. P. Friederich.)

"The Reception of Some Nineteenth-Century American Authors in Europe." Chapter in *The American Writer and the European Tradition.* Minneapolis: University of Minnesota Press, 1950, pp. 106–120; reprinted New York: McGraw-Hill, 1964.

"The Ku Klux Klan and the Classics." *The Georgia Review*, VII (Spring, 1953), 18–24.

"The Foreign Book in the United States, 1901–1930." *Yearbook of Comparative and General Literature*, III (1954), 51–53.

"A Comment on Section 5 of Whitman's 'Song of Myself.'" *Modern Language Notes*, LXIX (Dec., 1954), 583–586.

"Soviet Literary Doctrine as Illustrated in a Communist Magazine." *The Georgia Review*, IX (Winter, 1955), 443–451.

"Hunting in the Old South." *Southwest Review*, XLII (Winter, 1957), 69–72.

"Heine in America: A Cursory Survey." *The Georgia Review*, XI (Spring, 1957), 44–49.

"The *Atlantic* Celebrates Its Hundredth Birthday." *The South Atlantic Quarterly*, LVII (Spring, 1958), 163–167.

"Nationalism and Cosmopolitanism in Whitman's 'Leaves of Grass.'" In *Comparative Literature: Proceedings of the Second Congress of the International Comparative Literature Association* (Chapel Hill, N.C., 1959), II, 472–479. Also printed in *Walt Whitman Review*, V (March, 1959), 3–7 and in *Salon 13* (Guatemala), I (Feb., 1960), 53–58.

"American Liquor Lingo of Days Gone By." *The Georgia Review*, XIII (Spring, 1959); 53–58.

"Section 50 of Whitman's 'Song of Myself.'" *Modern Language Notes*, LXXV (Dec., 1960), 654–656.

"Whitman as 'One of the Roughs.'" *Walt Whitman Review*, VIII (March, 1962), 18.

"Some Remarks on Programs for Graduate Students in the Field of Recent Literature." In *Approaches to the Study of Twentieth-Century Literature: Proceedings of the Conference on the Study of Twentieth-Century Literature.* First Session, East Lansing, Michigan, 1962, pp. 147–154 *et passim.*

"Driving a Drag in Old New York." *Bulletin of the New York Public Library*, LXVI (June, 1962), 386–388.

"Whitman and the 'Good Old Cause.'" *American Literature*, XXXIV (Nov., 1962), 400–403.

"The Literature and Theatre of Hawaii: A Tentative Checklist." *Bulletin of the New York Public Library*, LXVII (Nov., 1963), 574–578.

"Hunting in the Old South: Original Narratives of the Hunters." *The Georgia Review*, XVIII (Fall, 1964), 255–265; XVIII (Winter, 1964), 463–478; XIX (Spring, 1965), 93–120; XIX (Summer, 1965), 226–238; XIX (Fall, 1965), 350–359; XX (Spring, 1966), 99–107; XX (Fall, 1966), 352–369.

"What 'South' Are They Talking About in the U.S.A.?" *American Litera-*

ture (Tokyo), I (Oct., 1964), 85–98; *Westerly* (Australia), No. 3, pp. 50–56 (1964); *Americana-Austriaca: Festschrift des Amerika-Instituts der universität Innsbruck*, Vienna, 1966, pp. 158–169.

"The Earliest Description of 'Western' Fiction?" *American Literature*, XXXVII (March, 1965), 70–71.

"The Theatre in New York: A Tentative Checklist." *Bulletin of the New York Public Library*, LXIX (April, 1965), 232–246.

"Wicked Old New York." *Huntington Library Bulletin*, XXIX (Feb., 1966), 171–181.

"Foreword" to *Mark Twain's Library of Humor*, New York: Garrett Press, 1969, pp. vii–x.

Other Editorial Assignments

Colliers Encyclopedia, first ed., New York, 1950. Editor of all materials on American authors.

The Muckrakers, 40 vols. Upper Saddle River, N.J.: Gregg Press, 1969. Editor of series.

The American Short Story Series, 87 vols. New York: Garrett Press, 1969. Editor of series.

The American Humorists, 28 vols. Upper Saddle River, N.J.: Gregg Press, 1970. Editor of Series.

Index